Fill in the blank with < or > to make each statement true.

1. 6,120,438,625,503 __<__ 6,120,438,625,530
2. 27,411,068,734 __>__ 27,411,068,374
3. 718,699,043,226 _____ 71,869,904,322
4. 98,104,327,665 _____ 98,104,237,665
5. 1,400,623,522,477 _____ 140,623,522,477
6. 322,446,771,879 _____ 322,446,771,987
7. 68,716,525,337 _____ 687,165,253,374
8. 418,998,566,545 _____ 418,998,566,554
9. 5,661,734,992,213 _____ 5,661,734,992,123
10. 81,102,356,672 _____ 811,023,566,723
11. 2,221,397,846,519 _____ 2,221,397,846,195
12. 587,923,443,126 _____ 587,923,434,126
13. 47,003,592,652 _____ 470,035,926,524
14. 209,762,154 _____ 209,762,153
15. 3,861,243,717,506 _____ 3,861,243,717,560

Put in increasing order.

16.	432,799,800,041	432,798,900,041	432,789,900,041
	_____	_____	_____
17.	2,501,623,765	2,510,632,765	2,512,630,765
	_____	_____	_____
18.	9,817,633,201,006	9,817,633,102,006	9,817,633,021,006
	_____	_____	_____
19.	50,739,662,443	5,073,966,244	507,296,624,433
	_____	_____	_____
20.	732,465,003,583	732,465,030,583	732,465,030,538
	_____	_____	_____

Put in decreasing order.

21.	64,710,239,885	64,710,329,885	64,710,239,588
	_____	_____	_____
22.	299,654,438,112	299,654,843,121	299,654,438,121
	_____	_____	_____
23.	10,354,011,998	1,035,401,199	103,540,119,987
	_____	_____	_____
24.	4,327,005,986,331	4,327,005,689,331	4,327,005,869,331
	_____	_____	_____
25.	9,663,012,245,638	9,663,012,254,638	9,663,012,245,368
	_____	_____	_____

Math IF8771

Rounding

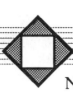

Name _____

Total Problems __**40**__
Problems Correct _____
Percent Correct _____

Round to the nearest:

ten-million
1. 4,003,445,629,808 _____
2. 226,884,502 _____
3. 752,899,483,342 _____
4. 63,443,005,632 _____

hundred-billion
1. 254,612,045,588 _____
3. 3,000,577,628,999 _____
2. 854,891,113,205 _____
4. 9,783,666,555,989 _____

thousand
1. 5,426,514 _____
3. 628,562,444,416 _____
2. 8,713,000,895,428 _____
4. 999,999 _____

billion
1. 16,322,682,111 _____
3. 897,577,469,555 _____
2. 5,555,444,333 _____
4. 7,000,687,004,987 _____

hundred-thousand
1. 280,799,445,612 _____
3. 900,047,888 _____
2. 6,498,652,003 _____
4. 1,111,111,111,111 _____

trillion
1. 5,555,555,555,555 _____
3. 6,481,110,236,773 _____
2. 9,526,666,122,808 _____
4. 5,399,899,599,799 _____

million
1. 628,509,348 _____
3. 5,433,489,512 _____
2. 6,540,999,976,004 _____
4. 54,489,566 _____

ten-thousand
1. 6,011,378,996,125 _____
3. 5,777,818,052 _____
2. 4,008,436 _____
4. 6,998,324,698 _____

hundred-million
1. 14,446,986,610 _____
3. 5,003,005,680,003 _____
2. 987,626,530,988 _____
4. 7,806,039,819,672 _____

ten-billion
1. 43,688,739,606 _____
3. 3,349,825,677,522 _____
2. 989,467,772,522 _____
4. 4,825,600,499,730 _____

Math IF8771

Name _____

Total Problems __**20**__

Problems Correct ____

Percent Correct _____

Add.

1.	50,987,625	2.	7,105
	9,860,008		862,430
	48,909,378		79,992
	28,009		314
	8,666,542		973,566
	+ 77,045,613		+ 8,666,542

3.	52,809,763	4.	4,682,003	5.	4,138,626	6.	78
	115,620		53,792,456		907,005		5,522
	9,766		1,119,363		3,881		987
	32,488		48,776,221		28,937,066		16,430
	7,001,537		238,456		56,420,823		489,376
	+ 662,348		+ 8,926,348		+ 22,440		+ 5,628

7.	3,408,970	8.	22,346,718	9.	61,589,733	10.	387
	560,889		4,005,613		52,111,003		4,520
	5,632		9,999		49,875,624		29,866
	111,818		875,802		88,006,424		492,039
	4,003,212		47,366		91,018,531		6,287,668
	+ 40,899		+ 37,508,202		+ 28,743,235		+ 72,011,653

11.	8,982,612	12.	88,888,888	13.	506,298,612	14.	324,562
	65,088		77,777,777		13,598		3,887
	7,123,456		66,666,666		1,110,566		113,540
	53,488		55,555,555		28,975,761		3,009,888
	9,300,246		44,444,444		344,347,655		44,505,005
	+ 89,044		+ 33,333,333		+ 881,009		+ 223,220,003

15.	3,999	16.	83,421,565	17.	26,980,723	18.	727,643
	26,999		62,317,692		45,629		8,102,111
	514,999		17,141,584		638		38,726
	6,888,999		28,756,487		482,111		5,437
	+ 18,900,999		+ 39,268,968		+ 722		+ 897,300

19. 63,428 + 99,420,018 + 561,443 + 8,704,552 + 23,489,733 + 826,515,555 = _____

20. 8,907,825 + 64,787,003 + 91,324,866 + 420,555 + 148,921,620 = _____

Math IF8771

Addition

Name _____

Check the addition problems using subtraction.
Circle the problems that are correct.

Total Problems __**38**__

Problems Correct _____

Percent Correct _____

1. 987,623
    + 710,754
    1,698,377

2. 872,455
    + 51,368
    823,823

3. 487,603
    + 39,877
    517,480

4. 5,678,629
    + 86,989
    5,765,618

5. 566,320
    + 111,999
    678,319

6. 865,412
    + 3,640,755
    4,506,167

7. 42,360
    + 58,865
    102,225

8. 988,756
    + 718,008
    1,706,764

9. 15,662,118
    + 3,997
    15,666,115

10. 34,612,568
    + 14,977,029
    49,589,597

11. 2,434,115
    + 788,627
    3,322,742

12. 8,612,544
    + 897,632
    9,510,176

13. 233,422,518
    + 321,211,521
    564,633,039

14. 681,236
    + 4,877,515
    5,558,751

15. 43,726
    + 87,899
    121,625

16. 4,311,988
    + 5,479,661
    9,801,649

17. 78,688,815
    + 65,565,698
    1,342,54413

18. 918,526
    + 79,442
    1,007,968

19. 32,766,187
    + 435,899,083
    468,665,270

20. 6,151,444
    + 3,222,312
    9,373,756

21. 414,112,397
    + 202,055,185
    616,167,582

22. 6,787,999
    + 40,123
    6,827,122

23. 28,976,314
    + 56,020,263
    74,996,577

24. 333,426
    + 231,117
    564,543

25. 5,618,977,634
    + 896,412,307
    6,514,389,941

26. 1,319,634,555
    + 3,027,519,815
    5,147,154,370

27. 2,516,788,651
    + 39,554,783
    2,546,343,434

28. 817,562,009
    + 526,765,001
    1,354,329,010

29. 660,576,781
    + 239,932,452
    900,509,233

30. 634,476,665
    + 515,666,019
    1,150,142,684

31. 8,881,811,888
    + 181,888,118
    9,063,700,006

32. 446,525,116
    + 789,009,999
    1,235,535,115

33. 583,340,119
    + 689,516,999
    1,372,857,118

34. 3,507,626,323
    + 8,898,787
    3,516,525,110

35. 58,402,989
    + 31,597,011
    80,000,000

36. 317,612,919
    + 496,738,555
    814,351,474

37. 618,987,635
    + 987,620,506
    1,606,608,141

38. 9,899,887,625
    + 28,661,587
    9,928,549,212

Math IF8771

©Instructional Fair, Inc.

Subtraction

Name _____

Total Problems __**40**__

Problems Correct _____

Percent Correct _____

Subtract.

1. 18,765,449
    − 9,810,566

2. 1,111,103
    − 5,624

3. 3,000,000
    − 28,977

4. 52,773,210
    − 19,895,333

5. 45,063
    − 38,775

6. 810,134
    − 2,666

7. 32,051,689
    − 23,863,799

8. 135,411
    − 942

9. 821,004
    − 69,367

10. 5,822,214
    − 3,997,651

11. 20,000,006
    − 13,732,897

12. 787,662
    − 515,515

13. 3,440,212
    − 566,529

14. 901,870
    − 633,509

15. 7,003,414
    − 5,289,088

16. 26,501,111
    − 18,626,777

17. 1,000,000
    − 927,602

18. 202,338,612
    − 6,441,058

19. 62,414,500
    − 15,389,772

20. 616,577
    − 604,988

21. 4,712,560
    − 98,799

22. 33,300,000
    − 27,425,767

23. 101,233,451
    − 100,122,566

24. 71,302,612
    − 558,999

25. 19,880,114
    − 17,903,434

26. 399,488,121
    − 308,599,333

27. 397,000,000
    − 28,727,313

28. 500,000
    − 213,996

29. 6,273,411
    − 6,215,699

30. 111,234,997
    − 97,455,998

31. 42,910,000
    − 879,612

32. 568,703,424
    − 29,888,888

33. 600,000,000
    − 537,826,919

34. 37,144,062
    − 19,256,709

35. 111,011,001
    − 1,101,110

36. 87,613,421
    − 896,555

37. 231,002,567
    − 5,627,189

38. 73,826,113
    − 9,997,345

39. 123,499,718
    − 46,798,935

40. 5,000,000,000
    − 312,135,244

Math IF8771

Check the subtraction problems using addition.
Circle the problems that are correct.

Total Problems __**38**__

Problems Correct _____

Percent Correct _____

1.
```
  306,221
- 198,360
  117,861
```

2.
```
   72,000
 - 68,355
    3,645
```

3.
```
  418,720
-  97,843
  417,877
```

4.
```
  1,450,006
- 1,388,972
     61,034
```

5.
```
  6,004,300
-   199,588
  5,804,712
```

6.
```
  32,616,424
-    977,005
  31,639,419
```

7.
```
  5,001,101
- 4,328,232
    672,869
```

8.
```
  431,651
-  98,777
  342,874
```

9.
```
  26,313,004
- 18,563,899
   7,749,205
```

10.
```
  7,349,612
- 7,258,988
     80,624
```

11.
```
  500,121
- 189,444
  310,677
```

12.
```
  300,000,000
- 123,717,888
  176,282,112
```

13.
```
  521,334
- 498,766
   21,568
```

14.
```
  718,872
-   9,799
  708,073
```

15.
```
  8,100,000
- 6,388,413
  1,811,587
```

16.
```
  7,100,245
-   587,666
  6,512,579
```

17.
```
  223,476,111
- 218,588,990
    5,887,121
```

18.
```
  910,111
-  88,088
  822,023
```

19.
```
  58,122
-  9,389
  49,733
```

20.
```
  234,515
- 217,909
   16,606
```

21.
```
  4,180,005
- 3,766,215
    413,790
```

22.
```
  5,101,625
-   983,411
  4,118,214
```

23.
```
  511,009,447
-  89,766,567
  421,242,880
```

24.
```
  28,568,009
- 19,779,221
   8,788,788
```

25.
```
  32,461,718
- 18,356,899
  14,104,819
```

26.
```
  500,000,000
-  49,602,313
  450,397,687
```

27.
```
  66,518,987
- 42,673,189
  13,845,798
```

28.
```
  54,332,141
- 16,414,322
  37,917,819
```

29.
```
  627,010,000
-  59,900,623
  568,109,377
```

30.
```
  41,200,144
-  3,122,666
  38,077,478
```

31.
```
  62,909,816
- 19,817,633
  43,092,183
```

32.
```
  18,410,008
-  6,222,119
  12,287,889
```

33.
```
  20,000,000
- 11,111,111
   8,888,889
```

34.
```
  333,110,087
- 198,233,448
  134,876,639
```

35.
```
  618,755,009
-     914,766
  617,840,243
```

36.
```
  99,877,650
- 81,986,777
  17,890,873
```

37.
```
  23,480,008
-  5,599,612
  18,880,396
```

38.
```
  390,621,334
-     972,806
  389,748,528
```

Math IF8771

©Instructional Fair, Inc.

Estimation

Name _____

Estimate the sums and differences by rounding to the largest place value.

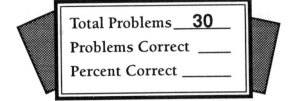

Total Problems __**30**__

Problems Correct _____

Percent Correct _____

1.
```
   5,498,786
+ 4,511,620
```

2.
```
   876,104
-  64,337
```

3.
```
  36,789,271
-  8,733,412
```

4.
```
   367,823
   444,529
+ 936,328
```

5.
```
  9,873,005
-  687,511
```

6.
```
   1,983,244
   4,476,322
+ 5,811,326
```

7.
```
   9,042,332
-  3,816,457
```

8.
```
   3,277,514
-   984,202
```

9.
```
    454,454
  1,066,999
+   983,260
```

10.
```
   3,566,208
+ 8,677,222
```

11.
```
  468,717,633
  809,999,512
+ 643,403,702
```

12.
```
   9,326,540
-  7,457,893
```

13.
```
   25,623,912
-  19,788,804
```

14.
```
   8,245,626
+ 5,513,726
```

15.
```
   644,912,999
-  432,877,814
```

16.
```
   3,541,116
   4,666,878
   5,991,003
+ 8,442,199
```

17.
```
       56,719
   36,781,004
      542,588
+ 515,117,439
```

18.
```
    723,520
    964,313
  3,526,245
+    68,723
```

19.
```
  436,542,512
-   8,783,666
```

20.
```
   2,568,729
   5,498,552
+ 6,312,118
```

21.
```
   4,488,973
-  2,377,616
```

22.
```
   8,762,311
-  3,451,212
```

23.
```
   9,410,562
-  8,726,673
```

24.
```
  766,832,632
+ 123,450,519
```

25.
```
   1,803,468,212
-  1,267,514,522
```

26.
```
  560,723,418
- 271,988,666
```

27.
```
   62,471,800
  336,900,787
+   5,562,313
```

28.
```
  346,712,987
-  54,620,666
```

29.
```
   2,814,399,415
   3,366,288,716
     444,555,612
+    768,900,755
```

30.
```
   56,728,555
  340,829,999
  296,766,544
+  18,221,101
```

Name _____

Multiply. Show your work on another piece of paper.
Write your answers here.

Total Problems __38__
Problems Correct ____
Percent Correct _____

1. 16,524
    x   83

2. 201,002
    x   93

3. 8,704,355
    x   71

4. 626,350
    x   36

5. 40,788
    x   413

6. 736,478
    x   679

7. 5,422
    x 908

8. 618
    x 927

9. 340,069
    x   541

10. 496
    x 518

11. 17,654
    x   255

12. 8,777
    x 198

13. 719
    x 637

14. 6,773
    x 545

15. 29,116
    x   993

16. 720,063
    x   440

17. 5,311
    x 4,668

18. 6,088
    x 3,515

19. 27,215
    x 8,443

20. 32,446
    x 7,919

21. 6,009
    x 3,671

22. 7,801
    x 6,439

23. 9,743
    x 7,658

24. 12,876
    x 5,445

25. 33,499
    x 5,668

26. 52,319
    x 7,777

27. 63,781
    x 6,005

28. 74,543
    x 3,376

29. 45,609
    x 8,817

30. 69,715
    x 8,566

31. 79,843
    x 8,901

32. 92,515
    x 9,845

33. 325,725
    x   5,555

34. 981,104
    x   3,389

35. 773,266
    x   6,551

36. 511,223
    x   3,244

37. 101,234
    x   5,661

38. 566,732
    x   8,899

Math IF8771
©Instructional Fair, Inc.

Name _____

Check the multiplication problems using division. Circle the problems that are correct. Show your work on another piece of paper.

Total Problems __**38**__

Problems Correct _____

Percent Correct _____

1. 68,727
    x   449
    30,858,423

2. 920,663
    x   88
    81,018,344

3. 7,805
    x   663
    5,074,715

4. 899
    x   710
    638,290

5. 4,566
    x   415
    1,794,890

6. 91,236
    x   83
    7,572,588

7. 8,617
    x   38
    337,446

8. 14,656
    x   73
    1,069,888

9. 522,544
    x   121
    63,227,824

10. 14,520
    x   3,223
    46,797,960

11. 631,224
    x   755
    476,574,120

12. 6,005
    x   2,442
    14,674,210

13. 67,999
    x   2,140
    145,517,860

14. 7,892
    x   8,181
    65,564,452

15. 5,545
    x   666
    3,692,970

16. 892,346
    x   718
    640,704,428

17. 73,464
    x   865
    64,546,360

18. 610,022
    x   454
    276,949,988

19. 512,344
    x   612
    313,554,528

20. 213,466
    x   392
    83,678,672

21. 300,019
    x   185
    55,503,515

22. 59,872
    x   999
    59,812,128

23. 341,187
    x   543
    185,605,728

24. 788,632
    x   329
    258,671,296

25. 8,114
    x   9,753
    79,135,842

26. 7,223
    x   1,145
    8,270,335

27. 3,289
    x   5,877
    19,229,453

28. 23,466
    x   1,982
    46,509,612

29. 67,233
    x   4,995
    335,828,835

30. 41,661
    x   5,702
    237,551,022

31. 68,723
    x   3,402
    233,795,646

32. 47,622
    x   3,477
    165,580,694

33. 91,202
    x   2,333
    212,774,266

34. 80,018
    x   8,810
    714,958,580

35. 18,918
    x   7,766
    146,917,188

36. 418,977
    x   2,065
    85,518,755

37. 988,662
    x   3,456
    3,416,815,872

38. 431,205
    x   7,866
    3,391,858,530

Multiply.

1. 4,000 x 800,000

2. 30 x 4,000,000,000

3. 20,000 x 90,000,000

4. 60,000 x 800,000

5. 120,000 x 40,000

6. 900 x 3,000,000,000

7. 700,000 x 70,000

8. 2,500 x 40,000

9. 5,000,000 x 60,000

10. 400 x 500,000,000

11. 20,000 x 100,000

12. 600,000,000 x 700

13. 3,000 x 900,000

14. 500,000 x 50,000

15. 2,000 x 1,500,000

16. 3,000 x 90,000

17. 200,000 x 2,000

18. 10,000 x 800,000

19. 7,000 x 50,000

20. 200 x 700,000

21. 60,000 x 6,000

22. 8,000 x 8,000

23. 900 x 7,000,000

24. 300 x 30,000,000

25. 5,000 x 8,000,000

26. 7,000 x 9,000,000

27. 40 x 40,000,000

28. 50 x 3,000,000,000

29. 80,000 x 300,000

30. 90,000 x 200,000,000

31. 20 x 50,000,000

32. 7,000 x 30,000,000

33. 1,100,000 x 500

34. 2,500,000 x 20

35. 15,000 x 40,000

36. 310,000 x 2,000

37. 120,000 x 30,000

38. 130,000 x 3,000

39. 40,000 x 2,500

40. 70,000 x 110,000

41. 210,000 x 30

42. 5,000 x 2,500,000

43. 160,000,000 x 20,000

44. 40,000 x 12,000,000

45. 300,000 x 3,300,000

46. 200 x 630,000,000

47. 20,000 x 24,000

48. 900,000 x 110

49. 510,000 x 30,000

50. 40,000 x 2,100,000,000

Name _____

Check the boxes on the chart that apply.

Total Problems **25**
Problems Correct ____
Percent Correct _____

Divisible by:

Number	2	3	4	5	6	8	9	10
1. 12								
2. 18								
3. 52								
4. 65								
5. 76								
6. 90								
7. 105								
8. 304								
9. 481								
10. 530								
11. 720								
12. 1,342								
13. 2,008								
14. 3,500								
15. 5,896								
16. 1,485								
17. 3,744								
18. 51,840								
19. 15,550								
20. 62,937								
21. 32,768								
22. 59,049								
23. 31,250								
24. 60,480								
25. 98,415								

Math IF8771

Name _____

Divide. Show your work on another piece of paper.
Write your answers here.

Total Problems __44__
Problems Correct _____
Percent Correct _____

1. $3,142 \overline{)6,888,972}$

2. $599 \overline{)5,236,458}$

3. $6,311 \overline{)70,113,102}$

4. $973 \overline{)41,737,808}$

5. $1,514 \overline{)6,998,004}$

6. $872 \overline{)81,624,503}$

7. $549 \overline{)9,032,119}$

8. $2,133 \overline{)10,681,218}$

9. $607 \overline{)7,914,063}$

10. $865 \overline{)85,637,595}$

11. $4,422 \overline{)32,603,406}$

12. $2,111 \overline{)6,337,899}$

13. $2,877 \overline{)13,098,981}$

14. $4,911 \overline{)662,308,915}$

15. $988 \overline{)70,568,888}$

16. $3,020 \overline{)654,302,198}$

17. $6,012 \overline{)58,983,732}$

18. $2,981 \overline{)342,766,752}$

19. $736 \overline{)90,112,354}$

20. $439 \overline{)2,651,560}$

21. $1,998 \overline{)14,897,088}$

22. $3,566 \overline{)723,056,009}$

23. $718 \overline{)404,459,452}$

24. $7,143 \overline{)988,453,612}$

25. $1,111 \overline{)69,267,517}$

26. $3,432 \overline{)278,517,096}$

27. $5,466 \overline{)201,300,444}$

28. $6,432 \overline{)47,802,624}$

29. $2,153 \overline{)68,392,114}$

30. $988 \overline{)47,188,856}$

31. $881 \overline{)235,008,512}$

32. $917 \overline{)142,699,812}$

33. $925 \overline{)193,301,875}$

34. $4,566 \overline{)5,421,733,612}$

35. $2,099 \overline{)11,414,362}$

36. $1,986 \overline{)1,004,612,337}$

37. $720 \overline{)31,999,680}$

38. $912 \overline{)88,723,321}$

39. $5,125 \overline{)46,140,375}$

40. $4,019 \overline{)6,616,008,512}$

41. $3,202 \overline{)68,670,092}$

42. $3,111 \overline{)8,990,119,876}$

43. $789 \overline{)77,914,539}$

44. $3,192 \overline{)161,942,928}$

Name _____

Check the division problems using multiplication.
Circle the problems that are correct. Remember to add
the remainders. Show your work on another piece of paper.

Total Problems	**38**
Problems Correct	___
Percent Correct	___

1. $663 \overline{\smash{)}59{,}825{,}142}$ 90,243

2. $720 \overline{\smash{)}63{,}428{,}511}$ 88,095 R211

3. $3{,}421 \overline{\smash{)}22{,}773{,}597}$ 6,657

4. $1{,}889 \overline{\smash{)}42{,}877{,}657}$ 22,698 R1,135

5. $665 \overline{\smash{)}21{,}944{,}338}$ 32,999 R3

6. $889 \overline{\smash{)}53{,}240{,}432}$ 59,888

7. $5{,}021 \overline{\smash{)}64{,}080{,}587}$ 12,762 R2,585

8. $917 \overline{\smash{)}30{,}157{,}379}$ 32,877

9. $494 \overline{\smash{)}80{,}009{,}006}$ 161,961 R272

10. $1{,}021 \overline{\smash{)}3{,}845{,}086}$ 3,766

11. $3{,}456 \overline{\smash{)}28{,}315{,}008}$ 8,093

12. $863 \overline{\smash{)}24{,}778{,}599}$ 28,712 R143

13. $921 \overline{\smash{)}77{,}122{,}008}$ 83,737 R221

14. $754 \overline{\smash{)}68{,}736{,}902}$ 91,163

15. $2{,}718 \overline{\smash{)}99{,}219{,}877}$ 36,504 R2,005

16. $5{,}426 \overline{\smash{)}35{,}909{,}268}$ 6,718

17. $2{,}348 \overline{\smash{)}59{,}800{,}686}$ 25,468 R1,922

18. $568 \overline{\smash{)}87{,}044{,}381}$ 153,247 R95

19. $825 \overline{\smash{)}6{,}433{,}201}$ 7,797 R666

20. $2{,}663 \overline{\smash{)}20{,}121{,}988}$ 7,556 R361

21. $1{,}873 \overline{\smash{)}82{,}518{,}761}$ 44,047

22. $857 \overline{\smash{)}50{,}028{,}763}$ 58,376 R531

23. $1{,}943 \overline{\smash{)}23{,}506{,}414}$ 12,098

24. $777 \overline{\smash{)}18{,}888{,}899}$ 24,310 R39

25. $4{,}718 \overline{\smash{)}89{,}599{,}538}$ 18,991

26. $548 \overline{\smash{)}30{,}809{,}656}$ 56,232

27. $2{,}305 \overline{\smash{)}60{,}111{,}323}$ 26,078 R1,533

28. $1{,}917 \overline{\smash{)}73{,}428{,}919}$ 38,304 R141

29. $7{,}216 \overline{\smash{)}52{,}776{,}509}$ 7,313 R5,901

30. $2{,}894 \overline{\smash{)}221{,}419{,}634}$ 76,509 R2,589

31. $877 \overline{\smash{)}60{,}525{,}612}$ 69,014 R343

32. $5{,}604 \overline{\smash{)}272{,}707{,}452}$ 48,663

33. $3{,}113 \overline{\smash{)}73{,}201{,}627}$ 23,514 R2,455

34. $8{,}917 \overline{\smash{)}2{,}091{,}652{,}968}$ 234,569 R1,195

35. $7{,}766 \overline{\smash{)}350{,}370{,}856}$ 45,116

36. $7{,}783 \overline{\smash{)}5{,}653{,}966{,}891}$ 726,450 R6,542

37. $4{,}502 \overline{\smash{)}398{,}741{,}487}$ 92,689 R2,013

38. $6{,}143 \overline{\smash{)}4{,}271{,}977{,}347}$ 695,422

Math IF8771

Name _____

Divide.

1. 6,300,000,000 ÷ 90,000

2. 48,000,000,000 ÷ 800,000,000

3. 490,000 ÷ 700

4. 180,000,000 ÷ 20,000

5. 21,000,000,000 ÷ 300,000

6. 54,000,000 ÷ 900,000

7. 36,000,000,000 ÷ 6,000

8. 4,000,000 ÷ 50

9. 1,600,000,000 ÷ 400,000

10. 8,100,000,000 ÷ 9,000,000

11. 250,000,000 ÷ 5,000,000

12. 56,000,000,000 ÷ 700,000

13. 90,000,000,000 ÷ 900

14. 350,000,000,000 ÷ 500,000

15. 640,000,000 ÷ 80

16. 10,000,000 ÷ 200

17. 4,200,000,000 ÷ 6,000,000

18. 320,000,000,000 ÷ 4,000,000

19. 120,000,000 ÷ 400,000

20. 3,000,000,000 ÷ 60

21. 2,700,000,000 ÷ 3,000

22. 24,000,000,000 ÷ 80,000,000

23. 600,000,000 ÷ 200

24. 9,000,000,000,000 ÷ 30,000,000,000

25. 15,000,000,000 ÷ 500,000

26. 280,000,000 ÷ 700

27. 7,2000,000,000 ÷ 90,000

28. 4,500,000,000 ÷ 500,000

29. 240,000,000 ÷ 40

30. 80,000,000,000 ÷ 20

31. 40,000,000,000 ÷ 2,000

32. 200,000,000 ÷ 40,000

33. 20,000,000,000,000 ÷ 250,000

34. 600,000,000 ÷ 40,000

35. 770,000,000 ÷ 1,100

36. 360,000,000,000 ÷ 1,200,000

37. 3,900,000,000 ÷ 13,000

38. 990,000,000 ÷ 33,000

39. 480,000,000,000 ÷ 40,000

40. 6,000,000,000 ÷ 50,000

41. 7,500,000,000 ÷ 150,000

42. 15,000,000,000 ÷ 750,000

43. 51,000,000 ÷ 30,000

44. 460,000,000 ÷ 200,000

45. 880,000 ÷ 200

46. 4,400,000,000 ÷ 110,000,000

47. 700,000,000 ÷ 1,400,000

48. 75,000,000,000 ÷ 300,000

49. 90,000,000 ÷ 3,000

50. 100,000,000 ÷ 2,500

Math IF8771

©Instructional Fair, Inc.

Estimation

Name _____

Estimate the products and quotients by rounding. Show your work on another sheet of paper. Write your answers here.

Total Problems __45__
Problems Correct _____
Percent Correct _____

1. 284 x 467,892

2. 36,348,720 ÷ 38

3. 7,329 x 77,885

4. 59,887 ÷ 12

5. 166 x 871,123

6. 2,378,619 ÷ 434

7. 444 x 3,875,562

8. 417,360,511 ÷ 6,299

9. 5,322 x 67,233

10. 403,564,302 ÷ 189

11. 64 x 7,549,986

12. 40,326,119 ÷ 43

13. 983 x 82,478

14. 59,980,333 ÷ 2,276

15. 756 x 9,432,886

16. 3,992,546,002 ÷ 522

17. 741 x 681,123

18. 11,810,435 ÷ 34

19. 635 x 86,677

20. 10,213,980 ÷ 2,435

21. 351 x 76,553

22. 24,663,432 ÷ 4,893

23. 2,608 x 94,212

24. 13,826,972 ÷ 219

25. 1,750 x 4,325

26. 23,745,677 ÷ 32

27. 5,417 x 85,627

28. 35,678,087 ÷ 625

29. 7,658 x 83,661

30. 34,785,606 ÷ 5,155

31. 333 x 73,468

32. 273,766,542 ÷ 888

33. 53 x 1,327,655

34. 158,711,223 ÷ 7536

35. 4,178 x 682,999

36. 6,998,991 ÷ 678

37. 3,727 x 46,878

38. 198,721,541 ÷ 432

39. 3,476 x 33,760

40. 183,877,524 ÷ 5,681

41. 66 x 9,288,764

42. 62,733,115 ÷ 8,842

43. 97 x 32,438

44. 48,322,718 ÷ 553

45. 513 x 6,244

Math IF8771

Name _____

Total Problems __48__
Problems Correct ____
Percent Correct _____

Find the powers.

1. 4^4 _____ 4 16 64 _____

2. 9^2 __81__

3. 2^3 _____ 8 _____

4. 10^2 _____

5. 3^4 _____

6. 12^2 _____

7. 4^3 _____

8. 11^2 _____

9. 5^2 __25__

10. 6^2 __36__

11. 5^5 _____

12. 10^5 __10,000__

13. 12^3 _____

14. 7^2 _____

15. 2^6 _____

16. 8^2 __64__

17. 3^6 _____

18. 2^5 _____

19. 7^3 ____49____

20. 6^3 _____

21. 5^3 _____

22. 14^2 __196__

23. 17^2 __289__

24. 13^2 __169__

Find the roots.

25. $\sqrt[3]{729}$ _____

26. $\sqrt{144}$ _____

27. $\sqrt{49}$ _____

28. $\sqrt{36}$ _____

29. $\sqrt[3]{64}$ _____

30. $\sqrt[4]{81}$ _____

31. $\sqrt{121}$ _____

32. $\sqrt[5]{32}$ _____

33. $\sqrt{225}$ _____

34. $\sqrt{400}$ _____

35. $\sqrt[3]{216}$ _____

36. $\sqrt[3]{343}$ _____

37. $\sqrt[3]{27}$ _____

38. $\sqrt{900}$ _____

39. $\sqrt[7]{128}$ _____

40. $\sqrt[4]{256}$ _____

41. $\sqrt{625}$ _____

42. $\sqrt[5]{243}$ _____

43. $\sqrt{2,500}$ _____

44. $\sqrt[9]{512}$ _____

45. $\sqrt[3]{125}$ _____

46. $\sqrt{256}$ _____

47. $\sqrt{484}$ _____

48. $\sqrt[8]{256}$ _____

Math IF8771

Factors, Primes and Composites

Name _____

Circle the prime numbers and list all the factors of the composite numbers.

54

1. (29) _____

2. 30 _5,6_____

3. 55 _115_____

4. 60 _____

5. 75 _15,5 25,3_____

6. 18 _____

7. 16 _8,2,4_____

8. 17 _____

9. 51 _____

10. 100 _50,2 25,4___

11. 12 _____

12. 25 _____

13. 28 _2,14_____

14. 36 _____

15. 23 _____

16. (49) _7_____

17. 77 _____

18. 57 _____

19. (73) _____

20. 64 _____

21. 24 _____

22. 65 _13,5_____

23. 50 _____

24. 61 _____

25. 14 _7,2_____

26. 97 _____

27. 80 _____

28. (11) _____

29. 72 _____

30. 15 _____

31. (19) _____

32. 140 _____

33. 47 _____

34. 20 _5,4,10,2___

35. 103 _____

36. 59 _____

37. 35 _7,5_____

38. 89 _____

39. 39 _____

40. (79) _____

41. 95 _____

42. 42 _____

43. 125 _____

44. 33 _____

45. 66 _____

46. 93 _____

47. 63 _____

48. 85 _____

49. 54 _9,6_____

50. 43 _____

Math IF8771

©Instructional Fair, Inc.

Name _____

| Total Problems __**40**__ |
| Problems Correct _____ |
| Percent Correct _____ |

Find the prime factorization of the following numbers.

1. 325	2. 420		
3. 200	4. 564		
5. 616	6. 240	7. 286	8. 270
9. 150	10. 476	11. 1,323	12. 264
13. 320	14. 500	15. 432	16. 104
17. 352	18. 1,539	19. 1,000	20. 1,372
21. 224	22. 792	23. 858	24. 1,020
25. 1,125	26. 8,624	27. 30,030	28. 3,036
29. 900	30. 3,971	31. 3,375	32. 6,732
33. 296	34. 1,435	35. 5,824	36. 10,404
37. 5,929	38. 16,170	39. 18,711	40. 120,050

Math IF8771

Find the GCF and LCM of each pair of numbers.

Total Problems __**40**__

Problems Correct _____

Percent Correct _____

1. 25, 45

2. 85, 51

3. 18, 21

4. 72, 26

5. 58, 12

6. 15, 65

7. 66, 44

8. 24, 52

9. 42, 40

10. 84, 68

11. 70, 60

12. 64, 28

13. 35, 77

14. 55, 20

15. 60, 75

16. 32, 24

17. 44, 33

18. 24, 46

19. 76, 57

20. 56, 84

21. 16, 20

22. 55, 22

23. 50, 65

24. 77, 66

25. 50, 30

26. 90, 63

27. 80, 28

28. 81, 18

29. 38, 57

30. 48, 36

31. 35, 50

32. 49, 28

33. 36, 81

34. 56, 70

35. 40, 70

36. 81, 27

37. 52, 32

38. 24, 64

39. 18, 90

40. 81, 90

Math IF8771

©Instructional Fair, Inc.

Name _____

Write the number.

1. 9.6×10^{-11} _____

2. 8.0054×10^{18} _____

3. 4.77×10^{10} _____

4. 1.11346×10^{8} _____

5. 6.0112×10^{-15} _____

6. 5.052×10^{14} _____

7. 2.2×10^{-13} _____

8. 6.0044×10^{17} _____

9. 4.433433×10^{19} _____

10. 1.99818×10^{26} _____

11. 9.17×10^{24} _____

12. 5.511×10^{-19} _____

13. 4.14×10^{18} _____

14. 2.102×10^{-18} _____

15. 5.01×10^{-23} _____

Write in scientific notation.

16. 4,432,000,000,000,000,000 _____

17. 0.00000000000000000000000000079961 _____

18. 605,000,000,000,000,000,000,000,000 _____

19. 0.0000000000000000723 _____

20. 9,999,000,000,000,000,000,000,000,000 _____

21. 0.0000000000000002391 _____

22. 514,100,000,000,000,000,000,000,000 _____

23. 0.00000000001888 _____

24. 666,660,000,000,000,000,000,000,000 _____

25. 0.0000000000000000882 _____

26. 0.00000000000000000000000000003918 _____

27. 87,160,000,000,000,000,000,000,000 _____

28. 934,100,000,000,000,000,000,000,000,000 _____

29. 0.0000000000000000664 _____

30. 0.000000000000000089118 _____

31. 5,499,600,000,000,000,000,000,000 _____

32. 71,310,000,000,000,000 _____

Name _____

Show your work on another piece of paper.
Write your answers here.

Total Problems __**24**__
Problems Correct ____
Percent Correct _____

1. $63 + \sqrt{81} \times {}^3\sqrt{27} + 44 + \sqrt{121}$ _____

2. $(3^2 + \sqrt{4})^2 - 5 \times \sqrt{36} + (3^3 + \sqrt{16})$ _____

3. $(28 - 13) \times (\sqrt{4} \times \sqrt{100}) + (\sqrt{36} \times {}^3\sqrt{8})$ _____

4. $26 + 5 \times 6 - 75 + 15 \times 11 + \sqrt{64} \times 13$ _____

5. $125 + \sqrt{25} + (72 + 2^3)^2 - \sqrt{49} \times 13$ _____

6. $(117 + 13)^2 - 4^3 + (\sqrt{9} + {}^5\sqrt{32})^2$ _____

7. $\sqrt{9} (80 + 4^2 \times 15 + 24 - 80) + \sqrt{169}$ _____

8. $\sqrt{(55 + \sqrt{121})} \times (15^2 + 5^2) + (\sqrt{9} \times \sqrt{16} + \sqrt{49})$ _____

9. $(13 \times 5 + 15 \times 13 + 13 \times 2 + 8^2) + 7 \times 2^2 - 10^2$ _____

10. $\sqrt{49} \times 2^3 + \sqrt{25} (238 + 14 - \sqrt{36})$ _____

11. $\dfrac{\sqrt{5^2 + 2^2 \times 6} + \sqrt{121} \times 2 \times 23 + \sqrt{49} \times 3^2}{8}$ _____

12. $(33 - 27)^2 + \sqrt{144} \times (42 - 38 + 6)^2$ _____

13. $240 + (10 + 2) \times (8 - 5) \times 3 + 5$ _____

14. $(240 + 10 + 2 \times 8 - 5 \times 3) \div 5$ _____

15. $10^2 + \sqrt{121} \times \sqrt{81} - 80 + 5 + (45 - 33)^2 - \sqrt{169} \times \sqrt{225} + 9 (135 + 3^3)$ _____

16. $(75 + 3) \times (72 + 12) \times {}^8\sqrt{256} + \sqrt{400} \times (\sqrt{121} - \sqrt{16}) \times (\sqrt{144} + \sqrt{36}) + {}^3\sqrt{27}$ _____

17. $\sqrt{100} (50 + \sqrt{25} \times 6 + 15 \times 1^5 \times {}^3\sqrt{216}) + (13^2 - 11 \times 12 + 84 + 14 - 5^2 - {}^4\sqrt{16})$ _____

18. $(75 + 5 + 16 \times 3) - (10^2 - 93)^2 + 8 \times 3^2 + \sqrt{36} \times 2^3 - 11 \times \sqrt{25}$ _____

19. $5,600 + (\sqrt{49} \times \sqrt{36} + {}^3\sqrt{27} \times {}^3\sqrt{125}) - 24 \times 30 + 36 \times 5 + 4 - 11 (4 \times {}^3\sqrt{1000} + \sqrt{64})$ ____

20. $120 + \sqrt{100} + 14 \times 2^2 - 2^4 \times \sqrt{9} + 6^3 + 2^2 - (\sqrt{121} + \sqrt{144}) + (4 - 3 + 6)^2$ _____

21. $10^2 \times {}^3\sqrt{27} + {}^6\sqrt{64} + 50 \times \sqrt{49} \times \sqrt{100} + (2^5 - 5^2 - 1^4)$ _____

22. $(2 \times {}^3\sqrt{27})^2 \times \sqrt{100} + \sqrt{81} \times \sqrt{36} \div 2^3 + {}^3\sqrt{1000} \times {}^4\sqrt{625}$ _____

23. $(\sqrt{100} \times \sqrt{25} - {}^3\sqrt{27} \times \sqrt{36}) + {}^6\sqrt{64} \times {}^4\sqrt{81} + 2^3 \times \sqrt{121} + 33 \times 50 + 5^2$ _____

24. $(\sqrt{169} + 3^2) \times (\sqrt{36} - 1^4) \times (12^2 - 142) \times (\sqrt{16} - 1^6) \times (9^2 - 78) + (4^2 + \sqrt{100} - \sqrt{81} - {}^3\sqrt{216})$

Math IF8771

Range, Median, Mean and Mode

Name _____

Find the range, median, mean and mode of the following sets of numbers.

Total Problems __18__
Problems Correct _____
Percent Correct _____

1. 96, 90, 126, 112, 88, 90, 110, 125, 90

    range = _____   median = _____

    mean = _____   mode = _____

2. 585, 501, 399, 313, 424, 476, 501, 568, 355

    range = _____   median = _____   mean = _____   mode = _____

3. 1250, 1315, 1020, 1315, 1442, 1442, 1250, 1442, 1017

    range = _____   median = _____   mean = _____   mode = _____

4. 53, 68, 6, 81, 23, 6, 57, 77, 57, 42, 57, 81, 68

    range = _____   median = _____   mean = _____   mode = _____

5. 94, 97, 98, 99, 94, 91, 95, 98, 90, 95, 98, 92, 96, 96, 92

    range = _____   median = _____   mean = _____   mode = _____

6. 235, 351, 217, 340, 367, 351, 223, 367, 223, 347, 367

    range = _____   median = _____   mean = _____   mode = _____

7. 55,866; 53,866; 57,662; 53,912; 55,866; 52,715; 56,772

    range = _____   median = _____   mean = _____   mode = _____

8. 3, 5, 13, 6, 1, 2, 3, 4, 7, 9, 3, 1, 6, 4, 7, 2, 1, 3, 7, 5, 9, 6, 8

    range = _____   median = _____   mean = _____   mode = _____

9. 100,111; 100,011; 100,001; 100,110; 100,100; 101,000; 100,008; 100,101; 100,110; 100,010; 100,110

    range = _____   median = _____   mean = _____   mode = _____

10. 2033, 2021, 2017, 2035, 2037, 2041, 2029, 2035, 2019, 2017, 2035, 2039, 2019

    range = _____   median = _____   mean = _____   mode = _____

11. 462,151; 462,511; 462,115; 462,115; 462,511; 462,151; 462,511

    range = _____   median = _____   mean = _____   mode = _____

12. 50,111; 51,105; 50,101; 50,113; 51,110; 51,110; 50,101; 51,115; 51,110

    range = _____   median = _____   mean = _____   mode = _____

13. 1621, 1620, 1611, 1621, 1616, 1605, 1606, 1621, 1613, 1621, 1611

    range = _____   median = _____   mean = _____   mode = _____

14. 310, 311, 315, 307, 310, 301, 305, 301, 313, 315, 311, 310, 303, 313, 310

    range = _____   median = _____   mean = _____   mode = _____

15. 44,040; 40,404; 40,444; 44,004; 44,044; 44,000; 40,400; 44,004; 40,440

    range = _____   median = _____   mean = _____   mode = _____

16. 569, 568, 566, 561, 567, 566, 567, 568, 563, 568, 563

    range = _____   median = _____   mean = _____   mode = _____

17. 21, 27, 11, 36, 38, 40, 44, 35, 23, 19, 19, 39, 21, 25, 33, 44, 43, 33, 19

    range = _____   median = _____   mean = _____   mode = _____

18. 771,711; 771,117; 771,007; 771,077; 771,170; 771,017; 771,171; 771,107; 771,711

    range = _____   median = _____   mean = _____   mode = _____

Math IF8771

Name _____

Total Problems __**30**__
Problems Correct _____
Percent Correct _____

Complete the chart.

	Measurement	Precision to the Nearest	GPE	Actual Length
1.	82 hm		0.5 hm	82 hm ± 0.5 hm
2.		decigram	0.5 dg	9 dg ± 0.5 dg
3.	247 L	liter		247 L ± 0.5 L
4.	35 cm	centimeter	0.5 cm	
5.	49 kg		0.5 kg	49 kg ± 0.5 kg
6.		milliliter	0.5 mL	112 mL ± 0.5 mL
7.	6 dam	dekameter		6 dam ± 0.5 dam
8.	75 kg	kilogram	0.5 kg	
9.	86 cL		0.5 cL	86 cL ± 0.5 cL
10.		hectometer	0.5 hm	14 hm ± 0.5 hm
11.	647 mm	millimeter		647 mm ± 0.5 mm
12.	51 mg	milligram	0.5 mg	
13.	33 dL		0.5 dL	33 dL ± 0.5 dL
14.		kilometer	0.5 km	240 km ± 0.5 km
15.	467 cg	centigram		467 cg ± 0.5 cg
16.	21.3 cm	0.1 centimeter	0.05 cm	
17.	346.09 L		0.005 L	346.09 L ± 0.005 L
18.		0.1 centimeter	0.05 cm	3.7 cm ± 0.05 cm
19.	29.88 g	0.01 gram		29.88 g ± 0.005 g
20.	9.2 hL	0.1 hectoliter	0.05 hL	
21.	10.17 dam		0.005 dam	10.17 dam ± 0.005 dam
22.		millimeter	0.5 mm	200 mm ± 0.5 mm
23.	918.01 cm	0.01 centimeter		918.01 cm ± 0.005 cm
24.	63.9 L	0.1 liter	0.05 L	
25.	4.003 g		0.0005 g	4.003 g ± 0.0005 g
26.		0.1 kilogram	0.05 kg	26.4 kg ± 0.05 kg
27.	30.7 m	0.1 meter		30.7 m ± 0.05 m
28.	16.42 kg	0.01 kilogram	0.005 kg	
29.	1.111 kL		0.0005 kL	1.111 kL ± 0.0005 kL
30.		0.01 decimeter	0.005 dm	114.14 dm ± 0.005 dm

Math IF8771

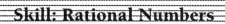

Name _____

Write as a rational number in the form $\frac{a}{b}$.

Total Problems **50**				
Problems Correct ____				
Percent Correct _____				

1. 0.6 _____

2. $3\frac{4}{7}$ _____

3. -10 _____

4. -0.82 _____

5. -3.33 _____

6. $-5\frac{5}{6}$ _____

7. 2.12 _____

8. 0.85 _____

9. 27 _____

10. -0.68 _____

11. -9 _____

12. -8.36 _____

13. -4.87 _____

14. $-8\frac{4}{7}$ _____

15. $12\frac{1}{2}$ _____

16. 0.44 _____

17. -0.16 _____

18. 10.3 _____

19. -2.99 _____

20. -0.24 _____

21. 5.25 _____

22. 72 _____

23. $7\frac{3}{10}$ _____

24. 0.28 _____

25. $-6\frac{2}{5}$ _____

Compare. Write >, < or =.

26. $-\frac{3}{5}$ ☐ -0.65

27. $-9\frac{1}{2}$ ☐ $-9\frac{1}{3}$

28. 3.42 ☐ $3\frac{2}{5}$

29. $4.1\overline{6}$ ☐ $4\frac{1}{6}$

30. $-0.2\overline{3}$ ☐ $-0.22\overline{3}$

31. $0.4\overline{6}$ ☐ $\frac{7}{16}$

32. $-\frac{2}{9}$ ☐ $-0.\overline{2}$

33. $-\frac{3}{11}$ ☐ $-\frac{2}{5}$

34. -2.2 ☐ -2.22

35. $-\frac{13}{14}$ ☐ $-\frac{13}{16}$

36. $-1\frac{3}{11}$ ☐ $-1.\overline{27}$

37. $-2\frac{5}{8}$ ☐ $-2.\overline{5}$

38. 6.625 ☐ $6\frac{5}{8}$

39. -21 ☐ -21.01

40. $-\frac{3}{7}$ ☐ $-0.\overline{42857}$

Put in increasing order.

41. $12\frac{3}{4}$, -12.74, 12.73, $12\frac{11}{15}$ _____

42. -4.19, -4.201, $-4\frac{2}{9}$, $-4\frac{1}{5}$ _____

43. $\frac{6}{25}$, $\frac{3}{11}$, $\frac{4}{15}$, 0.252 _____

44. $-1\frac{2}{5}$, -1.401, $-1\frac{3}{8}$, 1.389 _____

45. 15.151, $15\frac{3}{16}$, $15\frac{3}{20}$, 15.185 _____

46. $-\frac{2}{3}$, -0.66, $-\frac{5}{8}$, $\frac{7}{11}$ _____

47. 11.551, $11.\overline{15}$, $11\frac{11}{20}$, $11.\overline{5}$ _____

48. $\frac{3}{40}$, 0.0778, 0.081, $\frac{2}{25}$ _____

49. $-6\frac{9}{60}$, $-6.\overline{15}$, -6.145, $-6\frac{7}{50}$ _____

50. $-0.\overline{73}$, -0.777, $-\frac{11}{15}$, $-\frac{7}{9}$ _____

Real Numbers

Name _____

Circle the irrational numbers, express fractions as decimals, and write the repeating decimals with a bar over the repetend.

Total Problems __46__
Problems Correct ____
Percent Correct _____

1. $-6\frac{14}{15}$

2. 0.06627827927...

3. -3.024555555...

4. 27.138138138...

5. $20\frac{3}{32}$

6. $-11\frac{10}{11}$

7. 0.941941194111...

8. $\frac{7}{8}$

9. -0.1110626262...

10. $\frac{1}{13}$

11. -0.424424442...

12. 0.699999999...

13. -0.01723723723...

14. 1.1123111231111...

15. $-5\frac{2}{45}$

16. $-\frac{7}{60}$

17. $-\frac{2}{3}$

18. -0.488248824882...

19. 0.56071560715...

20. -3.0624106242...

21. 11.1172172172...

22. $-8\frac{15}{16}$

23. $-14\frac{2}{55}$

24. $-\frac{16}{125}$

25. $-\frac{3}{110}$

26. 28.0995109951...

27. -0.0563206532...

28. -33.0044556678...

29. $3\frac{5}{18}$

30. $1\frac{25}{160}$

Compare. Write >, < or =.

31. $-0.\overline{126}$ ☐ -0.126126216217

32. -0.233323323... ☐ $\frac{7}{30}$

33. 1.714285823... ☐ $1\frac{5}{7}$

34. $-4.00\overline{3248}$ ☐ -4.0032480328...

35. 0.8134792601... ☐ $0.8\overline{1347}$

36. $-33.8\overline{3}$ ☐ $-33\frac{5}{6}$

37. $-\frac{10}{11}$ ☐ -0.90919293...

38. 11.904760915... ☐ $11\frac{19}{21}$

39. $-0.0\overline{364}$ ☐ -0.0364363362...

40. $\frac{7}{60}$ ☐ 0.1166678029...

Put in increasing order.

41. $0.\overline{818}$, 0.818283..., $\frac{9}{11}$, $0.\overline{8182}$ _____

42. $-3\frac{19}{40}$, $-3.\overline{475}$, $-3.\overline{47}$, -3.47491682... _____

43. $0.\overline{316}$, 0.136135134..., $0.\overline{1361}$, $\frac{3}{22}$ _____

44. $-0.\overline{281}$, $\frac{9}{32}$, $-0.\overline{28125}$, -0.281259783... _____

45. -11.035038687..., $-11\frac{7}{200}$, $-11.\overline{035}$, $-11.03\overline{5}$ _____

46. 0.088789809..., $\frac{4}{45}$, $0.\overline{08}$, $0.\overline{088}$ _____

Math IF8771

Irrational Numbers

Skill: Irrational Numbers

Name _____

Circle the irrational numbers.

Total Problems	**45**
Problems Correct	_____
Percent Correct	_____

1. -3.4556173289985…
2. 6.123737373737…
3. -0.443655574433665…
4. 0.005680056800…
5. -3.973973973
6. 85.1436779981268…
7. 11.131114111151111116…
8. 88.888882573…
9. -92.989796959493…
10. 0.0587663663663…
11. -0.15115111511115…
12. -142.42917917917…
13. -0.865486548654
14. -3.965477320115
15. 488.93100672581…
16. 3.5136851368…
17. 149.650112762…
18. -0.431431143111…
19. -62.448931313131…
20. -5.623623624…
21. 0.882288228822…
22. -0.9817598175…
23. 0.8113662662…
24. -31.9545645632…
25. 59.006007008…
26. 0.9538753875…
27. 0.767515151…
28. 599.623625624…
29. -0.832883278326…
30. -18.143764376…

Compare. Write >, < or =.

31. -0.4366789967… ☐ -0.4366789867…
32. - 13.551038974… ☐ -13.515038974…
33. 0.63009467221… ☐ 0.6309467221…
34. 0.0412411241112… ☐ 0.0412411124112…
35. -8.87543375462… ☐ -8.87534375462…
36. 74.4000399625… ☐ 74.4000399655…
37. -0.6645302684… ☐ -0.6645320684…
38. -56.724724472444… ☐ -56.724724472444…
39. 915.15033150033… ☐ 915.15033315023…
40. 38.00578057857… ☐ 38.00578058758…

Put in increasing order.

41. -0.0673573473…, -0.0673573373…, -0.0673573483…, -0.0673574483…

_____

42. -4.1143111431111…, -4.1143111341111…, -4.143111431111…, -4.114311431111…

_____

43. 62.88787887…, 6.88787887…, 62.887787887…, 62.887878788…

_____

44. 0.7373536272…, 0.7733536272…, 0.7337536272…, 0.7733356272…

_____

45. -12.00000399824…, -12.0000399824…, -12.0000039824…, -12.0000398824…

_____

Math IF8771

Name _____

Find the value of each of the following. Show your work on another piece of paper. Write your answers here.

1. $3!$

2. $5!$

3. $(12 - 8)!$

4. $7! - 2!$

5. $6! - 4!$

6. $(16 - 9)!$

7. $(3!)\,(2!)$

8. $6!$

9. $(4!)\,(6!)$

10. $8!$

11. $(18 - 12)!$

12. $5! - 3!$

13. $10!$

14. $\dfrac{11!}{9!}$

15. $9!$

16. $\dfrac{12!}{8!}$

17. $\dfrac{9!}{7!}$

18. $(5!)\,(4!)$

19. $8! - 4!$

20. $(3!)\,(4!)$

21. $\dfrac{15!}{11!}$

22. $\dfrac{11!}{(20 - 15)!}$

23. $\dfrac{12!}{5!}$

24. $\dfrac{8!}{(12 - 9)!}$

How many ways can the letters of each of these words be arranged?
(Hint: The letters do not have to spell words.)

25. WORM

26. HORSE

27. FLOWER

28. DRAGONS

Evaluate. Show your work on another piece of paper. Write your answers here.

29. $_5P_2$

30. $_7P_3$

31. $_6P_2$

32. $_7P_4$

33. $_8P_1$

34. $_9P_4$

35. $_5P_1$

36. $_8P_5$

37. $_9P_6$

38. $_8P_3$

39. $_{10}P_3$

40. $_9P_2$

41. $_6P_4$

42. $_7P_5$

43. $_{10}P_7$

44. $_9P_4$

45. $_{11}P_3 + _9P_7$

46. $_5P_2 + _{12}P_8$

47. $_{13}P_2 - _8P_2$

48. $_9P_6 - _8P_5$

49. $\dfrac{_9P_4}{_4P_1}$

50. $\dfrac{_{10}P_3}{_6P_3}$

Math IF8771

©Instructional Fair, Inc.

Relatively Prime Numbers

Circle the pairs of numbers that are relatively prime.

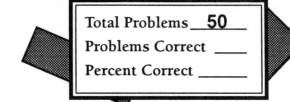
1. 14, 112

2. 106, 9

3. 40, 43

4. 107, 66

5. 111, 37

6. 46, 49

7. 10, 35

8. 78, 13

9. 95, 38

10. 133, 76

11. 77, 44

12. 85, 26

13. 33, 129

14. 64, 16

15. 38, 49

16. 115 46

17. 26, 125

18. 75, 6

19. 87, 118

20. 12, 51

21. 18, 21

22. 52, 39

23. 81, 74

24. 129, 18

25. 40, 57

26. 81, 54

27. 92, 15

28. 63, 20

29. 26, 91

30. 69, 32

31. 34, 129

32. 99, 70

33. 128, 21

34. 28, 49

35. 114, 55

36. 63, 84

37. 123, 26

38. 125, 20

39. 36, 117

40. 58, 87

41. 88, 17

42. 47, 7

43. 29, 129

44. 48, 15

45. 68, 9

46. 33, 35

47. 82, 123

48. 102, 55

49. 27, 81

50. 63, 8

Math IF8771

©Instructional Fair, Inc.

Name _____

Write the word form of each decimal.

Total Problems	**25**
Problems Correct	____
Percent Correct	_____

1. 2.600836 = _____
   _____
   _____

2. 4,669.3455 = _____
   _____

3. 0.000001 = _____
   _____

4. 11.23406 = _____
   _____

5. 807.005 = _____
   _____

6. 0.94103 = _____
   _____

7. 682.059 = _____
   _____

8. 5.5555 = _____
   _____

9. 0.003603 = _____
   _____

10. 9,167.22 = _____
    _____

Write the correct numeral for each number.

11. one hundred eighteen and four hundred ninety-seven hundred-thousandths _____

12. thirty-nine thousand, seventy-four and eighty-seven hundredths _____

13. five thousand eleven and nine thousandths _____

14. nine hundred and six hundred thirty-two thousandths _____

15. eight hundred ninety thousand, one millionths _____

16. forty thousand, six hundred two millionths _____

17. fourteen and sixty-eight thousand, nine hundred twenty-one millionths _____

18. fifty and one thousand ninety-three ten-thousandths _____

19. three hundred-thousandths _____

20. thirty-three thousand, four hundred thirteen hundred-thousandths _____

21. nine thousand, fifty-six and forty-eight ten-thousandths _____

22. nine and one hundred fifty-two ten-thousandths _____

23. five hundred forty-two and six hundred eighty-eight thousandths _____

24. seventeen and nineteen thousandths _____

25. one and eight hundred seventy-one thousand, eighteen millionths _____

On the following number:

4 , 1 3 9 . 6 5 0 1 2 2

Total Problems __40__

Problems Correct _____

Percent Correct _____

1. Circle the number in the tenth's place.
2. Put a triangle around the number in ten-thousandth's place.
3. Draw lips around the number in the millionth's place.
4. Put a star on the number in the one's place.
5. Make an X over the number that is in the hundred-thousandth's place.
6. Draw a heart around the number in the ten's place.
7. Give the number in the hundred's place a smiley face.
8. Make a sun out of the number in the thousand's place.
9. Draw flower petals around the number in the thousandth's place.
10. Put a check mark over the number in the hundredth's place.

The number 9,113.040872 has:

11. ____ hundredths
12. ____ ten-thousandths
13. ____ hundred
14. ____ hundred-thousandths

15. _____ ones
16. _____ millionths
17. _____ thousands

18. _____ tenths
19. _____ ten
20. _____ thousandths

(21-30) What number has:

4 ten-thousandths
8 thousands
9 millionths

0 ones
6 tens
1 hundred

9 hundredths
2 hundred-thousandths
5 thousandths
3 tenths

The number is ___, ___ ___ ___ . ___ ___ ___ ___ ___ ___

Use the numeral that holds the specified place value in each decimal below to create a number where it holds the same place value.

hundred-thousandths	4,062.983216	ones	624.567901
tens	918.42658	thousandths	18.722345
thousands	23,498.00542	tenths	127.156686
hundredths	13,568.006781	millionths	0.643112
ten-thousandths	2.34456	hundreds	91,875.2201

The number is ___, ___ ___ ___ . ___ ___ ___ ___ ___ ___

Math IF8771
©Instructional Fair, Inc.

Decimals

Name _____

Compare. Write <, > or =.

1. 39.00162 _____ 39.00126
2. 1,427.896205 _____ 1,247.896205
3. 0.057727 _____ 0.057772
4. 463.08888 _____ 463.088888
5. 0.00014 _____ 0.01014
6. 6.78799 _____ 6.78979
7. 8,223.67313 _____ 8,223.76313
8. 17.045893 _____ 17.045893
9. 0.0099761 _____ 0.099761
10. 382.18764 _____ 382.18674
11. 29.043652 _____ 29.43652
12. 991.036497 _____ 919.036437
13. 111.0101101 _____ 111.0101101
14. 0.0221221 _____ 0.0212212
15. 5,145.441545 _____ 5,145.44541516
16. 26,188.7658 _____ 26,818.7654
17. 6.431032 _____ 6.413032
18. 92.990913 _____ 92.909913
19. 732.145889 _____ 732.14589
20. 0.663201 _____ 0.6632

Put in increasing order.

21. 0.4689, 0.4698, 0.4869 _____
22. 3.45572, 3.45725, 3.45427 _____
23. 213.95002, 213.90552, 213.59992 _____
24. 0.0066763, 0.0066766, 0.007606 _____
25. 11.121121, 11.121211, 11.112222 _____
26. 8.899881, 8.89988, 8.89998 _____
27. 0.667321, 0.662731, 0.663726, 0.673216, 0.667231 _____
28. 0.0074432, 0.0074322, 0.00744232, 0.00744322, 0.0074342 _____
29. 3,401,782.0036; 3,401,728.0036; 3,401,782.00361 _____
30. 9.882086, 9.88286, 9.8826802, 9.2888888 _____

Put in decreasing order.

31. 89.07653, 89.70065, 89.70007 _____
32. 6.00498, 6.04009, 6.048809 _____
33. 0.112313, 0.1123201, 0.1123103 _____
34. 0.554545, 0.554554, 0.554455 _____
35. 0.631124, 0.63098, 0.631139 _____
36. 0.98062, 0.981, 0.980609 _____
37. 862.044302, 862.043402, 862.0443201, 862.0044989 _____
38. 0.004609, 0.004069, 0.004906, 0.04609, 0.0469 _____
39. 10,881.188118; 10,880.188818; 10,818.188118; 10,880.188188 _____
40. 47.707669, 47.707696, 47.770669, 47.77009 _____

Math IF8771

Name _____

Total Problems	**60**
Problems Correct	_____
Percent Correct	_____

Round to the nearest:

hundred-thousandth

1. 657.98086701 _____
2. 0.855432 _____
3. 3.440003 _____
4. 1,006.7892359 _____
5. 888.888888 _____   6. 46.600601 _____
7. 139.657775 _____   8. 91.152644 _____
9. 0.313003 _____   10. 8.000009 _____

tenth

11. 62.2856 _____   12. 0.0031 _____
13. 55.603603 _____   14. 8,973.689624 _____
15. 0.093844 _____   16. 14.53986 _____
17. 623.78906 _____   18. 74.6099 _____
19. 0.0568 _____   20. 3.2761 _____

ten-thousandth

21. 113.067562 _____   22. 0.000103 _____
23. 26.043167 _____   24. 4.411451 _____
25. 0.0113567 _____   26. 555.23999 _____
27. 13.73266 _____   28. 5.6113112 _____
29. 2,233.437001 _____   30. 0.6101167 _____

millionth

31. 3.4678113 _____   32. 0.5677809 _____
33. 26.7809651 _____   34. 0.6000004 _____
35. 3.8765333 _____   36. 1,042.06987218 _____
37. 9.8754305 _____   38. 0.2566609 _____
39. 4.41120612 _____   40. 36.69708265 _____

hundredth

41. 8,456.68923 _____   42. 0.006569 _____
43. 31.6375 _____   44. 0.89023 _____
45. 0.004999 _____   46. 2.3996 _____
47. 54.638206 _____   48. 10,091.03562 _____
49. 17.62983 _____   50. 826.8936 _____

thousandth

51. 2,051.063982 _____   52. 0.66666 _____
53. 3.05423 _____   54. 63.05499 _____
55. 14.00568 _____   56. 777.777777 _____
57. 20,053.10263 _____   58. 175.750009 _____
59. 0.00448 _____   60. 5.903999 _____

Math IF8771

Decimals

Name _____

Total Problems __**30**__

Problems Correct _____

Percent Correct _____

Add.

1.
```
    31.62394
  + 43.49863
```

2.
```
    0.046893
  + 0.988706
```

3.
```
    612.05466
  +  80.98802
```

4.
```
    132.0638
  +  99.542
```

5.
```
    1.39876
   26.8238
  + 0.666895
```

6.
```
    236.7842
      8.99999
  + 5,689.803
```

7.
```
    626.887762
       .000903
  +  44.44444
```

8.
```
    89.0006
     4.55
  +  0.368
```

9.
```
    638.421
      9.99808
  +  76.0039
```

10.
```
    6.890033
    2.689763
  + 5.589922
```

11.
```
    86.982683
     0.4036
  +  9.90832
```

12.
```
    46.325
    29.888
  + 98.634
```

13.
```
    638.26
     39.84
  + 119.08
```

14.
```
    162.894
    334.55
  + 712.203
```

15.
```
    9.0468
    0.3201
  + 14.5066
```

16.
```
    63.8907
     0.0655
  + 111.347
```

17.
```
    2.368
    1.114
  + 3.226
```

18.
```
      891.05637
      673.998
  + 1,487.009834
```

19.
```
    33.8912
     0.7436
  +  0.044
```

20.
```
    0.368811
    0.045332
  + 0.585857
```

21.
```
     47.0883
    681.119956
  + 700.8876
```

22.
```
    1,211.426789
    5,781.330042
  + 6,666.000455
```

23.
```
    565.889
    404.011
  + 300.979
```

24.
```
    0.663988
    0.700707
  + 0.301122
```

25.
```
     4.327
     0.689
  + 15.901
```

26.
```
    0.1111
    0.2222
    0.3333
  + 0.3334
```

27.
```
    28.43765
     0.002
     1.0934
  +  3.0
```

28.
```
    18
     0.00976
     5.703
  + 1,426.0008
```

29.
```
     162.009
      38.468
      89.001
  + 3,277.698
```

30.
```
    0.003486
    0.915541
    0.2389
  + 0.00687
```

Math IF8771

Subtract.

Total Problems	**38**
Problems Correct	_____
Percent Correct	_____

1. 92.6873
    − 89.0099

2. 0.90082
    − 0.89726

3. 3,427.67
    − 563.008

4. 0.99365
    − 0.112

5. 588.1188
    − 29.5979

6. 36.04
    − 0.9765

7. 11.111111
    − 10.101010

8. 3.98902
    − 1.19399

9. 6.537
    − 0.9688

10. 52.5
    − 50.75

11. 7.00006
    − 5.12349

12. 0.43683
    − 0.09817

13. 3.066666
    − 2.578899

14. 14.73402
    − 8.65211

15. 891.04
    − 763.57

16. 3.467
    − 2.00892

17. 2,657.8532
    − 1,748.9104

18. 666.78918
    − 423.88009

19. 99.123
    − 18.0566

20. 0.773286
    − 0.004499

21. 918.5
    − 2.665

22. 4,881.633
    − 9.808

23. 0.116102
    − 0.059333

24. 87.7654
    − 69.88888

25. 4.877681
    − 0.119991

26. 33.45688
    − 18.92111

27. 8.0076
    − 1.116542

28. 0.201
    − 0.11998

29. 386.44444
    − 189.98765

30. 1,100.88
    − 26.999

31. 3.87004
    − 1.98112

32. 19.6389
    − 0.9999

33. 0.661132
    − 0.450987

34. 63.00913
    − 58.11119

35. 4.59
    − 0.39986

36. 61.84344
    − 18.996

37. 1.6893
    − 0.9109

38. 419.00863
    − 98.74296

Math IF8771

©Instructional Fair, Inc.

 # Decimals

Name _____

Subtract. Show your work on another piece of paper. Write your answers here.

Total Problems	**40**
Problems Correct	____
Percent Correct	_____

1. 19 − 0.6819

2. 729 − 82.436

3. 6 − 0.9934

4. 18 − 16.00523

5. 1,003 − 2.567

6. 4 − 2.0008

7. 963 − 82.044

8. 3,000 − 2,268.836

9. 1 − 0.563892

10. 22 − 18.176

11. 3 − 1.111

12. 46 − 45.9817

13. 71 − 70.989

14. 5 − 0.10203

15. 438 − 419.05

16. 111 − 110.0023

17. 17 − 16.0315

18. 3 − 2.000009

19. 6,812 − 5,477.8

20. 5,006,892 − 0.04

21. 206 − 42.8818

22. 49 − 6.08172

23. 13 − 10.514

24. 7,862 − 912.75

25. 4 − 0.444

26. 81 − 80.796

27. 177 − 163.83

28. 99 − 27.6321

29. 7 − 5.8631

30. 12 − 11.111111

31. 3 − 0.00006

32. 453 − 447.609

33. 78 − 52.99

34. 194 − 87.0662

35. 26 − 18.0522

36. 6,000 − 0.0362

37. 489 − 3.3629

38. 5 − 2.202396

39. 18 − 3.342

40. 510 − 318.63112

Math IF8771

Name _____

Total Problems __37__
Problems Correct _____
Percent Correct _____

Solve.

1. 6,183.62
    − 5,812.897

2.   0.883621
    + 9.116379

3.   818
    − 807.66321

4.   6.891236
    − 5.723445

5.   214.68893
    + 98.51773

6.   26.8
    − 0.98712

7.   0.86102
    − 0.39445

8.   118
    − 106.0043

9.   53.0004
    − 19.5567

10.   82.065791
    + 29.554

11. 1,042.9896
    + 9,751.003654

12.   400.68033
    + 563.77141

13. 9,568 − 8,711.5

14.   4.68623
    + 89.632

15. 666,387.491632
    + 301,444.516339

16.   874.00689
    + 719.53654

17.   69.7864
    + 11.8913

18.   68.4388
    − 29.5595

19. 95 − 1.000041

20. 4,689
    + 93.684

21.   568.007
    − 491.63321

22.   0.798633
    − 0.509752

23.   36.81104
    + 13.18896

24.   5.06073
    + 93.684

25. 417 − 0.88

26.   91.66002
    − 72.65816

27.   388.36259
    − 163.445

28. 8 − 7.9562

29.   3.86214
       3.60023
    + 9.51669

30.   189.653
      445.22222
    + 208.303

31.   0.606312
       0.944561
    + 0.009999

32.   21.68102
       18.01334
    + 73.30564

33. 6,183.005
    − 5,317.72

34.   111.11111
      222.22222
    + 33.33333

35. 16 − 11.863415

36. 2,968 − 871.89

37. 348.632 − 192.78

Math IF8771

Decimals

Name _____

Estimate. Show your work on another piece of paper.
Write your answers here.

Total Problems	**38**
Problems Correct	_____
Percent Correct	_____

1.　　5.6804
　　+ 6.4918

2.　　364.980662
　　−　　1.06315

3.　　34.68119
　　− 14.98772

4.　　46.0098
　　+ 73.9776

5.　3,192.5689
　　− 814.6108

6.　　443.0261
　　+ 459.3095

7.　16,867.086
　− 11,309.99

8.　55,068.7274
　+ 38,942.3388

9.　　28.000014
　　+ 93.998762

10.　　9.04399
　　+ 4.5623

11.　　18.40462
　　−14.66

12.　3,298.4
　　− 765.3375

13.　4,569.0443
　　− 1,800.99

14.　　245.602
　　+ 918.55634

15.　　7.9892346
　　+ 22.023

16.　5,368.77
　　− 439.646

17.　　327.0963
　　− 183.8

18.　57,620.9187
　− 19,412.0006

19.　113,601.8543
　+ 47,788.9001

20.　1,230.976
　+ 7,681.005

21.　　9.48
　　− 3.76321

22.　　639.404
　　+ 54.555

23.　3,872.6004
　　− 987.75

24.　10,475.5
　+ 12,609.8

25.　　33.98876
　　+ 7.566

26.　4,114.4114
　+ 3,533.5533

27.　　138.006
　　− 132.98

28.　　55.78
　　− 42.00631

29.　678.005
　　− 7.99

30.　　93.5556
　　− 18.6611

31.　　42.818
　　+ 31.44

32.　51,412.77
　+ 3,899.001

33.　1,920.03
　− 1,212.66

34.　　498.0072
　　− 155.9

35.　10,730.201
　+ 48,666.444

36.　2,740.63
　+ 9,112.87

37.　　917.246
　　+ 874.3

38.　9,870.777
　+ 1,562.606

Decimals

Name _____

Multiply. Show your work on another piece of paper.
Write your answers here.

Total Problems __38__
Problems Correct _____
Percent Correct _____

1. 84.63
   x 7.64

2. 19.75
   x 4.3

3. 0.876
   x 0.54

4. 5.33
   x 46.7

5. 0.718
   x 9.2

6. 312.9
   x 0.63

7. 0.3443
   x 5.7

8. 99.6
   x 0.42

9. 1.115
   x 55.1

10. 2.04
    x 1.99

11. 713.26
    x 4.8

12. 88.3
    x 0.462

13. 264.3
    x 0.57

14. 340.22
    x 7.7

15. 2.005
    x 0.97

16. 631.8
    x 3.4

17. 0.698
    x 54.7

18. 802.6
    x 0.479

19. 66.5
    x 23.3

20. 84.11
    x 0.76

21. 0.981
    x 0.23

22. 4.468
    x 0.392

23. 0.688
    x 0.499

24. 0.5987
    x 0.83

25. 43.12
    x 98.7

26. 6.0083
    x 7.9

27. 0.4458
    x 0.81

28. 28.9
    x 0.103

29. 210.23
    x 0.654

30. 0.988
    x 0.99

31. 16.05
    x 35.6

32. 67.031
    x 0.52

33. 5.661
    x 1.03

34. 0.609
    x 0.732

35. 4.8912
    x 3.3

36. 65.7
    x 0.104

37. 0.70221
    x 0.66

38. 0.777
    x 34.6

Math IF8771

Decimals

Name _____

Multiply. Show your work on another piece of paper.
Write your answers here.

Total Problems **38**

Problems Correct _____

Percent Correct _____

1. 0.008
    x 0.073

2. 0.123
    x 0.42

3. 0.301
    x 0.104

4. 0.0399
    x 0.16

5. 0.2107
    x 0.34

6. 0.003
    x 0.005

7. 0.244
    x 0.15

8. 0.6732
    x 0.04

9. 0.213
    x 0.229

10. 0.078
    x 0.063

11. 0.21312
    x 0.44

12. 0.526
    x 0.12

13. 0.01098
    x 0.79

14. 0.3476
    x 0.025

15. 0.0566
    x 0.07

16. 0.188
    x 0.188

17. 0.903
    x 0.106

18. 0.00078
    x 0.65

19. 0.811
    x 0.062

20. 0.212
    x 0.323

21. 0.512
    x 0.123

22. 0.4041
    x 0.217

23. 0.099
    x 0.088

24. 0.30654
    x 0.25

25. 0.4432
    x 0.16

26. 0.309
    x 0.268

27. 0.7132
    x 0.11

28. 0.896
    x 0.017

29. 0.0866
    x 0.109

30. 0.24684
    x 0.36

31. 0.0039
    x 0.087

32. 0.517
    x 0.19

33. 0.521
    x 0.088

34. 0.621
    x 0.134

35. 0.3244
    x 0.27

36. 0.80162
    x 0.12

37. 0.0695
    x 0.04

38. 0.10389
    x 0.52

Math IF8771

Fill in the graph.

Total Problems __**25**__
Problems Correct ____
Percent Correct _____

Number	x	1,000	0.01	100	10,000	0.001	10	0.1
1. 27.9								
2. 0.0618								
3. 300.46								
4. 0.55								
5. 23.175								
6. 599.86								
7. 1.246								
8. 0.008								
9. 4,682.7								
10. 7.651								
11. 0.00049								
12. 86.3								
13. 9.72								
14. 0.8657								
15. 15,119.6								
16. 6.003								
17. 577.78								
18. 1,064.89								
19. 0.13246								
20. 3.992								
21. 12,981.4								
22. 0.0053								
23. 74.09								
24. 6.0003								
25. 9,086.5								

Math IF8771

Decimals

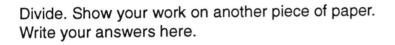

Name _____

Divide. Show your work on another piece of paper.
Write your answers here.

Total Problems __**40**__

Problems Correct _____

Percent Correct _____

1. 12)‾0.894

2. 34)‾2,318.8

3. 76)‾446.956

4. 42)‾294.84

5. 9)‾366.3

6. 55)‾39,119.3

7. 64)‾34.688

8. 29)‾99.789

9. 47)‾0.01034

10. 18)‾3.654

11. 81)‾530.55

12. 37)‾37.296

13. 52)‾10.4364

14. 26)‾256.62

15. 71)‾4.473

16. 90)‾636.3

17. 15)‾520.5

18. 44)‾4.3956

19. 57)‾4400.97

20. 70)‾11.711

21. 68)‾115.464

22. 31)‾6888.2

23. 86)‾410.22

24. 14)‾42.0658

25. 28)‾0.252

26. 95)‾134.045

27. 17)‾1,121.711

28. 22)‾0.0143

29. 50)‾875.2

30. 78)‾14.469

31. 65)‾50.193

32. 41)‾0.8282

33. 88)‾5.632

34. 13)‾0.3198

35. 91)‾778.05

36. 21)‾63.9366

37. 75)‾5783.325

38. 53)‾0.07102

39. 35)‾194.425

40. 61)‾195.2061

Math IF8771

Name _____

Divide. Show your work on another piece of paper.
Write your answers here.

Total Problems __40__
Problems Correct _____
Percent Correct _____

1. 3.6)‾0.4392

2. 0.414)‾3.17124

3. 0.59)‾0.00354

4. 1.8)‾179.19

5. 0.65)‾0.002665

6. 30.1)‾2,362.85

7. 0.91)‾7.28637

8. 0.08)‾0.36896

9. 7.3)‾0.00365

10. 1.21)‾101.6763

11. 22.2)‾0.9546

12. 0.34)‾0.306238

13. 0.41)‾0.008651

14. 0.07)‾3.941

15. 5.5)‾6.963

16. 0.85)‾8.024

17. 0.09)‾0.5994

18. 4.05)‾0.031185

19. 0.75)‾67.725

20. 6.2)‾0.00372

21. 1.12)‾10.08112

22. 0.291)‾0.012804

23. 3.9)‾0.6903

24. 0.58)‾0.32132

25. 0.86)‾77.83

26. 0.07)‾0.000441

27. 1.09)‾2.0492

28. 0.038)‾0.2109

29. 6.02)‾0.19866

30. 0.17)‾1.3583

31. 0.081)‾0.00405

32. 0.043)‾0.41538

33. 5.1)‾0.0357

34. 0.209)‾15.8004

35. 0.006)‾0.27798

36. 7.5)‾0.06975

37. 0.011)‾0.003784

38. 0.007)‾0.6335

39. 0.89)‾5.0196

40. 0.9)‾27.9198

Math IF8771

Name _____

Fill in the graph.

Total Problems **25**

Problems Correct _____

Percent Correct _____

Number	÷	0.01	10,000	100	0.0001	0.1	1,000	0.001
1. 63.8								
2. 0.0092								
3. 718.4								
4. 9.663								
5. 500.6								
6. 0.00081								
7. 8.005								
8. 40.067								
9. 7,100.5								
10. 0.06123								
11. 19.63								
12. 44.441								
13. 1,003.6								
14. 6.022								
15. 0.00055								
16. 21,560.3								
17. 0.1399								
18. 20.441								
19. 7,115.8								
20. 6.8897								
21. 17.099								
22. 321.05								
23. 69.4003								
24. 1.0008								
25. 555.11								

Math IF8771

Decimals

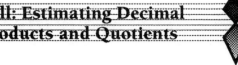

Estimate. Show your work on another piece of paper.
Write your answers here.

Total Problems __**40**__
Problems Correct _____
Percent Correct _____

1. 6.324 x 82.099

2. 70.862 x 67.934

3. 41,078.6211 ÷ 82.3678

4. 13,815.621 ÷ 7,456.008

5. 53,872.563 ÷ 609.717

6. 497.18 x 38.88

7. 310,814.366 ÷ 299.0063

8. 87.651 x 62.453

9. 27,900.6544 x 38.9881

10. 24,319.066 ÷ 5,894.57

11. 2,099.06 x 3.246

12. 1.9123 x 48,072.004

13. 381.786 x 8,132.704

14. 51,433.276 ÷ 10,387.655

15. 1,799,446.8 ÷ 8,777.0654

16. 9.4632 x 3,118.766

17. 8,888.888 ÷ 29.6354

18. 491.005 x 572.909

19. 98.0732 x 69.5621

20. 3,197.6042 ÷ 7.78063

21. 28.7119 x 7,232.604

22. 354.6328 ÷ 68.0435

23. 12,406.77112 ÷ 58.6337

24. 628.541 x 63.454

25. 1,759.6369 ÷ 8.8832

26. 53.276 x 676.543

27. 55,763.0032 ÷ 72.3009

28. 8.2478 x 8,642.987

29. 442.102 x 278.865

30. 63.0041 x 6,009.872

31. 2,460.31477 ÷ 45.78913

32. 7,218.044 ÷ 93.43006

33. 325.5678 x 5,411.8227

34. 6,018.405 ÷ 1.8976

35. 677.8045 x 760.554321

36. 1,587.4311 ÷ 37.6005

37. 41,890.6332 ÷ 68.552

38. 809.5563 ÷ 9.23877

39. 77.666 x 8,349.08667

40. 3,567.9982 x 14.7664

Metric

Name _____

Fill in the chart.

Total Problems __25__
Problems Correct _____
Percent Correct _____

	kilometer (km)	hectometer (hm)	dekameter (dam)	meter (m)	decimeter (dm)	centimeter (cm)	millimeter (mm)
1.		0.052					
2.				3.67			
3.					1.03		
4.			61				
5.							8,856
6.						32	
7.	0.73						
8.					406.9		
9.							3.8
10.	4.4						
11.				16			
12.		9.16					
13.						**0.05**	
14.			1.007				
15.			14.2				
16.					0.082		
17.						11.11	
18.				0.194			
19.		3					
20.							76.41
21.	90						
22.				7.03			
23.							118
24.	0.005						
25.						6.45	

Name _____

Total Problems __**50**__

Problems Correct _____

Percent Correct _____

Circle the equivalent fractions.

1. $\dfrac{12}{15} = \dfrac{28}{35}$ 2. $\dfrac{63}{72} = \dfrac{28}{32}$

3. $\dfrac{3}{18} = \dfrac{10}{60}$ 4. $\dfrac{16}{19} = \dfrac{17}{23}$

5. $\dfrac{18}{30} = \dfrac{24}{45}$ 6. $\dfrac{24}{34} = \dfrac{60}{85}$ 7. $\dfrac{60}{70} = \dfrac{8}{9}$ 8. $\dfrac{12}{27} = \dfrac{16}{36}$

9. $\dfrac{30}{42} = \dfrac{20}{28}$ 10. $\dfrac{47}{52} = \dfrac{33}{38}$ 11. $\dfrac{12}{33} = \dfrac{28}{77}$ 12. $\dfrac{16}{24} = \dfrac{6}{9}$

13. $\dfrac{36}{96} = \dfrac{27}{72}$ 14. $\dfrac{35}{50} = \dfrac{14}{20}$ 15. $\dfrac{9}{11} = \dfrac{72}{99}$ 16. $\dfrac{35}{42} = \dfrac{20}{28}$

17. $\dfrac{22}{25} = \dfrac{17}{20}$ 18. $\dfrac{18}{24} = \dfrac{6}{8}$ 19. $\dfrac{6}{45} = \dfrac{14}{105}$ 20. $\dfrac{36}{45} = \dfrac{42}{55}$

Simplify.

21. $\dfrac{16}{40}$ 22. $\dfrac{6}{42}$ 23. $\dfrac{20}{36}$ 24. $\dfrac{45}{54}$

25. $\dfrac{9}{30}$ 26. $\dfrac{39}{78}$ 27. $\dfrac{32}{48}$ 28. $\dfrac{45}{60}$

29. $\dfrac{24}{64}$ 30. $\dfrac{15}{36}$ 31. $\dfrac{8}{60}$ 32. $\dfrac{21}{39}$

33. $\dfrac{11}{66}$ 34. $\dfrac{16}{28}$ 35. $\dfrac{54}{60}$ 36. $\dfrac{12}{80}$

37. $\dfrac{12}{75}$ 38. $\dfrac{21}{48}$ 39. $\dfrac{20}{75}$ 40. $\dfrac{35}{98}$

41. $\dfrac{84}{108}$ 42. $\dfrac{22}{88}$ 43. $\dfrac{52}{65}$ 44. $\dfrac{28}{49}$

45. $\dfrac{30}{126}$ 46. $\dfrac{51}{60}$ 47. $\dfrac{92}{120}$ 48. $\dfrac{64}{88}$

49. $\dfrac{98}{112}$ 50. $\dfrac{8}{68}$

Math IF8771

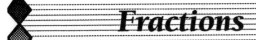

Name _____

Compare. Write >, = or <.

Total Problems __**40**__

Problems Correct _____

Percent Correct _____

1. $\dfrac{7}{9}$ _____ $\dfrac{5}{7}$ 2. $\dfrac{21}{25}$ _____ $\dfrac{9}{10}$

3. $\dfrac{4}{15}$ _____ $\dfrac{2}{5}$ 4. $\dfrac{22}{27}$ _____ $\dfrac{8}{9}$

5. $\dfrac{2}{3}$ _____ $\dfrac{3}{5}$ 6. $\dfrac{3}{8}$ _____ $\dfrac{7}{16}$ 7. $\dfrac{11}{12}$ _____ $\dfrac{23}{24}$ 8. $\dfrac{2}{3}$ _____ $\dfrac{13}{20}$

9. $\dfrac{8}{14}$ _____ $\dfrac{28}{49}$ 10. $\dfrac{12}{32}$ _____ $\dfrac{18}{48}$ 11. $\dfrac{3}{20}$ _____ $\dfrac{1}{5}$ 12. $\dfrac{3}{10}$ _____ $\dfrac{7}{25}$

13. $\dfrac{1}{4}$ _____ $\dfrac{1}{3}$ 14. $\dfrac{3}{14}$ _____ $\dfrac{2}{7}$ 15. $\dfrac{4}{21}$ _____ $\dfrac{2}{7}$ 16. $\dfrac{3}{10}$ _____ $\dfrac{4}{15}$

17. $\dfrac{8}{13}$ _____ $\dfrac{3}{4}$ 18. $\dfrac{3}{20}$ _____ $\dfrac{2}{15}$ 19. $\dfrac{3}{5}$ _____ $\dfrac{4}{7}$ 20. $\dfrac{5}{14}$ _____ $\dfrac{8}{21}$

Put in increasing order.

21. $\dfrac{3}{4}$, $\dfrac{2}{3}$, $\dfrac{19}{24}$ _____   22. $\dfrac{19}{20}$, $\dfrac{9}{10}$, $\dfrac{3}{4}$ _____

23. $\dfrac{3}{5}$, $\dfrac{5}{6}$, $\dfrac{11}{15}$ _____   24. $\dfrac{9}{20}$, $\dfrac{1}{2}$, $\dfrac{3}{5}$ _____

25. $\dfrac{11}{15}$, $\dfrac{7}{10}$, $\dfrac{2}{3}$ _____   26. $\dfrac{5}{6}$, $\dfrac{13}{18}$, $\dfrac{7}{9}$ _____

27. $\dfrac{1}{6}$, $\dfrac{2}{9}$, $\dfrac{1}{4}$ _____   28. $\dfrac{4}{9}$, $\dfrac{5}{12}$, $\dfrac{7}{18}$ _____

29. $\dfrac{3}{8}$, $\dfrac{7}{20}$, $\dfrac{3}{10}$ _____   30. $\dfrac{4}{7}$, $\dfrac{2}{3}$, $\dfrac{9}{14}$ _____

Put in decreasing order.

31. $\dfrac{9}{25}$, $\dfrac{3}{5}$, $\dfrac{4}{10}$ _____   32. $\dfrac{7}{8}$, $\dfrac{7}{12}$, $\dfrac{2}{3}$ _____

33. $\dfrac{4}{15}$, $\dfrac{1}{5}$, $\dfrac{7}{30}$ _____   34. $\dfrac{4}{5}$, $\dfrac{5}{6}$, $\dfrac{23}{20}$ _____

35. $\dfrac{5}{9}$, $\dfrac{8}{18}$, $\dfrac{1}{2}$ _____   36. $\dfrac{17}{20}$, $\dfrac{3}{4}$, $\dfrac{5}{8}$ _____

37. $\dfrac{11}{15}$, $\dfrac{2}{3}$, $\dfrac{5}{6}$ _____   38. $\dfrac{5}{21}$, $\dfrac{2}{7}$, $\dfrac{1}{3}$ _____

39. $\dfrac{5}{18}$, $\dfrac{1}{6}$, $\dfrac{5}{36}$ _____   40. $\dfrac{10}{33}$, $\dfrac{3}{11}$, $\dfrac{7}{22}$ _____

Fractions and Mixed Numbers

Skill: Mixed Numbers and Improper Fractions

Name _____Tyla_____

Total Problems __48__
Problems Correct ____
Percent Correct _____

Write as mixed numbers.

1. $\frac{51}{4}$ $12\,3/4$ $4\sqrt{51}$

2. $\frac{77}{6}$

3. $\frac{59}{10}$

4. $\frac{29}{3}$

5. $\frac{73}{11}$

6. $\frac{85}{6}$

7. $\frac{47}{5}$

8. $\frac{68}{3}$

9. $\frac{29}{5}$

10. $\frac{13}{4}$

11. $\frac{58}{3}$

12. $\frac{75}{6}$

13. $\frac{104}{9}$

14. $\frac{83}{10}$

15. $\frac{67}{11}$

16. $\frac{91}{2}$

17. $\frac{22}{3}$

18. $\frac{37}{7}$

19. $\frac{141}{8}$

20. $\frac{47}{15}$

21. $\frac{334}{15}$

22. $\frac{79}{9}$

23. $\frac{267}{16}$

24. $\frac{143}{20}$

Write as improper fractions.

25. $7\frac{2}{5}$

26. $12\frac{1}{2}$

27. $4\frac{5}{7}$

28. $3\frac{7}{9}$

29. $11\frac{2}{3}$

30. $8\frac{5}{9}$

31. $15\frac{2}{7}$

32. $21\frac{6}{7}$

33. $6\frac{3}{4}$

34. $8\frac{1}{8}$

35. $21\frac{1}{10}$

36. $50\frac{1}{3}$

37. $9\frac{2}{5}$

38. $11\frac{2}{3}$

39. $25\frac{1}{6}$

40. $2\frac{14}{15}$

41. $3\frac{4}{5}$

42. $7\frac{6}{7}$

43. $4\frac{2}{9}$

44. $3\frac{20}{21}$

45. $12\frac{5}{9}$

46. $6\frac{4}{5}$

47. $8\frac{9}{11}$

48. $13\frac{11}{13}$

Math IF8771

©Instructional Fair, Inc.

Fractions

Name _____

Write as decimals.

Total Problems	**48**
Problems Correct	_____
Percent Correct	_____

1. $9 \frac{7}{20}$

2. $\frac{3}{10}$

3. $\frac{1}{25}$

4. $8 \frac{5}{8}$

5. $\frac{4}{5}$

6. $\frac{5}{16}$

7. $\frac{19}{25}$

8. $4 \frac{7}{8}$

9. $11 \frac{1}{2}$

10. $\frac{3}{8}$

11. $\frac{17}{20}$

12. $3 \frac{5}{32}$

13. $\frac{17}{40}$

14. $6 \frac{5}{64}$

15. $\frac{21}{80}$

16. $3 \frac{11}{25}$

17. $112 \frac{7}{8}$

18. $\frac{13}{16}$

19. $1 \frac{9}{20}$

20. $2 \frac{9}{10}$

21. $\frac{21}{32}$

22. $5 \frac{3}{40}$

23. $22 \frac{2}{5}$

24. $1 \frac{1}{80}$

Write as fractions.

25. 3.65

26. 0.028

27. 0.16

28. 4.625

29. 0.075

30. 2.88

31. 0.321

32. 5.76

33. 6.0375

34. 16.004

35. 0.242

36. 8.089

37. 0.64

38. 1.48

39. 3.008

40. 0.886

41. 1.005

42. 0.362

43. 0.0008

44. 5.55

45. 0.012

46. 0.95

47. 0.11

48. 15.14

Math IF8771

©Instructional Fair, Inc.

 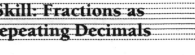

Name _____

Write as repeating decimals.

Total Problems	**46**	
Problems Correct	_____	
Percent Correct	_____	

1. $\dfrac{2}{11}$ 2. $\dfrac{5}{6}$ 3. $3\dfrac{8}{15}$

4. $1\dfrac{3}{22}$ 5. $\dfrac{5}{33}$ 6. $\dfrac{17}{44}$

7. $\dfrac{3}{7}$ 8. $\dfrac{23}{30}$ 9. $\dfrac{11}{24}$ 10. $2\dfrac{2}{27}$ 11. $13\dfrac{11}{18}$

12. $\dfrac{21}{27}$ 13. $\dfrac{2}{37}$ 14. $2\dfrac{5}{9}$ 15. $\dfrac{1}{48}$ 16. $6\dfrac{4}{11}$

17. $108\dfrac{2}{3}$ 18. $4\dfrac{1}{36}$ 19. $\dfrac{7}{22}$ 20. $2\dfrac{2}{15}$ 21. $\dfrac{11}{30}$

22. $4\dfrac{2}{3}$ 23. $14\dfrac{1}{6}$ 24. $5\dfrac{17}{33}$ 25. $\dfrac{1}{55}$ 26. $4\dfrac{19}{37}$

27. $1\dfrac{8}{9}$ 28. $\dfrac{7}{24}$ 29. $\dfrac{7}{45}$ 30. $\dfrac{17}{18}$ 31. $\dfrac{35}{36}$

32. $218\dfrac{5}{6}$ 33. $\dfrac{5}{66}$ 34. $1\dfrac{1}{99}$ 35. $54\dfrac{8}{11}$ 36. $\dfrac{5}{54}$

37. $\dfrac{28}{33}$ 38. $2\dfrac{9}{13}$ 39. $3\dfrac{11}{27}$ 40. $1\dfrac{7}{60}$ 41. $2\dfrac{7}{45}$

42. $12\dfrac{15}{22}$ 43. $2\dfrac{7}{30}$ 44. $\dfrac{5}{18}$ 45. $29\dfrac{2}{9}$ 46. $25\dfrac{1}{3}$

Math IF8771   ©Instructional Fair, Inc.

Name _____

Solve. Show your work on another piece of paper. Write your answers here.

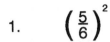

Total Problems __**40**__
Problems Correct ____
Percent Correct _____

1. $\left(\dfrac{5}{6}\right)^2$

2. $\left(\dfrac{7}{10}\right)^2$

3. $\left(\dfrac{3}{4}\right)^3$

4. $\left(\dfrac{9}{13}\right)^2$

5. $\left(\dfrac{1}{11}\right)^2$

6. $\left(\dfrac{4}{15}\right)^2$

7. $\left(\dfrac{1}{2}\right)^4$

8. $\left(\dfrac{1}{3}\right)^3$

9. $\left(\dfrac{5}{7}\right)^2$

10. $\left(\dfrac{2}{5}\right)^3$

11. $\left(\dfrac{3}{8}\right)^2$

12. $\left(\dfrac{7}{9}\right)^2$

13. $\left(\dfrac{3}{25}\right)^2$

14. $\left(\dfrac{1}{6}\right)^3$

15. $\left(\dfrac{5}{16}\right)^2$

16. $\left(\dfrac{4}{7}\right)^2$

17. $\left(\dfrac{7}{8}\right)^2$

18. $\left(\dfrac{5}{12}\right)^2$

19. $\left(\dfrac{4}{5}\right)^3$

20. $\left(\dfrac{11}{20}\right)^2$

21. $\left(\dfrac{3}{10}\right)^3$

22. $\left(\dfrac{1}{8}\right)^2$

23. $\left(\dfrac{3}{11}\right)^2$

24. $\left(\dfrac{1}{12}\right)^2$

25. $\left(\dfrac{1}{15}\right)^2$

26. $\left(\dfrac{5}{6}\right)^3$

27. $\left(\dfrac{3}{13}\right)^2$

28. $\left(\dfrac{1}{2}\right)^5$

29. $\left(\dfrac{1}{3}\right)^4$

30. $\left(\dfrac{3}{25}\right)^2$

31. $\left(\dfrac{7}{12}\right)^2$

32. $\left(\dfrac{3}{10}\right)^2$

33. $\left(\dfrac{3}{7}\right)^2$

34. $\left(\dfrac{1}{2}\right)^6$

35. $\left(\dfrac{2}{3}\right)^5$

36. $\left(\dfrac{5}{8}\right)^2$

37. $\left(\dfrac{1}{2} + \dfrac{1}{4}\right)^2$

38. $\left(\dfrac{1}{6} + \dfrac{1}{4}\right)^2$

39. $\left(\dfrac{2}{15} + \dfrac{1}{5}\right)^3$

40. $\left(\dfrac{1}{16} + \dfrac{3}{16}\right)^3$

Name _____

Add. Show your work on another piece of paper.
Write your answer here.

Total Problems __**40**__

Problems Correct ____

Percent Correct _____

1. $\frac{4}{7} + \frac{1}{3}$

2. $\frac{2}{5} + \frac{3}{4}$

3. $\frac{1}{2} + \frac{3}{10}$

4. $\frac{1}{4} + \frac{3}{8}$

5. $\frac{23}{30} + \frac{10}{15}$

6. $\frac{5}{6} + \frac{7}{9}$

7. $\frac{5}{12} + \frac{23}{24}$

8. $\frac{13}{15} + \frac{1}{3}$

9. $\frac{13}{20} + \frac{4}{5}$

10. $\frac{17}{18} + \frac{1}{6}$

11. $\frac{5}{14} + \frac{1}{2}$

12. $\frac{7}{10} + \frac{2}{3}$

13. $\frac{3}{4} + \frac{5}{6}$

14. $\frac{1}{6} + \frac{2}{9}$

15. $\frac{1}{4} + \frac{1}{5}$

16. $\frac{3}{4} + \frac{5}{6}$

17. $\frac{4}{5} + \frac{6}{12}$

18. $\frac{9}{10} + \frac{1}{3}$

19. $\frac{3}{7} + \frac{4}{5}$

20. $\frac{5}{8} + \frac{3}{4}$

21. $\frac{17}{20} + \frac{1}{4}$

22. $\frac{21}{25} + \frac{3}{5}$

23. $\frac{11}{15} + \frac{13}{25}$

24. $\frac{5}{11} + \frac{1}{2}$

25. $\frac{7}{9} + \frac{2}{5}$

26. $\frac{10}{11} + \frac{1}{3}$

27. $\frac{1}{8} + \frac{5}{6}$

28. $\frac{2}{3} + \frac{6}{7}$

29. $\frac{10}{15} + \frac{29}{30}$

30. $\frac{5}{18} + \frac{1}{3}$

31. $\frac{2}{5} + \frac{8}{15}$

32. $\frac{2}{9} + \frac{1}{7}$

33. $\frac{3}{11} + \frac{1}{3}$

34. $\frac{23}{25} + \frac{1}{4}$

35. $\frac{6}{24} + \frac{17}{18}$

36. $\frac{11}{16} + \frac{2}{3}$

37. $\frac{8}{15} + \frac{3}{4}$

38. $\frac{1}{18} + \frac{1}{12}$

39. $\frac{13}{15} + \frac{1}{2}$

40. $\frac{33}{40} + \frac{17}{20}$

Mixed Numbers

Name _____

Total Problems	**40**
Problems Correct	_____
Percent Correct	_____

Add. Show your work on another piece of paper.
Write your answers here.

1. $4 \frac{4}{5} + 3 \frac{2}{3}$ 2. $20 \frac{3}{8} + 14 \frac{1}{12}$

3. $16 \frac{17}{18} + 15 \frac{5}{6}$ 4. $25 \frac{13}{20} + 20 \frac{1}{4}$

5. $9 \frac{2}{7} + 6 \frac{1}{5}$ 6. $3 \frac{1}{5} + 2 \frac{3}{4}$ 7. $10 \frac{4}{7} + 11 \frac{5}{6}$ 8. $5 \frac{1}{2} + 3 \frac{2}{3}$

9. $7 \frac{5}{6} + 3 \frac{1}{3}$ 10. $51 \frac{3}{10} + 7 \frac{4}{5}$ 11. $8 \frac{4}{9} + 5 \frac{1}{6}$ 12. $33 \frac{3}{11} + 40 \frac{1}{2}$

13. $38 \frac{14}{15} + 19 \frac{1}{6}$ 14. $20 \frac{1}{25} + 1 \frac{4}{20}$ 15. $82 \frac{4}{9} + 3 \frac{1}{6}$ 16. $13 \frac{3}{4} + 4 \frac{14}{25}$

17. $16 \frac{3}{5} + 11 \frac{7}{8}$ 18. $16 \frac{3}{5} + 3 \frac{11}{15}$ 19. $9 \frac{2}{7} + 13 \frac{2}{3}$ 20. $10 \frac{3}{10} + 8 \frac{1}{8}$

21. $5 \frac{11}{15} + 3 \frac{9}{10}$ 22. $2 \frac{5}{12} + 4 \frac{11}{15}$ 23. $4 \frac{5}{8} + 3 \frac{1}{6}$ 24. $70 \frac{3}{5} + 5 \frac{2}{3}$

25. $16 \frac{3}{16} + 9 \frac{1}{4}$ 26. $25 \frac{3}{20} + 1 \frac{4}{15}$ 27. $26 \frac{7}{8} + 11 \frac{11}{12}$ 28. $41 \frac{1}{7} + 4 \frac{1}{9}$

29. $18 \frac{5}{8} + 23 \frac{2}{4}$ 30. $3 \frac{3}{14} + 9 \frac{6}{7}$ 31. $6 \frac{1}{4} + \frac{7}{9}$ 32. $17 \frac{3}{4} + 20 \frac{3}{10}$

33. $10 \frac{7}{10} + 8 \frac{5}{8}$ 34. $22 \frac{5}{22} + 13 \frac{19}{33}$ 35. $13 \frac{4}{5} + 3 \frac{11}{12}$ 36. $10 \frac{4}{5} + 9 \frac{5}{6}$

37. $7 \frac{1}{2} + 3 \frac{9}{13}$ 38. $60 \frac{20}{21} + 31 \frac{16}{18}$ 39. $38 \frac{1}{6} + \frac{23}{27}$ 40. $43 \frac{9}{11} + 16 \frac{1}{7}$

Math IF8771

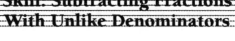

Subtract. Show your work on another piece of paper.
Write your answers here.

Total Problems __**40**__

Problems Correct _____

Percent Correct _____

1. $\frac{4}{5} - \frac{1}{3}$ 2. $\frac{20}{21} - \frac{2}{7}$

3. $\frac{10}{11} - \frac{1}{2}$ 4. $\frac{5}{6} - \frac{1}{12}$

5. $\frac{13}{15} - \frac{2}{3}$ 6. $\frac{19}{20} - \frac{1}{4}$ 7. $\frac{7}{10} - \frac{2}{25}$ 8. $\frac{4}{5} - \frac{3}{4}$

9. $\frac{11}{12} - \frac{1}{3}$ 10. $\frac{6}{7} - \frac{9}{14}$ 11. $\frac{9}{10} - \frac{1}{3}$ 12. $\frac{29}{30} - \frac{1}{6}$

13. $\frac{7}{8} - \frac{1}{4}$ 14. $\frac{17}{18} - \frac{1}{4}$ 15. $\frac{23}{25} - \frac{3}{50}$ 16. $\frac{21}{33} - \frac{5}{22}$

17. $\frac{4}{5} - \frac{7}{30}$ 18. $\frac{17}{30} - \frac{1}{10}$ 19. $\frac{21}{40} - \frac{1}{5}$ 20. $\frac{9}{10} - \frac{2}{7}$

21. $\frac{4}{9} - \frac{1}{4}$ 22. $\frac{7}{8} - \frac{5}{12}$ 23. $\frac{7}{10} - \frac{1}{3}$ 24. $\frac{1}{2} - \frac{3}{11}$

25. $\frac{18}{25} - \frac{3}{10}$ 26. $\frac{1}{4} - \frac{4}{25}$ 27. $\frac{15}{16} - \frac{2}{3}$ 28. $\frac{5}{6} - \frac{2}{7}$

29. $\frac{11}{15} - \frac{1}{2}$ 30. $\frac{6}{7} - \frac{2}{35}$ 31. $\frac{10}{11} - \frac{2}{3}$ 32. $\frac{46}{75} - \frac{2}{15}$

33. $\frac{1}{6} - \frac{1}{9}$ 34. $\frac{7}{12} - \frac{2}{9}$ 35. $\frac{13}{20} - \frac{3}{10}$ 36. $\frac{14}{35} - \frac{3}{10}$

37. $\frac{57}{80} - \frac{3}{40}$ 38. $\frac{1}{5} - \frac{1}{8}$ 39. $\frac{9}{10} - \frac{8}{45}$ 40. $\frac{19}{20} - \frac{17}{25}$

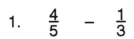
Math IF8771

Name _____

Total Problems __**40**__

Problems Correct _____

Percent Correct _____

Subtract. Show your work on another piece of paper.
Write your answers here.

1. $100 \frac{9}{10} - 3 \frac{1}{5}$

2. $29 \frac{1}{2} - 14 \frac{1}{3}$

3. $23 \frac{17}{20} - 4 \frac{7}{10}$

4. $18 \frac{3}{5} - 7 \frac{1}{4}$

5. $10 \frac{7}{9} - 3 \frac{1}{3}$

6. $20 \frac{5}{6} - 1 \frac{3}{8}$

7. $17 \frac{13}{15} - 10 \frac{4}{5}$

8. $43 \frac{3}{4} - 4 \frac{3}{10}$

9. $25 \frac{13}{16} - 11 \frac{1}{4}$

10. $66 \frac{5}{9} - 66 \frac{1}{6}$

11. $18 \frac{13}{15} - 6 \frac{3}{5}$

12. $3 \frac{19}{20} - 1 \frac{1}{10}$

13. $30 \frac{7}{9} - 5 \frac{1}{12}$

14. $125 \frac{8}{25} - 96 \frac{1}{5}$

15. $19 \frac{5}{12} - 11 \frac{1}{4}$

16. $29 \frac{23}{30} - 17 \frac{1}{15}$

17. $51 \frac{3}{4} - 26 \frac{1}{6}$

18. $96 \frac{19}{20} - 17 \frac{9}{10}$

19. $24 \frac{8}{15} - 19 \frac{1}{3}$

20. $18 \frac{15}{17} - 6 \frac{1}{2}$

21. $40 \frac{7}{8} - 1 \frac{1}{3}$

22. $22 \frac{14}{15} - 1 \frac{1}{2}$

23. $88 \frac{17}{18} - 14 \frac{5}{6}$

24. $11 \frac{7}{11} - 3 \frac{1}{2}$

25. $5 \frac{20}{33} - \frac{9}{22}$

26. $18 \frac{16}{25} - 4 \frac{7}{50}$

27. $11 \frac{11}{12} - 3 \frac{7}{8}$

28. $6 \frac{1}{2} - 2 \frac{2}{15}$

29. $38 \frac{4}{5} - 12 \frac{2}{7}$

30. $9 \frac{5}{6} - 2 \frac{2}{7}$

31. $26 \frac{7}{9} - 10 \frac{5}{12}$

32. $36 \frac{1}{3} - 4 \frac{2}{27}$

33. $7 \frac{41}{45} - 1 \frac{7}{10}$

34. $14 \frac{23}{25} - 6 \frac{13}{20}$

35. $42 \frac{23}{30} - 22 \frac{2}{5}$

36. $9 \frac{1}{4} - 3 \frac{1}{18}$

37. $19 \frac{9}{10} - 17 \frac{18}{25}$

38. $4 \frac{2}{3} - 3 \frac{3}{16}$

39. $3 \frac{7}{8} - 1 \frac{3}{5}$

40. $22 \frac{21}{25} - 7 \frac{3}{4}$

Name _____

Total Problems __**40**__

Problems Correct _____

Percent Correct _____

Subtract. Show your work on another piece of paper.
Write your answers here.

1. $33\frac{3}{16} - 13\frac{7}{16}$ 2. $16\frac{2}{7} - 3\frac{20}{21}$

3. $29\frac{1}{6} - 27\frac{2}{3}$ 4. $18\frac{1}{3} - 12\frac{3}{7}$

5. $17\frac{1}{8} - 12\frac{3}{8}$ 6. $11\frac{1}{8} - 3\frac{5}{12}$ 7. $10\frac{1}{9} - 9\frac{7}{45}$ 8. $76\frac{1}{6} - 19\frac{7}{9}$

9. $38\frac{1}{2} - 35\frac{13}{15}$ 10. $25\frac{5}{12} - 20\frac{8}{9}$ 11. $86\frac{3}{20} - 82\frac{7}{10}$ 12. $36\frac{9}{15} - 14\frac{11}{15}$

13. $2\frac{1}{25} - 1\frac{4}{5}$ 14. $88\frac{7}{20} - 62\frac{3}{5}$ 15. $100\frac{1}{4} - 99\frac{4}{5}$ 16. $15\frac{5}{18} - 4\frac{3}{4}$

17. $4\frac{3}{10} - 3\frac{6}{7}$ 18. $30\frac{9}{20} - 11\frac{17}{20}$ 19. $35\frac{1}{10} - 25\frac{2}{5}$ 20. $2\frac{3}{22} - 1\frac{7}{11}$

21. $16\frac{5}{28} - 2\frac{19}{28}$ 22. $20\frac{1}{4} - 13\frac{13}{15}$ 23. $19\frac{1}{4} - 2\frac{5}{6}$ 24. $51\frac{3}{10} - 22\frac{11}{10}$

25. $93\frac{1}{2} - 77\frac{4}{5}$ 26. $8\frac{3}{10} - 5\frac{12}{25}$ 27. $3\frac{1}{2} - 1\frac{8}{15}$ 28. $7\frac{1}{8} - 3\frac{2}{5}$

29. $55\frac{2}{9} - 13\frac{3}{4}$ 30. $11\frac{1}{6} - 8\frac{3}{10}$ 31. $14\frac{9}{50} - 11\frac{39}{50}$ 32. $48\frac{1}{3} - 45\frac{13}{18}$

33. $16\frac{5}{21} - 14\frac{6}{7}$ 34. $62\frac{23}{30} - 27\frac{29}{30}$ 35. $6\frac{1}{3} - 2\frac{7}{16}$ 36. $100\frac{8}{45} - 50\frac{9}{10}$

37. $80\frac{1}{75} - 6\frac{26}{75}$ 38. $2\frac{1}{4} - \frac{24}{25}$ 39. $40\frac{3}{20} - 39\frac{5}{6}$ 40. $13\frac{17}{33} - 10\frac{13}{22}$

Math IF8771

Mixed Numbers

Name _____

Estimate. Show your work on another piece of paper.
Write your answers here.

Total Problems __42__
Problems Correct _____
Percent Correct _____

1. $3\frac{5}{7} + 4\frac{6}{13}$

2. $18\frac{2}{3} - 15\frac{3}{5}$

3. $20\frac{1}{3} + 16\frac{3}{8}$

4. $20\frac{7}{10} - 18\frac{13}{20}$

5. $20\frac{9}{20} - 6\frac{5}{6}$

6. $12\frac{1}{2} + 13\frac{3}{5}$

7. $18\frac{2}{5} - 11\frac{7}{10}$

8. $6\frac{11}{15} + 3\frac{7}{18}$

9. $25\frac{7}{20} + 13\frac{11}{25}$

10. $49\frac{1}{3} - 47\frac{2}{7}$

11. $5\frac{4}{9} + 43\frac{11}{20}$

12. $20\frac{17}{30} - 20\frac{11}{15}$

13. $14\frac{7}{9} - 12\frac{3}{7}$

14. $10\frac{3}{10} + 5\frac{2}{5}$

15. $44\frac{9}{28} - 32\frac{16}{25}$

16. $29\frac{7}{12} + 14\frac{8}{15}$

17. $36\frac{3}{10} + 4\frac{9}{16}$

18. $50\frac{3}{8} - 16\frac{7}{9}$

19. $11\frac{7}{11} + 12\frac{9}{13}$

20. $41\frac{8}{15} - 39\frac{11}{16}$

21. $14\frac{3}{7} - 3\frac{9}{20}$

22. $15\frac{8}{19} + 93\frac{3}{4}$

23. $58\frac{1}{2} - 19\frac{7}{10}$

24. $6\frac{12}{25} + 18\frac{7}{18}$

25. $20\frac{17}{35} + 5\frac{17}{30}$

26. $5\frac{5}{9} - 1\frac{21}{50}$

27. $7\frac{11}{18} + 191\frac{7}{12}$

28. $31\frac{9}{17} - 11\frac{5}{13}$

29. $58\frac{4}{9} - 33\frac{5}{20}$

30. $40\frac{3}{5} + 31\frac{4}{9}$

31. $15\frac{11}{50} - 4\frac{11}{20}$

32. $5\frac{9}{16} + 16\frac{7}{16}$

33. $18\frac{34}{75} + 59\frac{13}{30}$

34. $22\frac{8}{15} - 18\frac{7}{16}$

35. $7\frac{9}{25} + 66\frac{3}{4}$

36. $14\frac{1}{2} - 9\frac{41}{100}$

37. $22\frac{7}{11} - 20\frac{2}{5}$

38. $14\frac{11}{30} + 6\frac{1}{2}$

39. $13\frac{15}{29} - 9\frac{17}{30}$

40. $80\frac{7}{17} + 61\frac{9}{22}$

41. $30\frac{3}{7} + 5\frac{3}{10}$

42. $50\frac{5}{12} - 10\frac{7}{18}$

Math IF8771

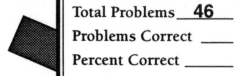

Name _____

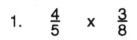

Multiply. Show your work on another piece of paper.
Write your answers here.

Total Problems	**46**
Problems Correct	_____
Percent Correct	_____

1. $\dfrac{4}{5}$ x $\dfrac{3}{8}$ 2. $\dfrac{4}{9}$ x $\dfrac{6}{7}$

3. $\dfrac{3}{5}$ x $\dfrac{1}{2}$ 4. $\dfrac{3}{10}$ x $\dfrac{1}{4}$ 5. $\dfrac{7}{20}$ x $\dfrac{5}{14}$ 6. $\dfrac{7}{10}$ x $\dfrac{2}{3}$

7. $\dfrac{3}{8}$ x $\dfrac{4}{21}$ 8. $\dfrac{1}{9}$ x $\dfrac{1}{2}$ 9. $\dfrac{1}{5}$ x $\dfrac{2}{7}$ 10. $\dfrac{8}{9}$ x $\dfrac{3}{4}$

11. $\dfrac{2}{3}$ x $\dfrac{3}{4}$ 12. $\dfrac{8}{15}$ x $\dfrac{5}{6}$ 13. $\dfrac{3}{4}$ x $\dfrac{5}{8}$ 14. $\dfrac{4}{5}$ x $\dfrac{11}{12}$

15. $\dfrac{3}{20}$ x $\dfrac{5}{12}$ 16. $\dfrac{3}{20}$ x $\dfrac{8}{9}$ 17. $\dfrac{49}{50}$ x $\dfrac{1}{4}$ 18. $\dfrac{5}{7}$ x $\dfrac{2}{3}$

19. $\dfrac{21}{25}$ x $\dfrac{2}{5}$ 20. $\dfrac{11}{16}$ x $\dfrac{4}{7}$ 21. $\dfrac{11}{14}$ x $\dfrac{2}{33}$ 22. $\dfrac{5}{8}$ x $\dfrac{16}{17}$

23. $\dfrac{5}{8}$ x $\dfrac{4}{5}$ 24. $\dfrac{7}{9}$ x $\dfrac{11}{20}$ 25. $\dfrac{7}{18}$ x $\dfrac{9}{10}$ 26. $\dfrac{2}{25}$ x $\dfrac{10}{11}$

27. $\dfrac{3}{11}$ x $\dfrac{3}{4}$ 28. $\dfrac{5}{12}$ x $\dfrac{8}{9}$ 29. $\dfrac{11}{30}$ x $\dfrac{15}{22}$ 30. $\dfrac{9}{10}$ x $\dfrac{3}{4}$

31. $\dfrac{21}{25}$ x $\dfrac{20}{21}$ 32. $\dfrac{7}{50}$ x $\dfrac{2}{9}$ 33. $\dfrac{3}{10}$ x $\dfrac{3}{10}$ 34. $\dfrac{14}{15}$ x $\dfrac{5}{7}$

35. $\dfrac{12}{13}$ x $\dfrac{13}{18}$ 36. $\dfrac{6}{7}$ x $\dfrac{9}{11}$ 37. $\dfrac{4}{5}$ x $\dfrac{5}{6}$ 38. $\dfrac{3}{20}$ x $\dfrac{10}{11}$

39. $\dfrac{13}{15}$ x $\dfrac{7}{8}$ 40. $\dfrac{7}{9}$ x $\dfrac{5}{14}$ 41. $\dfrac{2}{25}$ x $\dfrac{4}{5}$ 42. $\dfrac{17}{50}$ x $\dfrac{1}{2}$

43. $\dfrac{7}{20}$ x $\dfrac{5}{14}$ 44. $\dfrac{5}{6}$ x $\dfrac{8}{9}$ 45. $\dfrac{11}{16}$ x $\dfrac{9}{22}$ 46. $\dfrac{5}{7}$ x $\dfrac{7}{15}$

 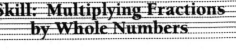
Multiply. Show your work on another piece of paper.
Write your answers here.

Total Problems __46__
Problems Correct ____
Percent Correct _____

1. $\dfrac{3}{10}$ x 25

2. $\dfrac{4}{5}$ x 35

3. $\dfrac{2}{3}$ x 15

4. $\dfrac{5}{6}$ x 14

5. $\dfrac{7}{8}$ x 26

6. $\dfrac{9}{11}$ x 44

7. $\dfrac{5}{12}$ x 34

8. $\dfrac{3}{7}$ x 63

9. $\dfrac{16}{25}$ x 55

10. $\dfrac{5}{9}$ x 20

11. $\dfrac{7}{18}$ x 12

12. $\dfrac{9}{14}$ x 3

13. $\dfrac{5}{14}$ x 21

14. $\dfrac{9}{10}$ x 45

15. $\dfrac{4}{15}$ x 40

16. $\dfrac{2}{11}$ x 13

17. $\dfrac{14}{35}$ x 5

18. $\dfrac{17}{20}$ x 8

19. $\dfrac{4}{5}$ x 7

20. $\dfrac{1}{6}$ x 32

21. $\dfrac{9}{16}$ x 36

22. $\dfrac{5}{21}$ x 14

23. $\dfrac{11}{18}$ x 12

24. $\dfrac{7}{8}$ x 18

25. $\dfrac{7}{19}$ x 3

26. $\dfrac{9}{20}$ x 15

27. $\dfrac{11}{18}$ x 7

28. $\dfrac{1}{12}$ x 30

29. $\dfrac{2}{15}$ x 45

30. $\dfrac{5}{6}$ x 21

31. $\dfrac{4}{7}$ x 20

32. $\dfrac{3}{11}$ x 44

33. $\dfrac{2}{3}$ x 23

34. $\dfrac{9}{10}$ x 55

35. $\dfrac{3}{8}$ x 28

36. $\dfrac{1}{4}$ x 101

37. $\dfrac{7}{30}$ x 2

38. $\dfrac{11}{14}$ x 21

39. $\dfrac{5}{6}$ x 14

40. $\dfrac{2}{5}$ x 28

41. $\dfrac{13}{22}$ x 33

42. $\dfrac{2}{3}$ x 65

43. $\dfrac{3}{8}$ x 27

44. $\dfrac{4}{9}$ x 39

45. $\dfrac{13}{14}$ x 5

46. $\dfrac{15}{26}$ x 4

Math IF8771

©Instructional Fair, Inc.

Mixed Numbers

Name _____

Total Problems __40__

Problems Correct _____

Percent Correct _____

Multiply. Show your work on another piece of paper.
Write your answers here.

1. $3\frac{3}{4}$ x $5\frac{1}{3}$ 2. $2\frac{6}{7}$ x $1\frac{4}{15}$

3. $1\frac{7}{10}$ x $5\frac{5}{6}$ 4. $1\frac{3}{10}$ x $1\frac{1}{20}$

5. $2\frac{5}{6}$ x $1\frac{2}{9}$ 6. $13\frac{1}{2}$ x $1\frac{5}{12}$ 7. $3\frac{2}{3}$ x $2\frac{4}{5}$ 8. $1\frac{7}{18}$ x $1\frac{1}{15}$

9. $2\frac{16}{25}$ x $3\frac{2}{11}$ 10. $11\frac{3}{7}$ x $2\frac{1}{5}$ 11. $5\frac{5}{9}$ x $2\frac{1}{20}$ 12. $1\frac{7}{11}$ x $2\frac{1}{2}$

13. $5\frac{3}{4}$ x $3\frac{3}{5}$ 14. $3\frac{1}{2}$ x $2\frac{1}{7}$ 15. $1\frac{13}{50}$ x $1\frac{11}{14}$ 16. $1\frac{13}{20}$ x $5\frac{5}{9}$

17. $2\frac{3}{16}$ x $1\frac{5}{14}$ 18. $2\frac{4}{7}$ x $1\frac{5}{16}$ 19. $7\frac{1}{2}$ x $1\frac{23}{25}$ 20. $1\frac{5}{13}$ x $2\frac{1}{4}$

21. $2\frac{2}{15}$ x $2\frac{5}{8}$ 22. $2\frac{1}{4}$ x $4\frac{1}{3}$ 23. $1\frac{1}{6}$ x $4\frac{4}{5}$ 24. $2\frac{8}{21}$ x $4\frac{9}{10}$

25. $1\frac{4}{5}$ x $13\frac{1}{3}$ 26. $2\frac{2}{5}$ x $10\frac{1}{2}$ 27. $2\frac{8}{11}$ x $2\frac{5}{14}$ 28. $2\frac{2}{3}$ x $7\frac{1}{2}$

29. $4\frac{1}{6}$ x $4\frac{1}{20}$ 30. $9\frac{1}{3}$ x $4\frac{2}{7}$ 31. $1\frac{4}{31}$ x $20\frac{2}{3}$ 32. $1\frac{1}{5}$ x $1\frac{17}{18}$

33. $1\frac{1}{12}$ x $5\frac{5}{7}$ 34. $2\frac{8}{9}$ x $5\frac{1}{4}$ 35. $3\frac{3}{4}$ x $7\frac{1}{5}$ 36. $2\frac{14}{25}$ x $4\frac{3}{8}$

37. $1\frac{1}{6}$ x $4\frac{1}{5}$ 38. $2\frac{13}{25}$ x $4\frac{2}{7}$ 39. $11\frac{1}{13}$ x $14\frac{1}{12}$ 40. $2\frac{2}{11}$ x $2\frac{14}{15}$

Math IF8771

Name _____

Total Problems __**40**__
Problems Correct ____
Percent Correct _____

Divide. Show your work on another piece of paper.
Write your answers here.

1. $\frac{8}{9} \div \frac{14}{15}$ 2. $\frac{3}{10} \div \frac{12}{25}$

3. $\frac{7}{50} \div \frac{21}{35}$ 4. $\frac{11}{18} \div \frac{5}{12}$

5. $\frac{4}{7} \div \frac{8}{9}$ 6. $\frac{9}{11} \div \frac{2}{3}$ 7. $\frac{13}{14} \div \frac{1}{2}$ 8. $\frac{11}{12} \div \frac{5}{8}$

9. $\frac{14}{15} \div \frac{3}{20}$ 10. $\frac{3}{4} \div \frac{13}{16}$ 11. $\frac{18}{33} \div \frac{15}{22}$ 12. $\frac{5}{6} \div \frac{2}{7}$

13. $\frac{3}{10} \div \frac{4}{11}$ 14. $\frac{5}{12} \div \frac{3}{5}$ 15. $\frac{17}{40} \div \frac{1}{4}$ 16. $\frac{4}{5} \div \frac{3}{35}$

17. $\frac{2}{3} \div \frac{5}{8}$ 18. $\frac{8}{9} \div \frac{11}{12}$ 19. $\frac{9}{10} \div \frac{7}{9}$ 20. $\frac{3}{7} \div \frac{12}{13}$

21. $\frac{17}{20} \div \frac{4}{5}$ 22. $\frac{15}{16} \div \frac{5}{14}$ 23. $\frac{7}{12} \div \frac{2}{11}$ 24. $\frac{2}{9} \div \frac{4}{11}$

25. $\frac{5}{16} \div \frac{5}{8}$ 26. $\frac{7}{9} \div \frac{2}{3}$ 27. $\frac{9}{10} \div \frac{15}{16}$ 28. $\frac{5}{8} \div \frac{5}{16}$

29. $\frac{14}{15} \div \frac{4}{5}$ 30. $\frac{22}{35} \div \frac{2}{35}$ 31. $\frac{2}{7} \div \frac{16}{21}$ 32. $\frac{21}{40} \div \frac{7}{24}$

33. $\frac{7}{18} \div \frac{5}{16}$ 34. $\frac{5}{8} \div \frac{4}{5}$ 35. $\frac{8}{15} \div \frac{12}{25}$ 36. $\frac{11}{12} \div \frac{1}{6}$

37. $\frac{25}{38} \div \frac{15}{32}$ 38. $\frac{3}{10} \div \frac{4}{5}$ 39. $\frac{18}{25} \div \frac{3}{10}$ 40. $\frac{22}{81} \div \frac{8}{9}$

Name _____

Divide. Show your work on another piece of paper.
Write your answers here.

Total Problems __**40**__
Problems Correct ____
Percent Correct _____

1. $4\frac{2}{7} \div 5\frac{1}{4}$ 2. $3\frac{1}{5} \div 1\frac{7}{15}$

3. $1\frac{13}{20} \div 6\frac{7}{8}$ 4. $12\frac{1}{2} \div 13\frac{1}{3}$

5. $1\frac{3}{16} \div 1\frac{1}{6}$ 6. $1\frac{19}{25} \div 1\frac{1}{10}$ 7. $2\frac{1}{12} \div 2\frac{2}{9}$ 8. $3\frac{6}{7} \div 7\frac{1}{5}$

9. $2\frac{14}{15} \div 4\frac{7}{12}$ 10. $3\frac{1}{8} \div 16\frac{2}{3}$ 11. $4\frac{4}{9} \div 6\frac{2}{3}$ 12. $5\frac{1}{5} \div 7\frac{3}{5}$

13. $4\frac{1}{6} \div 18\frac{1}{3}$ 14. $7\frac{1}{3} \div 1\frac{5}{6}$ 15. $3\frac{2}{3} \div 1\frac{1}{4}$ 16. $22\frac{1}{2} \div 4\frac{4}{9}$

17. $2\frac{1}{7} \div 8\frac{4}{7}$ 18. $11\frac{3}{5} \div 3\frac{1}{15}$ 19. $15\frac{3}{4} \div 5\frac{1}{7}$ 20. $6\frac{2}{9} \div 2\frac{1}{12}$

21. $9\frac{1}{6} \div 8\frac{1}{4}$ 22. $4\frac{7}{12} \div 2\frac{14}{15}$ 23. $4\frac{2}{3} \div 1\frac{7}{9}$ 24. $9\frac{3}{5} \div 4\frac{4}{15}$

25. $2\frac{11}{12} \div 7\frac{7}{8}$ 26. $7\frac{7}{10} \div 8\frac{1}{6}$ 27. $4\frac{6}{7} \div 1\frac{19}{21}$ 28. $5\frac{5}{11} \div 6\frac{2}{3}$

29. $3\frac{3}{5} \div 1\frac{3}{25}$ 30. $5\frac{1}{7} \div 5\frac{1}{3}$ 31. $23\frac{1}{3} \div 5\frac{5}{9}$ 32. $8\frac{4}{5} \div 4\frac{1}{8}$

33. $2\frac{11}{20} \div 3\frac{2}{5}$ 34. $28\frac{2}{3} \div 2\frac{14}{15}$ 35. $1\frac{11}{14} \div 1\frac{19}{21}$ 36. $5\frac{5}{6} \div 6\frac{1}{8}$

37. $3\frac{7}{8} \div 1\frac{2}{3}$ 38. $1\frac{37}{40} \div 1\frac{7}{15}$ 39. $3\frac{9}{10} \div 2\frac{1}{6}$ 40. $1\frac{3}{7} \div 18\frac{1}{3}$

Math IF8771

Fractions and Mixed Numbers

Skill: Dividing Whole Numbers by Fractions and Mixed Numbers

Name _____

Total Problems **40**

Problems Correct _____

Percent Correct _____

Divide. Show your work on another piece of paper. Write your answers here.

1. $18 \div 2\frac{1}{4}$ 2. $25 \div \frac{5}{13}$

3. $2 \div 1\frac{3}{5}$ 4. $44 \div \frac{11}{12}$

5. $21 \div 4\frac{2}{3}$ 6. $12 \div 4\frac{4}{5}$ 7. $10 \div 2\frac{6}{7}$ 8. $55 \div 6\frac{2}{3}$

9. $49 \div \frac{21}{45}$ 10. $13 \div 8\frac{2}{3}$ 11. $9 \div \frac{3}{4}$ 12. $32 \div \frac{1}{2}$

13. $18 \div 5\frac{1}{4}$ 14. $26 \div 3\frac{1}{4}$ 15. $51 \div 2\frac{5}{8}$ 16. $15 \div \frac{6}{11}$

17. $32 \div 2\frac{4}{5}$ 18. $27 \div \frac{3}{11}$ 19. $60 \div 2\frac{10}{13}$ 20. $6 \div \frac{5}{8}$

21. $75 \div 3\frac{3}{11}$ 22. $16 \div 1\frac{1}{5}$ 23. $21 \div \frac{7}{9}$ 24. $33 \div 4\frac{2}{5}$

25. $52 \div 2\frac{8}{9}$ 26. $24 \div \frac{9}{10}$ 27. $40 \div 5\frac{1}{3}$ 28. $22 \div \frac{7}{10}$

29. $64 \div 4\frac{4}{11}$ 30. $39 \div 5\frac{1}{4}$ 31. $60 \div 2\frac{1}{4}$ 32. $54 \div \frac{2}{9}$

33. $28 \div 1\frac{5}{13}$ 34. $64 \div 7\frac{3}{5}$ 35. $70 \div 4\frac{1}{6}$ 36. $12 \div \frac{7}{8}$

37. $5 \div 3\frac{1}{10}$ 38. $40 \div 3\frac{1}{3}$ 39. $81 \div 3\frac{3}{5}$ 40. $52 \div 9\frac{3}{4}$

Math IF8771   ©Instructional Fair, Inc.

Estimate. Show your work on another piece of paper.
Write your answers here.

Total Problems __42__

Problems Correct _____

Percent Correct _____

1. $47\frac{3}{5} \div 5\frac{5}{8}$ 2. $7\frac{7}{13} \times 4\frac{4}{7}$

3. $26\frac{7}{10} \div 9\frac{1}{3}$ 4. $6\frac{2}{5} \times 6\frac{5}{9}$ 5. $18\frac{5}{11} \div 1\frac{4}{7}$ 6. $10\frac{9}{16} \times 5\frac{7}{15}$

7. $41\frac{8}{15} \div 13\frac{7}{10}$ 8. $1\frac{7}{10} \times 7\frac{7}{12}$ 9. $12\frac{1}{6} \div 2\frac{4}{7}$ 10. $3\frac{9}{20} \times 9\frac{12}{25}$

11. $71\frac{8}{15} \div 7\frac{11}{20}$ 12. $6\frac{6}{11} \times 6\frac{3}{4}$ 13. $90\frac{5}{22} \div 2\frac{3}{4}$ 14. $21\frac{4}{7} \times 4\frac{1}{6}$

15. $36\frac{7}{16} \div 9\frac{10}{21}$ 16. $3\frac{2}{5} \times 25\frac{5}{12}$ 17. $76\frac{13}{25} \div 7\frac{10}{21}$ 18. $9\frac{23}{45} \times 9\frac{21}{50}$

19. $79\frac{19}{30} \div 9\frac{15}{28}$ 20. $8\frac{8}{15} \times 6\frac{5}{13}$ 21. $42\frac{3}{8} \div 6\frac{3}{5}$ 22. $20\frac{4}{9} \times 4\frac{11}{18}$

23. $31\frac{5}{9} \div 16\frac{3}{10}$ 24. $1\frac{5}{8} \times 10\frac{7}{10}$ 25. $44\frac{6}{11} \div 2\frac{7}{10}$ 26. $24\frac{7}{9} \times 2\frac{1}{3}$

27. $55\frac{17}{30} \div 8\frac{7}{20}$ 28. $14\frac{7}{12} \times 3\frac{8}{15}$ 29. $36\frac{5}{12} \div 6\frac{5}{14}$ 30. $13\frac{7}{20} \times 3\frac{9}{20}$

31. $49\frac{7}{15} \div 6\frac{11}{18}$ 32. $2\frac{11}{25} \times 13\frac{11}{14}$ 33. $60\frac{2}{21} \div 6\frac{13}{30}$ 34. $9\frac{21}{40} \times 9\frac{18}{35}$

35. $48\frac{9}{19} \div 7\frac{11}{17}$ 36. $9\frac{7}{30} \times 8\frac{7}{20}$ 37. $61\frac{7}{10} \div 2\frac{2}{5}$ 38. $5\frac{33}{50} \times 3\frac{5}{6}$

39. $99\frac{4}{7} \div 19\frac{6}{11}$ 40. $5\frac{2}{5} \times 7\frac{4}{9}$ 41. $25\frac{1}{6} \div 4\frac{8}{9}$ 42. $19\frac{3}{5} \times 3\frac{3}{10}$

Math IF8771

Decide if the two ratios are equal. If you check the "equal" box, finish the rest of the chart by writing the ratios in lowest terms three different ways. Follow the example.

Total Problems __**15**__

Problems Correct _____

Percent Correct _____

	Ratios		Are ratios equal?	3 ways to write ratios		
1.	$\frac{12}{28}$	$\frac{21}{49}$	✔	$\frac{3}{7}$	3 : 7	0.$\overline{428571}$
2.	$\frac{49}{70}$	$\frac{35}{50}$	✓	$\frac{7}{10}$	7 : 10	
3.	$\frac{6}{24}$	$\frac{5}{20}$				
4.	$\frac{45}{55}$	$\frac{18}{22}$				
5.	$\frac{2}{12}$	$\frac{9}{54}$				
6.	$\frac{85}{136}$	$\frac{15}{24}$				
7.	$\frac{12}{45}$	$\frac{28}{105}$				
8.	$\frac{18}{84}$	$\frac{22}{98}$				
9.	$\frac{85}{125}$	$\frac{51}{75}$				
10.	$\frac{42}{63}$	$\frac{30}{45}$				
11.	$\frac{39}{59}$	$\frac{52}{120}$				
12.	$\frac{52}{80}$	$\frac{78}{120}$				
13.	$\frac{36}{45}$	$\frac{28}{35}$				
14.	$\frac{21}{48}$	$\frac{49}{112}$				
15.	$\frac{32}{72}$	$\frac{12}{27}$				

Math IF8771

What is the unit rate? Show your work on another piece of paper. Write your answers here.

Total Problems __40__

Problems Correct _____

Percent Correct _____

1. 84 m in 6h _____

2. $92 for 23 books _____

3. 4500 km in 9 days _____

4. 198 in. in 9 days _____

5. $294 for 7 dresses _____

6. 36 dogs for 12 owners _____

7. 68 m in 4 s _____

8. 418 km in 38 days _____

9. 40 in. in 8 h _____

10. $1,200 for 4 plane tickets _____

11. 171 cm in 19 s _____

12. 468 m in 18 h _____

13. 63 m in 3 min _____

14. 90 toys for 6 babies _____

15. 12 exams in 6 days _____

16. 640 m in 80 days _____

17. $78 for 13 sandwiches _____

18. 98 km in 7 h _____

19. 64 travelers for 16 cars _____

20. $625 for 5 coats _____

21. 175 m in 7 h _____

22. 104 notebooks for 26 students _____

23. 48 km in 4 d _____

24. 162 km in 9 h _____

25. 112 candy bars for 14 students _____

26. $78 for 6 CD's _____

27. 159 in. in 53 s _____

28. 84 km in 12 h _____

29. 132 ft in 6 min _____

30. 288 marbles for 48 children _____

31. $38 for 19 hot dogs _____

32. 48 in. in 16 s _____

33. 72 km in 8 h _____

34. $49 for 7 pizzas _____

35. 66 m in 6 days _____

36. 361 km in 19 h _____

37. $26,000 for 2 cars _____

38. 21 m in 3 s _____

39. 42 classes in 7 days _____

40. $1,360 for 4 TV sets _____

Math IF8771

Proportions

Name _____

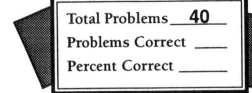

Total Problems __**40**__

Problems Correct _____

Percent Correct _____

Solve the proportions. Show your work on another piece of paper. Write your answers here.

1. $\dfrac{15}{n} = \dfrac{24}{128}$ 2. $\dfrac{n}{200} = \dfrac{28}{80}$

3. $\dfrac{15}{110} = \dfrac{24}{n}$ 4. $\dfrac{4}{5} = \dfrac{n}{20}$

5. $\dfrac{54}{63} = \dfrac{n}{49}$ 6. $\dfrac{5}{n} = \dfrac{2}{38}$ 7. $\dfrac{n}{12} = \dfrac{45}{108}$ 8. $\dfrac{42}{n} = \dfrac{8}{12}$

9. $\dfrac{8}{30} = \dfrac{28}{n}$ 10. $\dfrac{n}{108} = \dfrac{20}{72}$ 11. $\dfrac{7}{13} = \dfrac{n}{78}$ 12. $\dfrac{56}{n} = \dfrac{7}{31}$

13. $\dfrac{n}{22} = \dfrac{63}{154}$ 14. $\dfrac{120}{n} = \dfrac{40}{55}$ 15. $\dfrac{95}{110} = \dfrac{n}{22}$ 16. $\dfrac{33}{44} = \dfrac{132}{n}$

17. $\dfrac{9}{27} = \dfrac{n}{21}$ 18. $\dfrac{10}{22} = \dfrac{30}{n}$ 19. $\dfrac{n}{120} = \dfrac{15}{100}$ 20. $\dfrac{68}{n} = \dfrac{102}{108}$

21. $\dfrac{3}{n} = \dfrac{12}{76}$ 22. $\dfrac{15}{18} = \dfrac{n}{12}$ 23. $\dfrac{44}{77} = \dfrac{24}{n}$ 24. $\dfrac{n}{70} = \dfrac{36}{40}$

25. $\dfrac{84}{96} = \dfrac{35}{n}$ 26. $\dfrac{n}{27} = \dfrac{14}{63}$ 27. $\dfrac{32}{n} = \dfrac{28}{35}$ 28. $\dfrac{11}{12} = \dfrac{n}{60}$

29. $\dfrac{17}{20} = \dfrac{n}{120}$ 30. $\dfrac{30}{54} = \dfrac{20}{n}$ 31. $\dfrac{n}{24} = \dfrac{56}{64}$ 32. $\dfrac{11}{n} = \dfrac{44}{60}$

33. $\dfrac{18}{150} = \dfrac{15}{n}$ 34. $\dfrac{45}{72} = \dfrac{n}{56}$ 35. $\dfrac{77}{n} = \dfrac{42}{54}$ 36. $\dfrac{n}{56} = \dfrac{42}{49}$

37. $\dfrac{n}{41} = \dfrac{9}{123}$ 38. $\dfrac{35}{n} = \dfrac{5}{28}$ 39. $\dfrac{12}{52} = \dfrac{n}{39}$ 40. $\dfrac{40}{70} = \dfrac{32}{n}$

Math IF8771

Name _____

Write as a proportion and solve. Show your work on another piece of paper. Write your answers here.

Total Problems	**40**
Problems Correct	____
Percent Correct	____

1. What number is 17% of 200? _____

2. 16 is what percent of 80? _____

3. 25% of what number is 35? _____

4. What percent of 90 is 27? _____

5. 112 is what percent of 400? _____

6. What number is 140% of 280? _____

7. 12% of what number is 66? _____

8. What percent of 30 is 54? _____

9. What number is 15% of 40? _____

10. What percent of 90 is 72? _____

11. 495 is what percent of 500? _____

12. 125% of what number is 85? _____

13. 70% of what number is 42? _____

14. What number is 20% of 95? _____

15. 216 is what percent of 600? _____

16. What number is 230% of 40? _____

17. What percent of 900 is 792? _____

18. 27 is what percent of 90? _____

19. What number is 175% of 220? _____

20. 18% of what number is 117? _____

21. 42 is what percent of 120? _____

22. What percent of 260 is 247? _____

23. What percent of 315 is 63? _____

24. 40% of what number is 16? _____

25. 16 is what percent of 50? _____

26. What number is 65% of 80? _____

27. 325% of what number is 143? _____

28. What percent of 225 is 207? _____

29. 136 is what percent of 80? _____

30. What percent is 55% of 420? _____

31. What percent of 30 is 21? _____

32. 60% of what number is 72? _____

33. What number is 35% of 440? _____

34. 121 is what percent of 550? _____

35. What percent of 150 is 114? _____

36. 130% of what number is 78? _____

37. 12 is what percent of 80? _____

38. What number is 85% of 60? _____

39. 45% of what number is 54? _____

40. What percent of 165 is 198? _____

Math IF8771

Name _____

Total Problems __**40**__

Problems Correct ____

Percent Correct _____

Write the following ratios as percents. Show your work on another piece of paper. Write your answers here.

1. $\frac{2}{5}$

2. 15 : 16

3. $\frac{12}{25}$

4. 0.125

5. 17 : 20

6. $\frac{9}{10}$

7. 0.525

8. $\frac{3}{4}$

9. $\frac{11}{32}$

10. 7 : 50

11. 5 : 8

12. 0.8

13. 23 : 250

14. $\frac{137}{200}$

15. $\frac{17}{25}$

16. 17 : 80

17. 0.6875

18. 0.3

19. $\frac{7}{8}$

20. 9 : 40

21. $\frac{3}{5}$

22. 5 : 32

23. $\frac{333}{500}$

24. 3 : 8

25. 0.04

26. $\frac{1}{5}$

27. 33 : 40

28. $\frac{121}{250}$

29. 7 : 16

30. $\frac{19}{20}$

31. $\frac{23}{50}$

32. 0.748

33. 0.5625

34. 111 : 400

35. $\frac{21}{80}$

36. $\frac{8}{25}$

37. 0.7

38. $\frac{211}{500}$

39. 11 : 200

40. $\frac{27}{40}$

Math IF8771

Decimals, Percents and Fractions

Name _____

Total Problems __**40**__

Problems Correct _____

Percent Correct _____

Complete the charts by converting percents, decimals and fractions.

	Percent	Fraction	Decimal
1.		$1\frac{7}{8}$	
2.			0.18
3.	2%		
4.		$\frac{17}{20}$	
5.			1.2
6.	135%		
7.			0.204
8.		$\frac{89}{200}$	
9.			0.33
10.	77%		
11.	40%		
12.		$\frac{17}{40}$	
13.	5.5%		
14.			1.95
15.		$3\frac{47}{50}$	
16.	264%		
17.			0.88
18.		$1\frac{3}{10}$	
19.	12%		
20.			0.7175

	Percent	Fraction	Decimal
21.	19%		
22.		$\frac{7}{8}$	
23.		$1\frac{4}{5}$	
24.	128%		
25.		$\frac{1}{20}$	
26.			0.135
27.	86.5%		
28.			2.9
29.		$3\frac{13}{25}$	
30.			0.8125
31.	72%		
32.			1.44
33.		$\frac{61}{100}$	
34.			0.132
35.	27.6%		
36.		$\frac{151}{200}$	
37.			0.45
38.	87.5%		
39.		$\frac{111}{400}$	
40.			0.858

72

Name _____

Write as a percent rounded to the nearest:

Total Problems __**40**__
Problems Correct _____
Percent Correct _____

one of a percent

1. $\frac{4}{9}$ 2. $\frac{9}{16}$ 3. $\frac{3}{40}$

4. $\frac{2}{3}$ 5. $\frac{7}{8}$ 6. $\frac{17}{30}$ 7. $\frac{8}{15}$ 8. $\frac{8}{11}$

9. $\frac{27}{32}$ 10. $\frac{17}{80}$

tenth of a percent

11. $\frac{8}{9}$ 12. $\frac{22}{45}$ 13. $\frac{4}{7}$ 14. $\frac{5}{12}$ 15. $\frac{77}{80}$

16. $\frac{13}{30}$ 17. $\frac{111}{160}$ 18. $\frac{5}{16}$ 19. $\frac{19}{75}$ 20. $\frac{17}{18}$

hundredth of a percent

21. $\frac{7}{15}$ 22. $\frac{3}{11}$ 23. $\frac{5}{18}$ 24. $\frac{81}{160}$ 25. $\frac{6}{13}$

26. $\frac{21}{44}$ 27. $\frac{2}{9}$ 28. $\frac{97}{120}$ 29. $\frac{8}{21}$ 30. $\frac{6}{7}$

thousandth of a percent

31. $\frac{5}{19}$ 32. $\frac{13}{28}$ 33. $\frac{5}{26}$ 34. $\frac{13}{24}$ 35. $\frac{4}{21}$

36. $\frac{11}{12}$ 37. $\frac{2}{7}$ 38. $\frac{2}{13}$ 39. $\frac{1}{3}$ 40. $\frac{10}{11}$

Math IF8771

Write the percents with a decimal point instead of a fractional part, rounding to the nearest ten-thousandth of a percent when necessary. Then, write this new percent as a decimal.

Total Problems __48__

Problems Correct ____

Percent Correct _____

1. $1\frac{1}{2}\%$

2. $3\frac{3}{8}\%$

3. $18\frac{3}{4}\%$

4. $20\frac{17}{20}\%$

5. $9\frac{1}{5}\%$

6. $14\frac{2}{3}\%$

7. $66\frac{5}{6}\%$

8. $40\frac{5}{12}\%$

9. $55\frac{3}{7}\%$

10. $10\frac{11}{25}\%$

11. $180\frac{3}{10}\%$

12. $75\frac{39}{50}\%$

13. $14\frac{4}{5}\%$

14. $90\frac{8}{9}\%$

15. $33\frac{7}{15}\%$

16. $23\frac{1}{4}\%$

17. $120\frac{5}{8}\%$

18. $220\frac{11}{20}\%$

19. $8\frac{7}{18}\%$

20. $2\frac{9}{10}\%$

21. $11\frac{1}{12}\%$

22. $28\frac{9}{30}\%$

23. $12\frac{9}{10}\%$

24. $18\frac{7}{8}\%$

25. $110\frac{7}{12}\%$

26. $12\frac{1}{4}\%$

27. $450\frac{24}{25}\%$

28. $90\frac{1}{3}\%$

29. $72\frac{7}{12}\%$

30. $34\frac{3}{16}\%$

31. $17\frac{3}{5}\%$

32. $22\frac{7}{9}\%$

33. $8\frac{1}{8}\%$

34. $200\frac{1}{2}\%$

35. $50\frac{9}{25}\%$

36. $5\frac{1}{10}\%$

37. $88\frac{1}{2}\%$

38. $11\frac{1}{6}\%$

39. $99\frac{98}{99}\%$

40. $105\frac{1}{7}\%$

41. $45\frac{11}{25}\%$

42. $70\frac{11}{15}\%$

43. $89\frac{2}{17}\%$

44. $125\frac{2}{5}\%$

45. $65\frac{3}{20}\%$

46. $19\frac{11}{12}\%$

47. $62\frac{13}{16}\%$

48. $95\frac{7}{10}\%$

Math IF8771

©Instructional Fair, Inc.

Name _____

Solve. Show your work on another piece of paper.
Write your answers here.

Total Problems __**40**__
Problems Correct _____
Percent Correct _____

1. How much is 19% of 45? _____

2. 88% of 70 is how much? _____

3. 3.6% of 40 is how much? _____

4. How much is 125% of 72? _____

5. How much is 58% of 95? _____

6. 220% of 8 is how much? _____

7. 110% of 39 is how much? _____

8. How much is 12% of 130? _____

9. How much is 90% of 70? _____

10. 0.5% of 400 is how much? _____

11. 45% of 80 is how much? _____

12. How much is 60% of 30? _____

13. How much is 190% of 33? _____

14. 70% of 90 is how much? _____

15. 24% of 55 is how much? _____

16. How much is 215% of 420? _____

17. How much is 30% of 70? _____

18. 55% of 80 is how much? _____

19. 90% of 130 is how much? _____

20. How much is 4% of 16? _____

21. How much is 22% of 66? _____

22. 16% of 85 is how much? _____

23. 120% of 90 is how much? _____

24. How much is 35% of 44? _____

25. How much is 0.2% of 470? _____

26. 6% of 20 is how much? _____

27. 170% of 3 is how much? _____

28. How much is 2.5% of 140? _____

29. How much is 80% of 210? _____

30. 22% of 20 is how much? _____

31. 35% of 17 is how much? _____

32. How much is 14.8% of 50? _____

33. How much is 60% of 80? _____

34. 92% of 300 is how much? _____

35. 290% of 5 is how much? _____

36. How much is 105% of 25? _____

37. How much is 40% of 60? _____

38. 35.8% of 190 is how much? _____

39. 9% of 200 is how much? _____

40. How much is 150% of 150? _____

Math IF8771

©Instructional Fair, Inc.

Name _____

Solve. Show your work on another piece of paper.
Write your answers here.

1. What percent of 20 is 8? _____

2. 50 is what percent of 16? _____

3. 18 is what percent of 120? _____

4. What percent of 200 is 121? _____

5. What percent of 4 is 5? _____

6. 3 is what percent of 250? _____

7. 15 is what percent of 80? _____

8. What percent of 24 is 33? _____

9. What percent of 25 is 29? _____

10. 39 is what percent of 75? _____

11. 28 is what percent of 40? _____

12. What percent of 160 is 55? _____

13. What percent of 200 is 111? _____

14. 120 is what percent of 600? _____

15. 193 is what percent of 80? _____

16. What percent of 24 is 21? _____

17. What percent of 250 is 193? _____

18. 36 is what percent of 96? _____

19. 18 is what percent of 48? _____

20. What percent of 220 is 44? _____

21. What percent of 8 is 20? _____

22. 8 is what percent of 128? _____

23. 15 is what percent of 125? _____

24. What percent of 160 is 88? _____

25. What percent of 400 is 301? _____

26. 10 is what percent of 64? _____

27. 18 is what percent of 45? _____

28. What percent of 480 is 198? _____

29. What percent of 120 is 9? _____

30. 38 is what percent of 95? _____

31. 63 is what percent of 112? _____

32. What percent of 256 is 32? _____

33. What percent of 18 is 45? _____

34. 12 is what percent of 150? _____

35. 156 is what percent of 160? _____

36. What percent of 300 is 132? _____

37. What percent of 72 is 45? _____

38. 180 is what percent of 450? _____

39. 42 is what percent of 56? _____

40. What percent of 220 is 77? _____

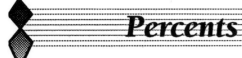

Name _____

Solve. Show your work on another piece of paper.
Write your answers here.

1. 6.48 is 18% of what number? _____

2. 360% of what number is 7.2? _____

3. 135% of what number is 99.9? _____   4. 3 is 15% of what number? _____

5. 59.4 is 90% of what number? _____   6. 38% of what number is 20.9? _____

7. 80% of what number is 24? _____   8. 404 is 101% of what number? _____

9. 192 is 240% of what number? _____   10. 11% of what number is 13.2? _____

11. 86% of what number is 184.9? _____   12. 79.9 is 85% of what number? _____

13. 28 is 40% of what number? _____   14. 70% of what number is 133? _____

15. 22% of what number is 27.5? _____   16. 10.6 is 265% of what number? _____

17. 114 is 95% of what number? _____   18. 325% of what number is 39? _____

19. 140% of what number is 42? _____   20. 39 is 20% of what number? _____

21. 18.2 is 28% of what number? _____   22. 250% of what number is 15? _____

23. 25% of what number is 40? _____   24. 122.1 is 185% of what number? _____

25. 98 is 35% of what number? _____   26. 60% of what number is 90? _____

27. 5% of what number is 9? _____   28. 105 is 25% of what number? _____

29. 645 is 215% of what number? _____   30. 75% of what number is 15? _____

31. 70% of what number is 56? _____   32. 76 is 95% of what number? _____

33. 9.24 is 14% of what number? _____   34. 120% of what number is 72? _____

35. 2% of what number is 1.92? _____   36. 9.2 is 8% of what number? _____

37. 288 is 144% of what number? _____   38. 92% of what number is 110.4? _____

39. 96% of what number is 144? _____   40. 79.2 is 198% of what number? _____

Math IF8771

Percents

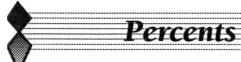

Skill: Percent Increase and Decrease

Name _____

Solve. Show your work on another piece of paper.
Write your answers here.

Total Problems **30**
Problems Correct ____
Percent Correct _____

1. What is the percent increase from 12 to 60? _____
2. What is 70 decreased by 20%? _____
3. What is 66 increased by 88%? _____
4. What is the percent decrease from 300 to 12? _____
5. What is the percent decrease from 72 to 45? _____
6. What is the percent increase from 120 to 150? _____
7. What is the percent increase from 80 to 95? _____
8. What is 200 increased by 18%? _____
9. What is 90 decreased by 13%? _____
10. What is 480 decreased by 95%? _____
11. What is the percent decrease from 105 to 42? _____
12. What is the percent increase from 16 to 93? _____
13. What is 120 increased by 13%? _____
14. What is 45 increased by 35%? _____
15. What is the percent increase from 20 to 30? _____
16. What is the percent decrease from 25 to 17? _____
17. What is 175 decreased by 80%? _____
18. What is 60 increased by 28%? _____
19. What is the percent decrease from 220 to 33? _____
20. What is the percent increase from 40 to 51? _____
21. What is 94 increased by 30%? _____
22. What is 16 decreased by 60%? _____
23. What is the percent increase from 35 to 56? _____
24. What is the percent decrease from 150 to 108? _____
25. What is 212 decreased by 11%? _____
26. What is 105 decreased by 15%? _____
27. What is the percent decrease from 168 to 63? _____
28. What is 90 increased by 95%? _____
29. What is 15 decreased by 4%? _____
30. What is the percent increase from 72 to 81? _____

78

Math IF8771

©Instructional Fair, Inc.

Sales Tax

Name _____

Complete the chart. Round to the nearest cent.

Total Problems __20__

Problems Correct _____

Percent Correct _____

	Cost of Item	% Sales Tax	Tax Paid	Total Cost
1.	$4.99	$3 \frac{1}{4}$ %		
2.	$12.50	5.65%		
3.	$.58	$6 \frac{3}{4}$ %		
4.	$372.48	12%		
5.	$111.20	$18 \frac{1}{8}$ %		
6.	$13.84	4.3%		
7.	$25.25	7.11%		
8.	$30.18	$8 \frac{5}{8}$ %		
9.	$441.89	9.0625%		
10.	$580.60	14%		
11.	$14.12	1.35%		
12.	$8.19	6.8%		
13.	$5.45	$5 \frac{1}{4}$ %		
14.	$613.20	22%		
15.	$125.50	$11 \frac{3}{8}$ %		
16.	$220.16	$9 \frac{1}{2}$ %		
17.	$8.12	2.625%		
18.	$9.00	8.9375%		
19.	$16.85	19%		
20.	$21.22	5.0375%		

Math IF8771

Simple Interest

Name _____

Complete the chart. Round to the nearest cent.

Total Problems __20__

Problems Correct _____

Percent Correct _____

	Principal	Interest Rate Per Year	Time	Interest Earned
1.	$625.00	16%	6 months	
2.	$720.50	$7\frac{1}{2}$ %	1 year	
3.	$5,670.80	22%	9 months	
4.	$4,112.20	$11\frac{1}{8}$ %	$4\frac{1}{4}$ years	
5.	$905.60	14%	$5\frac{1}{2}$ years	
6.	$814.75	$5\frac{3}{4}$ %	4 years	
7.	$1,100.50	15%	3 months	
8.	$870.20	$8\frac{3}{8}$ %	$9\frac{3}{4}$ years	
9.	$415.15	$6\frac{1}{2}$ %	5 months	
10.	$6,540.50	11%	$1\frac{1}{4}$ years	
11.	$11,140.25	5.0375%	8 years	
12.	$26,500.75	8%	6 months	
13.	$408.50	2.625%	4 months	
14.	$910.80	21%	3 years	
15.	$12,540.00	$14\frac{5}{8}$ %	7 months	
16.	$9,750.50	12.0625%	$11\frac{1}{2}$ years	
17.	$810.40	$10\frac{1}{2}$ %	6 years	
18.	$4,480.10	4.6875%	3 months	
19.	$33,500.00	33%	$4\frac{1}{4}$ years	
20.	$18,549.99	9.6%	5 years	

Interest

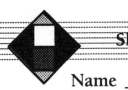

Name _____

Complete the chart. Round to the nearest cent.

Total Problems __**20**__
Problems Correct _____
Percent Correct _____

	Principal	Interest Rate	Compounded	Time	Interest
1.	$4,000.00	12.4%	semiannually	1 year	
2.	$650.00	8%	quarterly	1 year	
3.	$18,999.99	$7\frac{1}{4}$ %	annually	3 years	
4.	$525.25	$19\frac{3}{4}$ %	monthly	2 months	
5.	$27,428.20	21%	annually	2 years	
6.	$5,000.00	$8\frac{3}{8}$ %	quarterly	1 year	
7.	$16,888.75	14%	semiannually	18 months	
8.	$21,050.25	10.6%	semiannually	2 years	
9.	$9,420.55	16.2%	monthly	4 months	
10.	$625.00	$18\frac{1}{8}$ %	monthly	2 months	
11.	$718.99	20.5%	annually	2 years	
12.	$330.20	17.9%	quarterly	6 months	
13.	$890.15	$13\frac{7}{8}$ %	annually	2 years	
14.	$10,000.00	8.85%	quarterly	1 year	
15.	$15,980.00	9.8%	monthly	2 months	
16.	$25,400.00	12.35%	annually	2 years	
17.	$29,590.25	$19\frac{5}{8}$ %	semiannually	1 year	
18.	$18,670.20	$21\frac{1}{4}$ %	quarterly	9 months	
19.	$6,430.05	22.1%	annually	3 years	
20.	$780.10	$5\frac{3}{4}$ %	annually	4 years	

Math IF8771

Discounts and Markups

Name _____

Complete the last two columns of the chart using the discount rate or markup rate. Round to the nearest cent.

Total Problems __**20**__

Problems Correct _____

Percent Correct _____

	Cost/Price	Discount Rate	Markup Rate	Discount or Markup	Sale Price or Selling Price
1.	$35.00	25%			
2.	$42.00		18%		
3.	$68.00		20%		
4.	$24.99	70%			
5.	$50.00		65%		
6.	$20.00	35%			
7.	$17.50	5%			
8.	$110.90		33%		
9.	$240.50	60%			
10.	$89.75		28%		
11.	$64.25	40%			
12.	$19.99		88%		
13.	$595.00		8%		
14.	$616.80	12%			
15.	$200.00		15%		
16.	$450.50	55%			
17.	$38.90	64%			
18.	$14.98		70%		
19.	$5.65		95%		
20.	$717.20		18%		

Math IF8771

Name _____

Complete the charts. Round to the nearest cent.

Total Problems __**40**__

Problems Correct _____

Percent Correct _____

	Rate of Commission	Total Sales	Commission			Rate of Commission	Total Sales	Commission
1.	14%	$950.00		21.	$4\frac{7}{8}$ %	$412.13	
2.	22%	$412.75		22.	18%	$5,678.20	
3.	11%	$1,020.80		23.	5.6%	$718.65	
4.	25%	$428.66		24.	28%	$95.25	
5.	15%	$505.15		25.	$12\frac{1}{2}$ %	$648.29	
6.	9%	$3,496.98		26.	33.3%	$300.50	
7.	$10\frac{1}{2}$ %	$54.75		27.	8.2%	$982.17	
8.	30%	$104.73		28.	16%	$1,546.70	
9.	$13\frac{1}{4}$ %	$64.00		29.	$15\frac{1}{4}$ %	$3,009.75	
10.	16%	$89.11		30.	18.5%	$818.40	
11.	35%	$715.25		31.	14%	$335.25	
12.	44%	$300.50		32.	9.6%	$1,124.55	
13.	$8\frac{3}{8}$ %	$2,450.75		33.	12%	$39,428.00	
14.	$11\frac{1}{4}$ %	$918.75		34.	28%	$518.95	
15.	13%	$600.00		35.	$17\frac{3}{4}$ %	$499.99	
16.	24%	$818.95		36.	31%	$4,000.00	
17.	28%	$42.82		37.	42%	$780.99	
18.	$7\frac{1}{2}$ %	$348.60		38.	14.2%	$395.00	
19.	6%	$659.34		39.	14%	$488.62	
20.	5%	$205.12		40.	$8\frac{3}{4}$ %	$199.00	

Name _____

Complete the charts. Round to the nearest cent.

Total Problems __**40**__

Problems Correct _____

Percent Correct _____

	Purchase Price	Down Payment Percentage	Down Payment		Purchase Price	Down Payment Percentage	Down Payment
1.	$5,000.00	15%		21.	$750.00	8%	
2.	$1,125.00	20%		22.	$990.95	12%	
3.	$890.50	19%		23.	$4,508.85	20%	
4.	$7,500.00	14%		24.	$1,427.99	15%	
5.	$9,000.00	10%		25.	$843.75	$14\frac{1}{2}$%	
6.	$1,546.88	5%		26.	$6,000.00	12%	
7.	$2,999.99	25%		27.	$7,300.00	20%	
8.	$8,500.00	50%		28.	$640.25	25%	
9.	$7,400.00	40%		29.	$900.00	40%	
10.	$658.75	35%		30.	$415.50	$11\frac{3}{8}$%	
11.	$400.00	20%		31.	$21,750.00	22%	
12.	$925.50	15%		32.	$8,173.25	35%	
13.	$717.25	18%		33.	$767.20	$16\frac{3}{4}$%	
14.	$629.84	15%		34.	$2,480.25	45%	
15.	$3,985.15	10%		35.	$960.00	14.2%	
16.	$200.00	$12\frac{1}{2}$%		36.	$817.20	20.8%	
17.	$718.99	14%		37.	$415.10	16%	
18.	$515.20	25%		38.	$9,000.00	$9\frac{1}{2}$%	
19.	$7,600.00	40%		39.	$11,400.00	7%	
20.	$95,000.00	30%		40.	$880.15	6.8%	

Math IF8771

Name _____

Total Problems __50__
Problems Correct _____
Percent Correct _____

Is the number positive or negative?
Write positive or negative.

1. -44   2. 36   3. 51

4. -19   5. 26   6. 93

7. -12   8. -71   9. 86   10. -113   11. 225

12. -5   13. -16   14. 29   15. -85

Write the opposite of each number.

16. 42   17. -7   18. -12   19. -15   20. 21

21. 106   22. -230   23. -81   24. -60   25. 75

26. -111   27. 525   28. -65   29. -33   30. -2

Each symbol represents a number on the number line. Tell which integer is represented by each symbol.

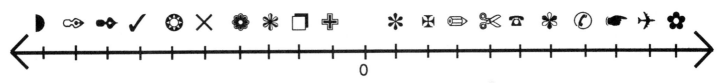

31. ⚙   32. ✳   33. ☎   34. ⬯   35. ❁

36. ✂   37. ◗   38. ✐   39. ✿   40. ✚

41. ✈   42. ✓   43. ✳   44. ✳   45. ⊞

46. ✕   47. ✆   48. ●➤   49. ☛   50. ▢

Math IF8771   ©Instructional Fair, Inc.

Integers

Name _____

Write which property is used.

1. $8 \times (3 + 6) = (8 \times 3) + (8 \times 6)$

2. $-55 + 0 = -55$

3. $-14 \times -8 = -8 \times -14$

4. $-18 \times (-5 \times -7) = (-18 \times -5) \times -7$

5. $8 + (11 + -5) = (8 + 11) + -5$

6. $-5 \times (-2 + 9) = (-5 \times -2) + (-5 \times 9)$

7. $0 + -16 = -16$

8. $-132 + 114 = 114 + -132$

9. $11 \times (-4 + -5) = (11 \times -4) + (11 \times -5)$

10. $-46 \times 1 = -46$

11. $(-12 \times 4) \times -3 = -12 \times (4 \times -3)$

12. $28 \times -5 = -5 \times 28$

13. $66 + -98 = -98 + 66$

14. $(13 + -12) + -39 = 13 + (-12 + -39)$

15. $1 \times -98 = -98$

16. $-7 \times (9 + 7) = (-7 \times 9) + (-7 \times 7)$

Use the properties to solve the equations.

17. $-36 + x = -36$

18. $(3 \times -7) + (3 \times n) = 3 \times (-7 + 9)$

19. $n \times -11 = -11 \times 9$

20. $-5 \times (4 \times -18) = (-5 \times 4) \times n$

21. $(-11 \times -5) + (-11 \times 6) = n \times (-5 + 6)$

22. $19 \times (n + -4) = (19 \times -5) + (19 \times -4)$

23. $14 + 17 = 17 + n$

24. $1 \times n = -55$

25. $(6 + -11) + n = 6 + (-11 + -13)$

26. $36 + -15 = n + 36$

27. $n \times -18 = -18$

28. $0 + n = -75$

29. $8 \times (4 + -10) = (8 \times n) + (8 \times -10)$

30. $n + (-12 + -13) = (-9 + -12) + -13$

Integers

Name _____

Total Problems __**52**__
Problems Correct _____
Percent Correct _____

Add.

1. 18 + 11

2. -13 + -11

3. -22 + -5

4. 19 + 5

5. -7 + -12

6. -8 + -6

7. -4 + -5

8. -13 + -2

9. -20 + -4

10. 8 + 13

11. 22 + 2

12. -15 + -1

13. -14 + -6

14. -3 + -9

15. 9 + 9

16. 8 + 31

17. -20 + -2

18. -9 + -7

19. 15 + 14

20. -19 + -8

21. -15 + -6

22. -18 + -3

23. 17 + 7

24. 16 + 5

25. -6 + -7

26. -34 + -5

27. 28 + 13

28. -25 + -1

29. -20 + -13

30. 30 + 30

31. 14 + 7

32. -17 + -8

33. -18 + -4

34. -50 + -5

35. -27 + -5

36. 16 + 13

37. -25 + -16

38. -28 + -9

39. 19 + 12

40. -11 + -18

41. -15 + -21

42. -8 + -80

43. -6 + -17

44. 4 + 62

45. -2 + -19

46. 35 + 62

47. -28 + -31

48. -19 + -23

49. -14 + -9

50. 16 + 24

51. -103 + -207

52. -244 + -244

Math IF8771

Name _____

Total Problems	**52**
Problems Correct	_____
Percent Correct	_____

Add.

1. 8 + -10

2. 19 + -20

3. -18 + 6

4. -17 + 7

5. 12 + -18

6. 33 + -12

7. -21 + 18

8. -15 + 11

9. 26 + -12

10. 34 + -15

11. -16 + 18

12. -14 + 22

13. 15 + -33

14. 17 + -16

15. 14 + -20

16. -18 + 22

17. -19 + 13

18. 18 + -28

19. 31 + -5

20. -42 + 41

21. 11 + -19

22. -4 + 20

23. -18 + 11

24. 26 + -29

25. 14 + -8

26. -48 + 96

27. 81 + -66

28. 28 + -90

29. -42 + 100

30. 88 + -140

31. -16 + 12

32. -90 + 72

33. 14 + -56

34. 20 + -35

35. -28 + 51

36. 17 + -42

37. 28 + -11

38. -53 + 62

39. -40 + 28

40. -93 + 105

41. 42 + -20

42. -80 + 64

43. 59 + -84

44. -4 + 89

45. -18 + 75

46. 71 + -44

47. 92 + -200

48. 22 + -63

49. 16 + -59

50. -94 + 163

51. -303 + 303

52. 422 + -109

Name _____

Total Problems __**52**__

Problems Correct ____

Percent Correct _____

Subtract.

1. $-70 - 42$

2. $18 - -12$

3. $-90 - -26$

4. $42 - 86$

5. $-38 - 14$

6. $49 - -58$

7. $-16 - 63$

8. $22 - -36$

9. $-33 - -51$

10. $-11 - 72$

11. $10 - 46$

12. $-13 - 48$

13. $28 - -94$

14. $-54 - -25$

15. $-38 - 65$

16. $-16 - -39$

17. $75 - 96$

18. $-81 - 105$

19. $-95 - -45$

20. $60 - -49$

21. $-35 - 20$

22. $-150 - 390$

23. $70 - 246$

24. $18 - -94$

25. $-39 - -59$

26. $50 - 120$

27. $9 - -30$

28. $-2 - 45$

29. $14 - -27$

30. $-98 - -43$

31. $-42 - 64$

32. $38 - 55$

33. $77 - -21$

34. $-60 - 40$

35. $-181 - -105$

36. $-10 - 28$

37. $8 - -25$

38. $-3 - 64$

39. $-5 - -38$

40. $15 - -202$

41. $21 - -9$

42. $-8 - 37$

43. $79 - -14$

44. $-84 - 28$

45. $-120 - -98$

46. $105 - -73$

47. $1 - -99$

48. $-4 - 86$

49. $50 - -43$

50. $-62 - -50$

51. $-84 - 84$

52. $212 - 506$

Name _____

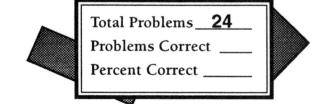

Total Problems **24**

Problems Correct _____

Percent Correct _____

Add and subtract. Show your work on another piece of paper. Write your answers here.

1. -9 + -11 − 4 + -8 − 10

2. 8 − 14 + 95 − -105 + -111 − 63

3. 111 + -128 − -98 − -74 + 110

4. -28 − -43 − 16 − -20 + 89 + -105

5. 89 − -62 − 49 + 68 + 3 − -41

6. 16 − -21 − 28 + -99 − -54 − -17

7. -400 − 32 − -58 + 63 + -94 − 6

8. 48 − 63 + -11 + 25 − -26 + -21

9. 78 − -23 − 49 + 63 + -98 − -19

10. -65 + -94 + 68 − 23 − -89 + -63

11. 36 − -42 + 6 − -28 − 43 − -81 − 6

12. -4 + 8 − 10 − -11 + -13 + 5 − 11 + 12 − -14

13. -90 − -27 + 105 − -230 + -64

14. 81 − 104 + 29 − -33 + -56 − 78

15. 42 + 40 + -89 − -64 − 76 + 91

16. -50 − -41 − -65 + 205 − 318 + -5

17. -18 − 29 − -60 + 58 + -70

18. 39 − -82 − 68 + 95 − 53 − -48 + -18

19. -193 − -205 + -68 − 211 − -150

20. 420 − 561 − -502 + 418 + -715 − -42

21. -73 − -68 − 52 + 19 + -105

22. 218 + 195 − 75 + -188 − -163

23. -50 + 77 − -84 − 93 + -60 − -22

24. 409 + -518 − -210 + -68 − -115 + 96

Math IF8771

Name _____

Multiply. Show your work on another piece of paper.
Write your answers here.

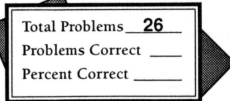

Total Problems __26__
Problems Correct ____
Percent Correct _____

1. -628
    x 433

2. -716
    x -87

3. 914
    x -533

4. -328
    x -319

5. 52,864
    x   -96

6. -7,862
    x   99

7. -64,515
    x   -980

8. 70,426
    x   88

9. -562
    x -198

10. 516
    x -293

11. -3,842
    x   19

12. 51,826
    x   -77

13. 8,265
    x -444

14. 54,178
    x   328

15. -665
    x -313

16. -908
    x 113

17. -7,268
    x   158

18. -60,170
    x   -425

19. 9,119
    x 205

20. -516
    x -39

21. 3,009
    x -717

22. -16,412
    x   -908

23. -28,110
    x   91

24. -5,648
    x   -99

25. -2,372
    x   71

26. -30,194
    x   -28

Math IF8771

Divide. Show your work on another piece of paper. Write your answers here.

Total Problems __36__
Problems Correct _____
Percent Correct _____

1. -828 ÷ -92

2. 308 ÷ -14

3. -608 ÷ 8

4. -612 ÷ -9

5. -2,958 ÷ 34

6. 3,234 ÷ -42

7. 2,548 ÷ 26

8. -1,504 ÷ -47

9. 6,888 ÷ -56

10. 40,572 ÷ 98

11. -5,610 ÷ 55

12. -8,892 ÷ -38

13. -23,408 ÷ 56

14. 6,480 ÷ -18

15. -9,252 ÷ -12

16. -33,048 ÷ 81

17. 37,668 ÷ -73

18. 56,482 ÷ 62

19. -6,902 ÷ -58

20. 28,576 ÷ -47

21. -6,176 ÷ -32

22. 8,236 ÷ -29

23. 13,536 ÷ -94

24. -56,712 ÷ 51

25. 13,158 ÷ -43

26. -46,260 ÷ -90

27. 33,538 ÷ 82

28. -6,150 ÷ -75

29. -16,188 ÷ -71

30. -9,021 ÷ 93

31. 15,447 ÷ -19

32. -4,624 ÷ 68

33. 6,372 ÷ -59

34. -37,584 ÷ -58

35. 35,388 ÷ 36

36. -29,232 ÷ -48

Math IF8771

©Instructional Fair, Inc.

Multiply and divide. Show your work on another piece of paper. Write your answers here.

Total Problems __**30**__

Problems Correct _____

Percent Correct _____

1. -18 x -45 ÷ 54 x -40 ÷ -30

2. 588 ÷ 14 x -6 ÷ 21 x 20 ÷ -8 x 5

3. 2,400 ÷ -15 x -3 ÷ -60 x 11

4. 21 x -2 ÷ -14 x 25 ÷ -15 x -9

5. -85 x -4 ÷ 17 x -22 ÷ 55 x 8

6. -1,584 ÷ 44 x -21 ÷ 6 x -5 ÷ -90

7. -216 ÷ 18 x -13 ÷ 2 x 5 ÷ 39

8. 90 x 35 ÷ 210 x -8 ÷ 60 x 17

9. 81 x -15 ÷ 27 x -4 ÷ 60 x -14

10. 540 ÷ -18 x 16 ÷ 24 x 11 ÷ -4 x 6 ÷ -33

11. -270 ÷ -18 x 16 ÷ -15 x -22 ÷ -44

12. -81 x 75 ÷ -15 x -4 ÷ 27 x -11 ÷ -4

13. 22 x -55 ÷ 10 x -36 ÷ 33 x 4

14. 195 x -2 ÷ 26 x -12 ÷ 9 x -5 ÷ -25

15. -528 ÷ 24 x -9 ÷ -11 x 50 ÷ -45

16. 1,000 ÷ -40 x 21 ÷ 15 x -2 ÷ 7

17. 28 x -15 ÷ 21 x -35 ÷ 28 x -6

18. -210 ÷ -14 x 21 ÷ -35 x 16 ÷ -12 x -5

19. -504 ÷ -42 x -33 ÷ 2 x -21 ÷ 77

20. -36 x 25 ÷ -4 x 7 ÷ -63 x 3 ÷ 5

21. 72 x 11 ÷ -12 x 18 ÷ 4 x 5 ÷ 33

22. 750 ÷ -5 x 6 ÷ 75 x 12 ÷ -8 x 3

23. 156 ÷ -2 x -5 ÷ 13 x -7 ÷ -35 x -6

24. 18 x 28 ÷ 36 x -110 ÷ 2 x 3 ÷ 66

25. 33 x -56 ÷ -77 x 25 ÷ -300 x 27 ÷ -18

26. -1,080 ÷ -54 x 55 ÷ -44 x 12 ÷ -15

27. 2,640 ÷ -22 x 9 ÷ 24 x -5 ÷ 15

28. 64 x -9 ÷ 24 x 25 ÷ -15 x 11 ÷ -20

29. -26 x -20 ÷ 52 x -9 ÷ 5 x -7 ÷ -6

30. -360 ÷ -15 x -35 ÷ -28 x 40 ÷ -30

Evaluate.

	Total Problems __52__
	Problems Correct _____
	Percent Correct _____

1. $|-11|$ 2. $|28|$

3. $|33|$ 4. $|-110|$

5. $|-50|$ 6. $|35|$ 7. $|4|$ 8. $|-18|$

9. $|-72|$ 10. $|-18|$ 11. $|-25|$ 12. $|-71|$

13. $|-64|$ 14. $|44|$ 15. $|36|$ 16. $|-41|$

17. $|-8|$ 18. $|9|$ 19. $|214|$ 20. $|-510|$

Simplify. Show your work on another piece of paper. Write your answers here.

21. $|25| + |-15|$ 22. $|-63| - |12|$ 23. $|-52| + |-8|$ 24. $|-3| \times |-7|$

25. $|24| + |-6|$ 26. $|7| \times |-6|$ 27. $|-16| + |-9|$ 28. $|-7| + |15|$

29. $|43| - |-20|$ 30. $|-15| \div |3|$ 31. $|5| \times |-4|$ 32. $|-20| + |-34|$

33. $|-12| - |-7|$ 34. $|-22| + |-2|$ 35. $|-2| \times |20|$ 36. $|70| - |-51|$

37. $|-18| \div |-3|$ 38. $|-40| - |-17|$ 39. $|8| \times |-8|$ 40. $|50| \div |-5|$

41. $|36 - 50|$ 42. $|-6 \times 5|$ 43. $|-7 + -2|$ 44. $|-36 \div -6|$

45. $|5 + -10|$ 46. $|-11 - -3|$ 47. $|40 \div -4|$ 48. $|-50 \times -2|$

49. $|-12 + 15|$ 50. $|4 \times -7|$ 51. $|-81| \times |-16|$ 52. $|-301 + 296|$

Math IF8771   ©Instructional Fair, Inc.

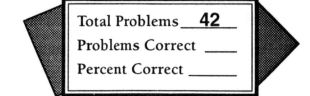

Name _____

Total Problems __**42**__

Problems Correct ____

Percent Correct _____

Evaluate. Show your work on another piece of paper.
Write your answers here.

1. 3^{-4} 2. 4^0

3. 12^{-1} 4. 9^{-2} 5. $(-5)^2$ 6. 8^{-2}

7. $(-3)^{-3}$ 8. 10^{-3} 9. 19^0 10. $(-4)^{-2}$

11. $(-6)^{-2}$ 12. 30^{-1} 13. $(-3)^{-4}$ 14. 17^{-1}

15. 4^{-2} 16. 16^0 17. 2^{-5} 18. $(-6)^2$

19. 11^{-2} 20. $(-5)^{-3}$ 21. 22^{-1} 22. 14^0

23. $(-2)^{-4}$ 24. $(-9)^2$ 25. 5^{-3} 26. 4^{-3}

27. 18^{-1} 28. 3^{-3} 29. $(-13)^{-2}$ 30. $(-10)^{-2}$

31. 24^0 32. 2^{-6} 33. $(-2)^{-5}$ 34. 15^{-2}

35. $(-2)^{-6}$ 36. $(-10)^{-3}$ 37. 12^{-2} 38. 18^0

39. $(-4)^{-3}$ 40. 26^{-1} 41. $(-8)^{-2}$ 42. -4^5

Math IF8771

Name _____

Total Problems	**48**
Problems Correct	____
Percent Correct	_____

Evaluate the expressions. Use a=6, b=5 and c=4.

1. $b + 9$ 2. $a - c$

3. $a + 8$ 4. $\dfrac{12}{c}$

5. $\dfrac{15}{b}$ 6. $c - 1$ 7. bc 8. $a + \text{-}c$

9. $4b - a$ 10. $4(b + c)$ 11. $8 + c$ 12. b^2

13. $c^3 - a^2$ 14. $\dfrac{33}{a + b}$ 15. $6a + \text{-}8c$ 16. $ca + b$

17. $\dfrac{26 - a}{c}$ 18. $a^2 + b$ 19. $\dfrac{2b + 2}{a}$ 20. $\dfrac{a^2}{c}$

Evaluate the expressions. Use x=2, y=7 and z=-5.

21. $z - y$ 22. $2y + x$ 23. xz 24. y^2

25. $4xy - z$ 26. $xy + 1$ 27. $28 \div y$ 28. $6z$

29. $3(x + y)$ 30. $2xyz$ 31. x^3 32. 3^x

33. 10^x 34. xz^x 35. $\dfrac{y - z}{x}$ 36. $\dfrac{16 - x}{y}$

37. $y^x - 6y$ 38. $4^x - y$ 39. z^x 40. $yz + 40$

41. $\dfrac{25}{\text{-}z}$ 42. x^y 43. $10y \div z$ 44. $\text{-}3xz$

45. $\dfrac{x + \text{-}z}{y}$ 46. $\dfrac{77}{\text{-}y}$ 47. z^3 48. $x^2(x + y)$

Math IF8771

Name _____

Is the given number a solution of the equation? Show your work on another piece of paper. Write yes or no here.

Total Problems __**38**__
Problems Correct _____
Percent Correct _____

1. $13 = x - 20$; 7

2. $88 = 8x$; 11

3. $a - 15 = 8$; 23

4. $\frac{n}{15} = -3$; -45

5. $9x = -72$; 8

6. $22 = y + 14$; 7

7. $9 = \frac{x}{8}$; 81

8. $20a = 80$; 4

9. $-4 = x + 23$; -27

10. $16 = b - 4$; 20

11. $-13c = -65$; 6

12. $6 = \frac{a}{-11}$; -95

13. $-12 = \frac{m}{6}$; -70

14. $6 = c + 28$; 22

15. $y - 6 = -1$; 7

16. $c + 10 = 33$; 23

17. $r - 18 = 26$; 44

18. $3a + 5 = 14$; 3

19. $\frac{c}{-9} = 8$; 72

20. $8a = -64$; 8

21. $\frac{y}{7} = -6$; -42

22. $49 = 7m$; 7

23. $b + 11 = -8$; 19

24. $n - 9 = -6$; 3

25. $-6y = 60$; -10

26. $40 = x - 11$; 29

27. $5 = \frac{n}{-21}$; -105

28. $-5 = r + 26$; -33

29. $\frac{a}{-13} = -4$; 52

30. $20 = 4n + 12$; 3

31. $3 = c - 22$; 26

32. $12c = 48$; -3

33. $a - 35 = -12$; 23

34. $19 = \frac{x}{-5}$; -85

35. $m + 15 = 4$; -11

36. $-75 = 15x$; -3

37. $-99 = -33b$; 3

38. $40 = 5x + 15$; 5

Math IF8771

©Instructional Fair, Inc.

Name _____

Solve.

1. $5 + x = 8$

2. $m - 11 = 19$

3. $-6 = -a + 3$

4. $a + 20 = 33$

5. $-4 = 13 + b$

6. $150 + b = 163$

7. $n - 14 = -11$

8. $x + 8 = -5$

9. $21 + c = 30$

10. $18 - x = 3$

11. $-15 = x - 20$

12. $18 = x + 13$

13. $x + -9 = 15$

14. $-15 = c - 7$

15. $44 + x = 56$

16. $19 - c = 11$

17. $n + 14 = -11$

18. $6 = a - 25$

19. $y + 7 = -14$

20. $b + 25 = 4$

21. $b + 9 = -11$

22. $-20 = d - 8$

23. $x - 10 = -8$

24. $-14 + y = -3$

25. $12 - y = 1$

26. $19 = c + 30$

27. $b - 13 = -25$

28. $4 = y - 16$

29. $45 + a = 22$

30. $-20 = a + 11$

31. $13 = 38 + x$

32. $-45 = d - 50$

33. $-14 = a - 39$

34. $8 + y = -30$

35. $11 - y = 5$

36. $15 = -22 + y$

37. $-5 = 16 + x$

38. $a - 63 = 7$

39. $-7 + y = -4$

40. $-16 = c - 22$

Math IF8771

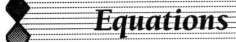

Solve.

Total Problems __**40**__
Problems Correct ____
Percent Correct _____

1. $4x = -20$

2. $\dfrac{n}{6} = 3$

3. $64 = 8y$

4. $11 = \dfrac{a}{-4}$

5. $\dfrac{n}{-14} = 2$

6. $49 = -7x$

7. $-10 = \dfrac{b}{4}$

8. $36 = 4y$

9. $6 = \dfrac{c}{7}$

10. $3a = -45$

11. $\dfrac{x}{-11} = -9$

12. $-5x = 80$

13. $-48 = -12c$

14. $\dfrac{c}{-8} = 9$

15. $7b = -77$

16. $\dfrac{x}{5} = 13$

17. $-8y = 120$

18. $-12 = \dfrac{y}{-6}$

19. $120 = 20n$

20. $\dfrac{n}{-10} = 13$

21. $-8 = \dfrac{y}{11}$

22. $-52 = -13m$

23. $15 = \dfrac{a}{9}$

24. $60 = 6x$

25. $-39 = -3n$

26. $5 = \dfrac{m}{8}$

27. $\dfrac{n}{-12} = -4$

28. $2a = -90$

29. $81 = 9b$

30. $\dfrac{x}{25} = -8$

31. $-10m = 110$

32. $\dfrac{y}{-9} = -9$

33. $12 = \dfrac{x}{7}$

34. $-63 = 21x$

35. $8y = 56$

36. $-4 = \dfrac{m}{20}$

37. $-99 = -11a$

38. $4 = \dfrac{b}{21}$

39. $72 = 9c$

40. $\dfrac{a}{-13} = 2$

Name _____

Solve. Show your work on another piece of paper.
Write your answers here.

Total Problems __**38**__

Problems Correct _____

Percent Correct _____

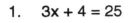

1. $3x + 4 = 25$

2. $\dfrac{x}{4} + 3 = 11$

3. $8 = 6x - 4$

4. $\dfrac{p}{-5} + 6 = -5$

5. $-55 = -8n + 9$

6. $5x + 1 = 21$

7. $-20 = -11s + 24$

8. $\dfrac{r}{8} + 5 = 4$

9. $7x - 11 = 3$

10. $8r - 7 = 17$

11. $20w + 5 = 85$

12. $12c - 16 = 44$

13. $13r - 11 = 28$

14. $\dfrac{c}{-3} + 16 = -5$

15. $3x - 8 = 28$

16. $\dfrac{c}{8} + 9 = 15$

17. $-33 = -6r + 9$

18. $7x - 3 = 18$

19. $8n + 21 = -43$

20. $63 = 9a - 27$

21. $8 - 2r = -12$

22. $\dfrac{x}{7} - 5 = 6$

23. $9s + 13 = 85$

24. $22 = 11 + \dfrac{x}{-4}$

25. $\dfrac{a}{-5} + 2 = -13$

26. $20b - 93 = 7$

27. $\dfrac{n}{-12} + 8 = 10$

28. $7a - 28 = 21$

29. $\dfrac{n}{10} - 3 = 8$

30. $40 - 7x = -16$

31. $-28 = -9x + 17$

32. $16 = \dfrac{c}{20} + 19$

33. $12r + 33 = 81$

34. $\dfrac{n}{15} - 13 = -18$

35. $61 = 16 + 15a$

36. $18 = 22 - \dfrac{n}{5}$

37. $\dfrac{x}{-15} - 160 = -32$

38. $21x + 42 = -378$

Math IF8771

Name _____

Complete the tables.

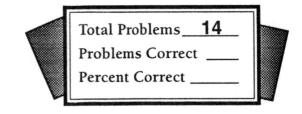

Total Problems __14__
Problems Correct _____
Percent Correct _____

1. 2x + y = 6

x	y	(x, y)
-2	10	(-2, 10)
-1	8	(-1,)
0		(0,)
1		(1,)
2		(2,)

2. y = x + 3

x	y	(x, y)
-2		
-1		
0		
2		
3		

3. y = 4x

x	y	(x, y)
-3		
-1		
0		
2		
4		

4. y = 2x + 3

x	y	(x, y)
-4		
-2		
0		
1		
3		

5. y = x − 2

x	y	(x, y)
-5		
-3		
0		
1		
2		

6. x − y = 5

x	y	(x, y)
-3		
-1		
0		
2		
4		

7. x + y = 6

x	y	(x, y)
-1		
0		
1		
2		
3		

8. y = 7x − 3

x	y	(x, y)
-2		
0		
3		
5		
7		

9. y = -4x

x	y	(x, y)
-3		
-2		
-1		
0		
1		
2		
3		

10. y = -x

x	y	(x, y)
-5		
-3		
-1		
0		
2		
4		
6		

11. y = - x − 2

x	y	(x, y)
-4		
-2		
0		
1		
3		
5		
7		

12. y = x − 5

x	y	(x, y)
-3		
-2		
-1		
0		
1		
2		
3		

13. y = 5x − 4

x	y	(x, y)
-3		
-2		
-1		
0		
2		
4		

14. y = -20x + 15

x	y	(x, y)
-1		
0		
1		
2		
3		
4		

Math IF8771

Name _____

Find the ordered pair that is a solution of the systems of equations. To do this, first make and complete an (x, y) table for each equation. Then, draw each equation on the graph given. Where the two lines intersect is the solution.

Total Problems __12__

Problems Correct ____

Percent Correct _____

1. $y - x = 4$
    $y = \dfrac{x}{-3}$

2. $-11 = x + 2y$
    $3y - 2x = -6$

3. $x - 5y = 14$
    $y = \dfrac{-x}{2}$

4. $8x + 3y = -15$
    $y = -x$

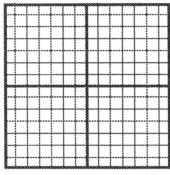 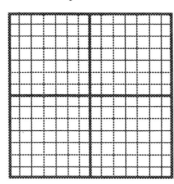 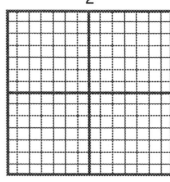 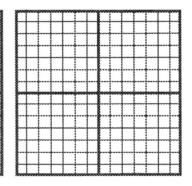

5. $-3y = -21 - x$
    $5x + 2y = -20$

6. $y - 2x = 2$
    $3x = y$

7. $8 = x + y$
    $3y = x$

8. $x + 4y = 12$
    $y = \dfrac{x}{2}$

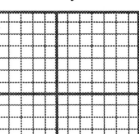 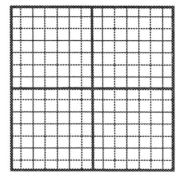 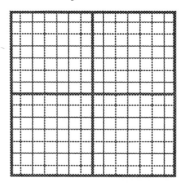

9. $2 = 3x + y$
    $y = -5x$

10. $4x - 2y = 4$
    $3x = y$

11. $3y + x = 7$
    $2x = y$

12. $2x + y = -7$
    $-3y = x + 11$

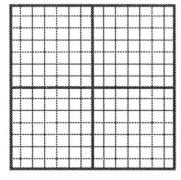 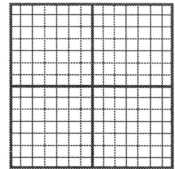 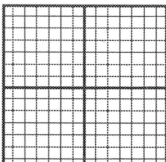 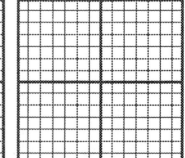

Reading & Writing Numbers

Skill: Reading and Writing Through Trillions

Name _____

Total Problems __20__
Problems Correct _____
Percent Correct _____

Write the word name for each numeral.

1. five trillion, four hundred three billion, two hundred sixty-nine million, one hundred thirty-three thousand, four hundred twelve

2. two hundred ninety-eight billion, five hundred five million, six hundred seventy-two thousand, one hundred eighty-seven

3. seven billion, four hundred fifty-three million, sixty-eight

4. nine trillion, six hundred eighty billion, forty-three million, one hundred twenty-three thousand, five hundred seventy-seven

5. fifty-two billion, sixty-six million, four hundred fifty-two thousand, one hundred eleven

6. one trillion, three billion, four hundred six million, seven hundred thousand, four

7. eight hundred ninety billion, three hundred thirty-three million, two

8. two hundred forty-five million, six hundred ninety-eight thousand, seven hundred forty-six

9. three billion, forty-one million, five hundred sixty-seven thousand, eight hundred ninety-two

10. six trillion, four hundred twenty-one billion, one hundred thirty-five million, six hundred seventy-nine thousand, eight hundred eighty

Write the correct numeral for each number.

11. 5,403,222,006,713

12. 931,426,502

13. 13,001,284,005

14. 417,670,060,252

15. 9,000,876,000,962

16. 80,537,222,039

17. 1,101,011,110,001

18. 613,200,056,506

19. 5,418,229,506

20. 3,472,567,511,653

Place Value

Skill: Place Value Through Trillions

Name _____

Total Problems __58__
Problems Correct _____
Percent Correct _____

In the number 3,024,598,136,670, what is the place value for:
1= hundred-thousands
2= ten-billions
3= ten-thousands
and trillions
4= billions
5= hundred-millions
6= hundreds
7= tens
8= millions
9= ten-millions
0= ones

and thousands

and hundred-billions

The number 9,438,722,017,654 has:
2 ten-millions
4 ones
0 hundred-thousands
8 billions
3 ten-billions
7 thousands
6 hundreds
7 hundred-millions
9 trillions
5 tens
2 millions
4 hundred-billions
1 ten-thousand

What number has:
0 billions   6 trillions   2 ten-billions
3 tens   4 hundred-thousands   7 millions
9 thousands   5 ten-millions   8 hundreds
8 hundred-millions   4 ones   3 ten-thousands
1 hundred-billion

The number is 6,120,857,439,834

In the numbers 5,603,447,628,515 and 6,613,436,528,017, which place values have the same numbers in each?
tens   hundred-millions
thousands   billions
ten-thousands hundred billions

Pick the numeral of the specified place values, and fill in the appropriate blanks below.
hundred-millions   6,023,478,929,555   thousands   5,866,111,327,420
tens   8,100,322,568,115   millions   7,897,144,628,404
hundred-billions   4,602,335,777,999   ones   9,991,087,655,222
trillions   3,436,791,199,345   hundred-thousands   8,000,000,432,006
ten-millions   1,998,002,304,511   hundreds   4,444,374,623,632
billions   5,312,344,576,104   ten-thousands   2,577,696,827,328
ten-billions   9,102,004,566,721

3,602,404,427,612

Comparing & Ordering

Skill: Comparing and Ordering Whole Numbers Through Trillions

Name _____

Total Problems __25__
Problems Correct _____
Percent Correct _____

Fill in the blank with < or > to make each statement true.
1. 6,120,438,625,503 < 6,120,438,625,530
2. 27,411,068,734 > 27,411,068,374
3. 718,699,043,226 > 71,869,904,322
4. 98,104,327,665 > 98,104,237,665
5. 1,400,623,522,477 > 140,623,522,477
6. 322,446,771,879 < 322,446,771,987
7. 68,716,525,337 < 687,165,253,374
8. 418,998,566,545 < 418,998,566,554
9. 5,661,734,992,213 > 5,661,734,992,123
10. 81,102,356,672 < 811,023,566,723
11. 2,221,397,846,519 > 2,221,397,846,195
12. 587,923,443,126 > 587,923,434,126
13. 47,003,592,652 < 470,035,926,524
14. 209,762,154 > 209,762,153
15. 3,861,243,717,506 < 3,861,243,717,560

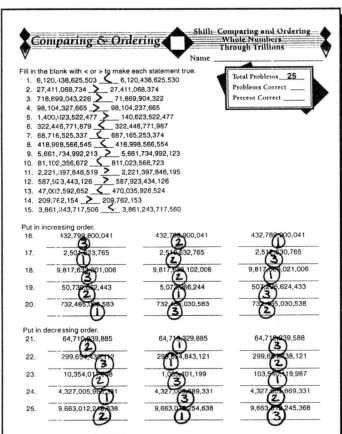

Put in increasing order.
16.
17.
18.
19.
20.

Put in decreasing order.
21.
22.
23.
24.
25.

Rounding

Skill: Rounding Whole Numbers

Name _____

Total Problems __40__
Problems Correct _____
Percent Correct _____

Round to the nearest:

ten-million
1. 4,003,450,000,000
2. 230,000,000
3. 752,900,000,000
4. 63,440,000,000

hundred-billion
1. 300,000,000,000   2. 800,000,000,000
3. 3,000,000,000,000   4. 9,800,000,000,000

thousand
1. 5,427,000   2. 8,713,000,895,000
3. 628,562,444,000   4. 1,000,000

billion
1. 16,000,000,000   2. 6,000,000,000
3. 898,000,000,000   4. 7,001,000,000,000

hundred-thousand
1. 280,799,400,000   2. 6,498,700,000
3. 900,000,000   4. 1,111,111,100,000

trillion
1. 6,000,000,000,000   2. 10,000,000,000,000
3. 6,000,000,000,000   4. 5,000,000,000,000

million
1. 629,000,000   2. 6,541,000,000,000
3. 5,433,000,000   4. 54,000,000

ten-thousand
1. 6,011,379,000,000   2. 4,010,000
3. 5,777,820,000   4. 6,998,320,000

hundred-million
1. 14,400,000,000   2. 987,600,000
3. 5,003,000,000,000   4. 7,806,000,000,000

ten-billion
1. 40,000,000,000   2. 990,000,000
3. 3,350,000,000,000   4. 4,830,000,000,000

Math IF8771   ©Instructional Fair, Inc.

Addition — Skill: Adding Greater Numbers

Name _____

Total Problems **20**
Problems Correct ____
Percent Correct ____

Add.

1.	2.
50,987,625 9,860,008 48,909,378 28,009 8,666,542 + 77,045,613 **195,497,175**	7,105 862,430 79,992 314 973,566 + 8,666,542 **10,589,949**

3.	4.	5.	6.
52,809,763 115,620 9,766 32,488 7,001,537 + 662,348 **60,631,522**	4,682,003 53,792,456 1,119,363 48,776,221 238,456 + 8,926,348 **117,534,847**	4,138,626 907,005 3,881 28,937,066 56,420,823 + 22,440 **90,429,841**	78 5,522 987 16,430 489,376 + 5,628 **518,021**

7.	8.	9.	10.
3,408,970 560,889 5,632 111,818 4,003,212 + 40,899 **8,131,420**	22,346,718 4,005,613 9,999 875,802 47,366 + 37,508,202 **64,793,700**	61,589,733 52,111,003 49,875,624 86,006,424 91,018,531 + 28,743,235 **371,344,550**	387 4,520 29,866 492,039 6,287,668 + 72,011,653 **78,826,133**

11.	12.	13.	14.
8,982,612 65,088 7,123,456 53,488 9,300,246 + 89,044 **25,613,934**	88,888,888 77,777,777 66,666,666 55,555,555 44,444,444 + 33,333,333 **366,666,663**	506,298,612 13,598 1,110,566 28,975,761 344,347,655 + 881,009 **881,627,201**	324,562 3,887 113,540 3,009,888 44,505,005 + 223,220,003 **271,176,885**

15.	16.	17.	18.
3,999 26,999 514,999 6,888,999 + 18,900,999 **26,335,995**	83,421,565 62,317,692 17,141,584 28,756,487 + 39,268,968 **230,906,296**	26,980,723 45,629 638 482,111 + 722 **27,509,823**	727,643 8,102,111 38,726 5,437 + 897,300 **9,771,217**

19. 63,428 + 99,420,018 + 561,443 + 8,704,552 + 23,489,733 + 826,515,555 = **958,754,729**

20. 8,907,825 + 64,787,003 + 91,324,866 + 420,555 + 148,921,620 = **314,361,869**

Addition — Skill: Checking Addition Using Subtraction

Name _____

Total Problems **38**
Problems Correct ____
Percent Correct ____

Check the addition problems using subtraction.
Circle the problems that are correct.

(1.)	2.	3.	(4.)	(5.)	(6.)
987,623 + 710,754 1,698,377	872,455 + 51,368 823,823	487,603 + 39,877 517,480	5,678,629 + 86,989 5,765,618	566,320 + 111,999 678,319	865,412 + 3,640,755 4,506,167

7.	(8.)	(9.)	(10.)
42,360 + 58,865 102,225	988,756 + 718,008 1,706,764	15,662,118 + 3,997 15,666,115	34,612,568 + 14,977,029 49,589,597

11.	12.	13.	(14.)
2,434,115 + 788,627 3,322,742	8,612,544 + 897,632 9,510,176	233,422,518 + 321,211,521 564,633,039	681,236 + 4,877,515 5,558,751

15.	16.	17.	18.
43,726 + 87,899 121,625	4,311,988 + 5,479,661 9,801,649	78,688,815 + 65,565,698 1,342,54413	918,526 + 79,442 1,007,968

(19.)	20.	(21.)	22.
32,766,187 + 435,899,083 468,665,270	6,151,444 + 3,222,312 9,373,756	414,112,397 + 202,055,185 616,167,582	6,787,999 + 40,123 6,827,122

23.	24.	25.	26.
28,976,314 + 56,020,263 74,996,577	333,426 + 231,117 564,543	5,618,977,634 + 896,412,307 6,514,389,941	1,319,634,555 + 3,027,519,815 5,147,154,370

27.	28.	(29.)	(30.)
2,516,788,651 + 39,554,783 2,546,343,434	817,562,009 + 526,765,001 1,354,329,010	660,576,781 + 239,932,452 900,509,233	634,476,665 + 515,666,019 1,150,142,684

(31.)	32.	33.	(34.)
8,881,811,888 + 181,888,118 9,063,700,006	446,525,116 + 789,009,999 1,235,535,115	583,340,119 + 689,516,999 1,372,857,118	3,507,626,323 + 8,898,787 3,516,525,110

35.	(36.)	(37.)	38.
58,402,989 + 31,597,011 80,000,000	317,612,919 + 496,738,555 814,351,474	618,987,635 + 987,620,506 1,606,608,141	9,899,887,625 + 28,661,587 9,928,549,212

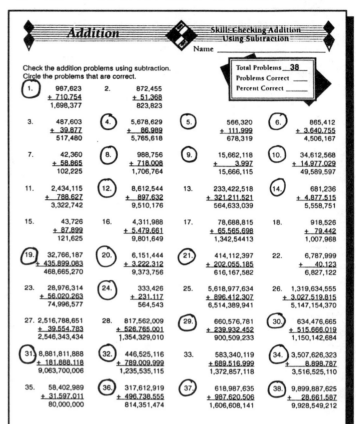

Subtraction — Skill: Subtracting Greater Numbers

Name _____

Total Problems **40**
Problems Correct ____
Percent Correct ____

Subtract.

1.	2.
18,765,449 - 9,810,566 **8,954,883**	1,111,103 - 5,624 **1,105,479**

3.	4.
3,000,000 - 28,977 **2,971,023**	52,773,210 - 19,895,333 **32,877,877**

5.	6.	7.	8.
45,063 - 38,775 **6,288**	810,134 - 2,666 **807,468**	32,051,689 - 23,863,799 **8,187,890**	135,411 - 942 **134,469**

9.	10.	11.	12.
821,004 - 69,367 **751,637**	5,822,214 - 3,997,651 **1,824,563**	20,000,006 - 13,732,897 **6,267,109**	787,662 - 515,515 **272,147**

13.	14.	15.	16.
3,440,212 - 566,529 **2,873,683**	901,870 - 633,509 **268,361**	7,003,414 - 5,289,088 **1,714,326**	26,501,111 - 18,626,777 **7,874,334**

17.	18.	19.	20.
1,000,000 - 927,602 **72,398**	202,338,612 - 6,441,058 **195,897,554**	62,414,500 - 15,389,772 **47,024,728**	616,577 - 604,988 **11,589**

21.	22.	23.	24.
4,712,560 - 98,799 **4,613,761**	33,300,000 - 27,425,767 **5,874,233**	101,233,451 - 100,122,566 **1,110,885**	71,302,612 - 558,999 **70,743,613**

25.	26.	27.	28.
19,880,114 - 17,903,434 **1,976,680**	399,488,121 - 308,599,333 **90,888,788**	397,000,000 - 28,727,313 **368,272,687**	500,000 - 213,996 **286,004**

29.	30.	31.	32.
6,273,411 - 6,215,699 **57,712**	111,234,997 - 97,455,998 **14,778,999**	42,910,000 - 879,612 **42,030,388**	568,703,424 - 29,888,888 **538,814,536**

33.	34.	35.	36.
600,000,000 - 537,826,919 **62,173,081**	37,144,062 - 19,256,709 **17,887,353**	111,011,001 - 1,101,110 **109,909,891**	87,613,421 - 896,555 **86,716,866**

37.	38.	39.	40.
231,002,567 - 5,627,189 **225,375,378**	73,826,113 - 9,997,345 **63,828,768**	123,499,718 - 46,798,935 **76,700,783**	5,000,000,000 - 312,135,244 **4,687,864,756**

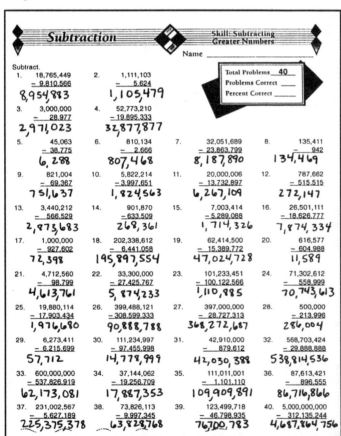

Subtraction — Skill: Checking Subtraction Using Addition

Name _____

Total Problems **38**
Problems Correct ____
Percent Correct ____

Check the subtraction problems using addition.
Circle the problems that are correct.

(1.)	(2.)
306,221 - 198,360 117,861	72,000 - 68,355 3,645

3.	(4.)	(5.)	6.
418,720 - 97,843 417,877	1,450,006 - 1,388,972 61,034	6,004,300 - 199,588 5,804,712	32,616,424 - 977,005 31,639,419

(7.)	8.	9.	10.
5,001,101 - 4,328,232 672,869	431,651 - 98,777 342,874	26,313,004 - 18,563,899 7,749,205	7,349,612 - 7,258,988 80,624

(11.)	(12.)	13.	14.
500,121 - 189,444 310,677	300,000,000 - 123,717,888 176,282,112	521,334 - 498,766 21,568	718,872 - 9,799 708,073

15.	16.	17.	(18.)
8,100,000 - 6,388,413 1,811,587	7,100,245 - 587,666 6,512,579	223,476,111 - 218,588,990 5,887,121	910,111 - 88,088 822,023

19.	(20.)	(21.)	22.
58,122 - 9,389 49,733	234,515 - 217,909 16,606	4,180,005 - 3,766,215 413,790	5,101,625 - 983,411 4,118,214

(23.)	(24.)	(25.)	26.
511,009,447 - 89,766,567 421,242,880	28,568,009 - 19,779,221 8,788,788	32,461,718 - 18,356,899 14,104,819	500,000,000 - 49,602,313 450,397,687

27.	28.	29.	30.
66,518,987 - 42,673,189 13,845,798	54,332,141 - 16,414,322 37,917,819	627,010,000 - 59,900,623 568,109,377	41,200,144 - 3,122,666 38,077,478

(31.)	32.	(33.)	(34.)
62,909,816 - 19,817,633 43,092,183	18,410,008 - 6,222,119 12,287,889	20,000,000 - 11,111,111 8,888,889	333,110,087 - 198,233,448 134,876,639

(35.)	(36.)	37.	38.
618,755,009 - 914,766 617,840,243	99,877,650 - 81,986,777 17,890,873	23,480,008 - 5,599,612 18,880,396	390,621,334 - 972,806 389,748,528

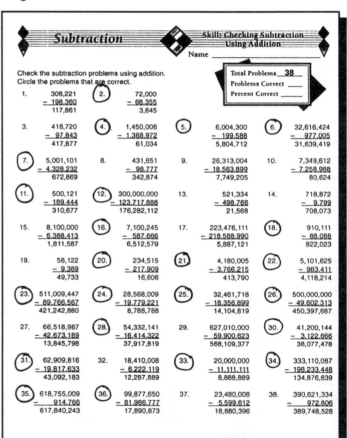

Math IF8771

Estimation

Skill: Estimating Whole Number Sums and Differences

Name _____

Estimate the sums and differences by rounding to the largest place value.

Total Problems __30__
Problems Correct ____
Percent Correct ____

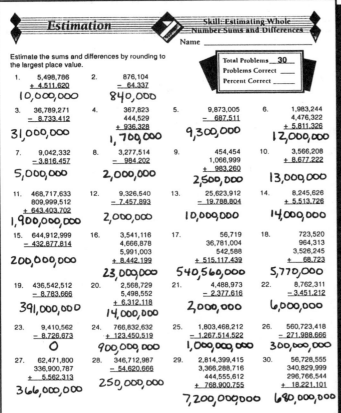

1. 5,498,786 + 4,511,620 = **10,000,000**
2. 876,104 − 64,337 = **840,000**
3. 36,789,271 − 8,733,412 = **31,000,000**
4. 367,823 + 444,529 + 936,328 = **1,700,000**
5. 9,873,005 − 687,511 = **9,300,000**
6. 1,983,244 + 4,476,322 + 5,811,326 = **12,000,000**
7. 9,042,332 − 3,816,457 = **5,000,000**
8. 3,277,514 − 984,202 = **2,000,000**
9. 454,454 + 1,066,999 + 983,260 = **2,500,000**
10. 3,566,208 + 8,677,222 = **13,000,000**
11. 468,717,633 + 809,999,512 + 643,403,702 = **1,900,000,000**
12. 9,326,540 − 7,457,893 = **2,000,000**
13. 25,623,912 − 19,788,804 = **10,000,000**
14. 8,245,626 + 5,513,726 = **14,000,000**
15. 644,912,999 − 432,877,814 = **200,000,000**
16. 3,541,116 + 4,666,878 + 5,991,003 + 8,442,199 = **23,000,000**
17. 56,719 + 36,781,004 + 542,588 + 515,117,439 = **540,560,000**
18. 723,520 + 964,313 + 3,526,245 + 68,723 = **5,770,000**
19. 436,542,512 − 8,783,666 = **391,000,000**
20. 2,568,729 + 5,498,552 + 6,312,118 = **14,000,000**
21. 4,488,973 − 2,377,616 = **2,000,000**
22. 8,762,311 − 3,451,212 = **6,000,000**
23. 9,410,562 − 8,726,673 = **0**
24. 766,832,632 − 123,450,519 = **900,000,000**
25. 1,803,468,212 − 1,267,514,522 = **1,000,000,000**
26. 560,723,418 − 271,988,666 = **300,000,000**
27. 62,471,800 + 336,900,787 + 5,562,313 = **366,000,000**
28. 346,712,987 − 54,620,666 = **250,000,000**
29. 2,814,399,415 + 3,366,288,716 + 444,555,612 + 768,900,755 = **7,200,000,000**
30. 56,728,555 + 340,829,999 + 296,766,544 + 18,221,101 = **680,000,000**

Multiplication

Skill: Multiplying Whole Numbers

Name _____

Multiply. Show your work on another piece of paper. Write your answers here.

Total Problems __38__
Problems Correct ____
Percent Correct ____

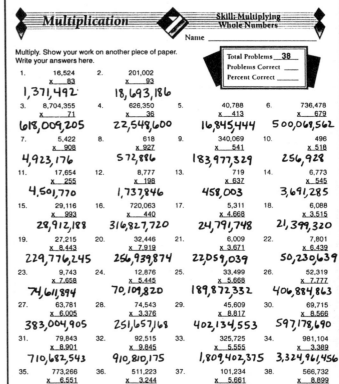

1. 16,524 × 83 = **1,371,492**
2. 201,002 × 93 = **18,693,186**
3. 8,704,355 × 71 = **618,009,205**
4. 626,350 × 36 = **22,548,600**
5. 40,788 × 413 = **16,845,444**
6. 736,478 × 679 = **500,068,562**
7. 5,422 × 908 = **4,923,176**
8. 618 × 927 = **572,886**
9. 340,069 × 541 = **183,977,329**
10. 496 × 518 = **256,928**
11. 17,654 × 255 = **4,501,770**
12. 8,777 × 198 = **1,737,846**
13. 719 × 637 = **458,003**
14. 6,773 × 545 = **3,691,285**
15. 29,116 × 993 = **28,912,188**
16. 720,063 × 440 = **316,827,720**
17. 5,311 × 4,668 = **24,791,748**
18. 6,088 × 3,515 = **21,399,320**
19. 27,215 × 8,443 = **229,776,245**
20. 32,446 × 7,919 = **256,939,874**
21. 6,009 × 3,671 = **22,059,039**
22. 7,801 × 6,439 = **50,230,639**
23. 9,743 × 7,658 = **74,611,894**
24. 12,876 × 5,445 = **70,109,820**
25. 33,499 × 5,668 = **189,872,332**
26. 52,319 × 7,777 = **406,884,863**
27. 63,781 × 6,005 = **383,004,905**
28. 74,543 × 3,376 = **251,657,168**
29. 45,609 × 8,817 = **402,134,553**
30. 69,715 × 8,566 = **597,178,690**
31. 79,843 × 8,901 = **710,682,543**
32. 92,515 × 9,845 = **910,810,175**
33. 325,725 × 5,555 = **1,809,402,375**
34. 981,104 × 3,389 = **3,324,961,456**
35. 773,266 × 6,551 = **5,065,665,566**
36. 511,223 × 3,244 = **1,658,407,412**
37. 101,234 × 5,661 = **573,085,674**
38. 566,732 × 8,899 = **5,043,348,068**

Multiplication

Skill: Checking Multiplication Using Division

Name _____

Check the multiplication problems using division. Circle the problems that are correct. Show your work on another piece of paper.

Total Problems __38__
Problems Correct ____
Percent Correct ____

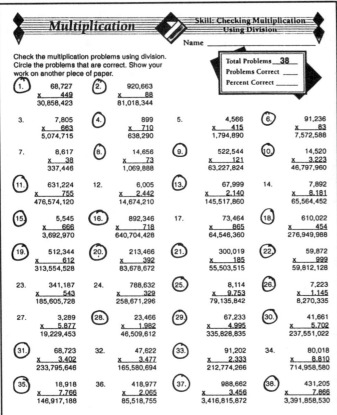

1. (circled) 68,727 × 449 = 30,858,423
2. (circled) 920,663 × 88 = 81,018,344
3. 7,805 × 663 = 5,074,715
4. (circled) 899 × 710 = 638,290
5. 4,566 × 415 = 1,794,890
6. (circled) 91,236 × 83 = 7,572,588
7. 8,617 × 38 = 337,446
8. (circled) 14,656 × 73 = 1,069,888
9. (circled) 522,544 × 121 = 63,227,824
10. (circled) 14,520 × 3,223 = 46,797,960
11. (circled) 631,224 × 755 = 476,574,120
12. 6,005 × 2,442 = 14,674,210
13. (circled) 67,999 × 2,140 = 145,517,860
14. 7,892 × 8,181 = 65,564,452
15. (circled) 5,545 × 666 = 3,692,970
16. (circled) 892,346 × 718 = 640,704,428
17. 73,464 × 865 = 64,546,360
18. (circled) 610,022 × 454 = 276,949,988
19. (circled) 512,344 × 612 = 313,554,528
20. (circled) 213,466 × 392 = 83,678,672
21. (circled) 300,019 × 185 = 55,503,515
22. (circled) 59,872 × 999 = 59,812,128
23. 341,187 × 543 = 185,605,728
24. 788,632 × 329 = 258,671,296
25. (circled) 8,114 × 9,753 = 79,135,842
26. (circled) 7,223 × 1,145 = 8,270,335
27. 3,289 × 5,877 = 19,229,453
28. (circled) 23,466 × 1,982 = 46,509,612
29. 67,233 × 4,995 = 335,828,835
30. (circled) 41,661 × 5,702 = 237,551,022
31. (circled) 68,723 × 3,402 = 233,795,646
32. 47,622 × 3,477 = 165,580,694
33. (circled) 91,202 × 2,333 = 212,774,266
34. 80,018 × 8,810 = 714,958,580
35. (circled) 18,918 × 7,766 = 146,917,188
36. 418,977 × 2,065 = 85,518,755
37. (circled) 988,662 × 3,456 = 3,416,815,872
38. (circled) 431,205 × 7,866 = 3,391,858,530

Multiplication

Skill: Multiplying by Multiples of 10

Name _____

Multiply.

Total Problems __50__
Problems Correct ____
Percent Correct ____

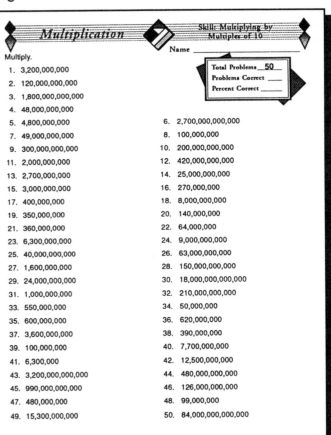

1. 3,200,000,000
2. 120,000,000,000
3. 1,800,000,000
4. 48,000,000,000
5. 4,800,000,000
6. 2,700,000,000,000
7. 49,000,000,000
8. 100,000,000
9. 300,000,000,000
10. 200,000,000,000
11. 2,000,000,000
12. 420,000,000,000
13. 2,700,000,000
14. 25,000,000,000
15. 3,000,000,000
16. 270,000,000
17. 400,000,000
18. 8,000,000,000
19. 350,000,000
20. 140,000,000
21. 360,000,000
22. 64,000,000
23. 6,300,000,000
24. 9,000,000,000
25. 40,000,000,000
26. 63,000,000,000
27. 1,600,000,000
28. 150,000,000,000
29. 24,000,000,000
30. 18,000,000,000,000
31. 1,000,000,000
32. 50,000,000,000
33. 500,000,000
34. 50,000,000
35. 600,000,000
36. 620,000,000
37. 3,600,000,000
38. 390,000,000
39. 100,000,000
40. 7,700,000,000
41. 6,300,000
42. 12,500,000,000
43. 3,200,000,000,000
44. 480,000,000
45. 990,000,000,000
46. 126,000,000,000
47. 480,000,000
48. 99,000,000
49. 15,300,000,000
50. 84,000,000,000,000

Page 13

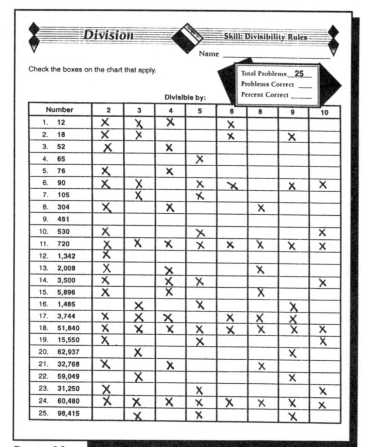

Division — Skill: Divisibility Rules

Name _____

Check the boxes on the chart that apply.

Total Problems __25__
Problems Correct ____
Percent Correct ____

Divisible by:

Number	2	3	4	5	6	8	9	10
1. 12	X	X	X		X			
2. 18	X	X			X		X	
3. 52	X		X					
4. 65				X				
5. 76	X		X					
6. 90	X	X		X	X		X	X
7. 105		X		X				
8. 304	X		X			X		
9. 481								
10. 530	X			X				X
11. 720	X	X	X	X	X	X	X	X
12. 1,342	X							
13. 2,008	X		X			X		
14. 3,500	X		X	X				X
15. 5,896	X		X			X		
16. 1,485		X		X			X	
17. 3,744	X	X	X		X	X	X	
18. 51,840	X	X	X	X	X	X	X	X
19. 15,550	X			X				X
20. 62,937		X					X	
21. 32,768	X		X			X		
22. 59,049		X					X	
23. 31,250	X			X				X
24. 60,480	X	X	X	X	X	X	X	X
25. 98,415		X		X			X	

Page 14

Division — Skill: Dividing Whole Numbers

Name _____

Divide. Show your work on another piece of paper.
Write your answers here.

Total Problems __44__
Problems Correct ____
Percent Correct ____

1. 3,142 | 6,888,972 = **2192 R1708**
2. 599 | 5,236,458 = **8742**
3. 6,311 | 70,113,102 = **11,109 R4203**
4. 973 | 41,737,808 = **42,896**
5. 1,514 | 6,998,004 = **4622 R296**
6. 872 | 81,624,503 = **93,606 R71**
7. 549 | 9,032,119 = **16,451 R520**
8. 2,133 | 10,681,218 = **5007 R1287**
9. 607 | 7,914,063 = **13,037 R604**
10. 865 | 85,637,595 = **99,003**
11. 4,422 | 32,603,406 = **7373**
12. 2,111 | 6,337,899 = **3002 R677**
13. 2,877 | 13,098,981 = **4553**
14. 4,911 | 662,308,915 = **134,862 R1633**
15. 988 | 70,568,888 = **71,426**
16. 3,020 | 654,302,198 = **216,656 R1078**
17. 6,012 | 58,983,732 = **9811**
18. 2,981 | 342,766,752 = **114,983 R2429**
19. 736 | 90,112,354 = **122,435 R194**
20. 439 | 2,651,560 = **6040**
21. 1,998 | 14,897,088 = **7456**
22. 3,566 | 723,056,009 = **202,763 R3351**
23. 718 | 404,459,452 = **563,314**
24. 7,143 | 988,453,612 = **138,380 R5,272**
25. 1,111 | 69,267,517 = **62,347**
26. 3,432 | 278,517,096 = **81,153**
27. 5,466 | 201,300,444 = **36,827 R4062**
28. 6,432 | 47,802,624 = **7432**
29. 2,153 | 68,392,114 = **31,765 R2069**
30. 988 | 47,188,856 = **47,762**
31. 881 | 235,008,512 = **266,752**
32. 917 | 142,699,812 = **155,615 R857**
33. 925 | 193,301,875 = **208,975**
34. 4,566 | 5,421,733,612 = **1,187,414 R1288**
35. 2,099 | 11,414,362 = **5438**
36. 1,986 | 1,004,612,337 = **505,847 R195**
37. 720 | 31,999,680 = **44,444**
38. 912 | 88,723,321 = **97,284 R313**
39. 5,125 | 46,140,375 = **9003**
40. 4,019 | 6,616,008,512 = **1,646,182 R3054**
41. 3,202 | 68,670,092 = **21,446**
42. 3,111 | 8,990,119,876 = **2,889,784 R1852**
43. 789 | 77,914,539 = **98,751**
44. 3,192 | 161,942,928 = **50,734**

Page 15

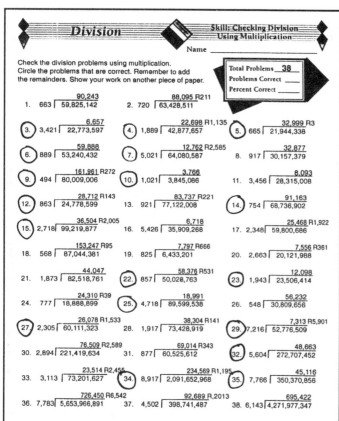

Division — Skill: Checking Division Using Multiplication

Name _____

Check the division problems using multiplication.
Circle the problems that are correct. Remember to add
the remainders. Show your work on another piece of paper.

Total Problems __38__
Problems Correct ____
Percent Correct ____

1. 663 | 59,825,142 = 90,243
2. 720 | 63,428,511 = 88,095 R211
3. (circled) 3,421 | 22,773,597 = 6,657
4. 1,889 | 42,877,657 = 22,698 R1,135
5. (circled) 665 | 21,944,338 = 32,999 R3
6. (circled) 889 | 53,240,432 = 59,888
7. 5,021 | 64,080,587 = 12,762 R2,585
8. 917 | 30,157,379 = 32,877
9. (circled) 494 | 80,009,006 = 161,961 R272
10. 1,021 | 3,845,086 = 3,766
11. 3,456 | 28,315,008 = 8,093
12. (circled) 863 | 24,778,599 = 28,712 R143
13. 921 | 77,122,008 = 83,737 R221
14. (circled) 754 | 68,736,902 = 91,163
15. (circled) 2,718 | 99,219,877 = 36,504 R2,005
16. 5,426 | 35,909,268 = 6,718
17. 2,348 | 59,800,686 = 25,468 R1,922
18. 568 | 87,044,381 = 153,247 R95
19. 825 | 6,433,201 = 7,797 R666
20. 2,663 | 20,121,988 = 7,556 R361
21. 1,873 | 82,518,761 = 44,047
22. (circled) 857 | 50,028,763 = 58,376 R531
23. (circled) 1,943 | 23,506,414 = 12,098
24. 777 | 18,888,899 = 24,310 R39
25. (circled) 4,718 | 89,599,538 = 18,991
26. 548 | 30,809,656 = 56,232
27. (circled) 2,305 | 60,111,323 = 26,078 R1,533
28. 1,917 | 73,428,919 = 38,304 R141
29. (circled) 7,216 | 52,776,509 = 7,313 R5,901
30. 2,894 | 221,419,634 = 76,509 R2,589
31. 877 | 60,525,612 = 69,014 R343
32. (circled) 5,604 | 272,707,452 = 48,663
33. 3,113 | 73,201,627 = 23,514 R2,455
34. (circled) 8,917 | 2,091,652,968 = 234,569 R1,195
35. (circled) 7,766 | 350,370,856 = 45,116
36. 7,783 | 5,653,966,891 = 726,450 R6,542
37. 4,502 | 398,741,487 = 92,689 R2,013
38. 6,143 | 4,271,977,347 = 695,422

Page 16

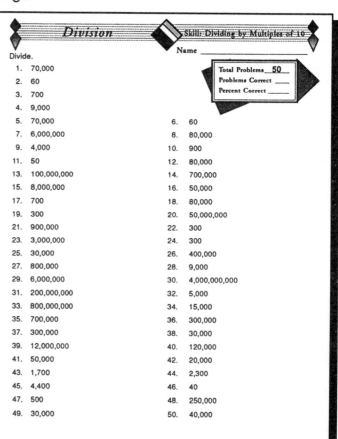

Division — Skill: Dividing by Multiples of 10

Name _____

Divide.

Total Problems __50__
Problems Correct ____
Percent Correct ____

1. 70,000
2. 60
3. 700
4. 9,000
5. 70,000
6. 60
7. 6,000,000
8. 80,000
9. 4,000
10. 900
11. 50
12. 80,000
13. 100,000,000
14. 700,000
15. 8,000,000
16. 50,000
17. 700
18. 80,000
19. 300
20. 50,000,000
21. 900,000
22. 300
23. 3,000,000
24. 300
25. 30,000
26. 400,000
27. 800,000
28. 9,000
29. 6,000,000
30. 4,000,000,000
31. 200,000,000
32. 5,000
33. 800,000,000
34. 15,000
35. 700,000
36. 300,000
37. 300,000
38. 30,000
39. 12,000,000
40. 120,000
41. 50,000
42. 20,000
43. 1,700
44. 2,300
45. 4,400
46. 40
47. 500
48. 250,000
49. 30,000
50. 40,000

Page 17

Estimation
Skill: Estimating Whole Number Products and Quotients

Name _____

Estimate the products and quotients by rounding. Show your work on another sheet of paper. Write your answers here.

Total Problems __45__
Problems Correct ____
Percent Correct ____

1. 284 x 467,892
150,000,000
2. 36,348,720 ÷ 38
900,000
3. 7,329 x 77,885
560,000,000
4. 59,887 ÷ 12
6,000
5. 166 x 871,123
180,000,000
6. 2,378,619 ÷ 434
6,000
7. 444 x 3,875,562
1,600,000,000
8. 417,360,511 ÷ 6,299
70,000
9. 5,322 x 67,233
350,000,000
10. 403,564,302 ÷ 189
2,000,000
11. 64 x 7,549,986
480,000,000
12. 40,326,119 ÷ 43
1,000,000
13. 983 x 82,478
80,000,000
14. 59,980,333 ÷ 2,276
30,000
15. 756 x 9,432,886
7,200,000,000
16. 3,992,546,002 ÷ 522
8,000,000
17. 741 x 681,123
490,000,000
18. 11,810,435 ÷ 34
400,000
19. 635 x 86,677
54,000,000
20. 10,213,980 ÷ 2,435
5,000
21. 351 x 76,553
32,000,000
22. 24,663,432 ÷ 4,893
5,000
23. 2,608 x 94,212
270,000,000
24. 13,826,972 ÷ 219
70,000
25. 1,750 x 4,325
8,000,000
26. 23,745,677 ÷ 32
800,000
27. 5,417 x 85,627
450,000,000
28. 35,678,087 ÷ 625
60,000
29. 7,658 x 83,661
640,000,000
30. 34,7865,606 ÷ 5,155
7,000
31. 333 x 73,468
21,000,000
32. 273,766,542 ÷ 888
300,000
33. 53 x 1,327,655
50,000,000
34. 158,711,223 ÷ 7536
20,000
35. 4,178 x 682,999
2,800,000,000
36. 6,998,991 ÷ 678
10,000
37. 3,727 x 46,878
200,000,000
38. 198,721,541 ÷ 432
500,000
39. 3,476 x 33,760
90,000,000
40. 183,877,524 ÷ 5,681
30,000
41. 66 x 9,288,764
630,000,000
42. 62,733,115 ÷ 8,842
7,000
43. 97 x 32,438
3,000,000
44. 48,322,718 ÷ 553
80,000
45. 513 x 6,244
3,000,000

Page 17

Page 18

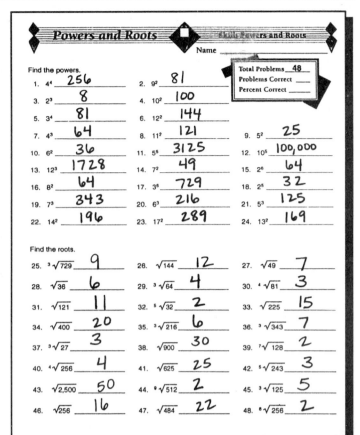

Powers and Roots
Skill: Powers and Roots

Name _____

Total Problems __48__
Problems Correct ____
Percent Correct ____

Find the powers.

1. 4^4 = 256
2. 9^2 = 81
3. 2^3 = 8
4. 10^2 = 100
5. 3^4 = 81
6. 12^2 = 144
7. 4^3 = 64
8. 11^2 = 121
9. 5^2 = 25
10. 6^2 = 36
11. 5^5 = 3125
12. 10^5 = 100,000
13. 12^3 = 1728
14. 7^2 = 49
15. 2^6 = 64
16. 8^2 = 64
17. 3^6 = 729
18. 2^5 = 32
19. 7^3 = 343
20. 6^3 = 216
21. 5^3 = 125
22. 14^2 = 196
23. 17^2 = 289
24. 13^2 = 169

Find the roots.

25. $\sqrt[3]{729}$ = 9
26. $\sqrt{144}$ = 12
27. $\sqrt{49}$ = 7
28. $\sqrt{36}$ = 6
29. $\sqrt[3]{64}$ = 4
30. $\sqrt[4]{81}$ = 3
31. $\sqrt{121}$ = 11
32. $\sqrt[5]{32}$ = 2
33. $\sqrt{225}$ = 15
34. $\sqrt{400}$ = 20
35. $\sqrt[3]{216}$ = 6
36. $\sqrt[3]{343}$ = 7
37. $\sqrt[3]{27}$ = 3
38. $\sqrt{900}$ = 30
39. $\sqrt[7]{128}$ = 2
40. $\sqrt[4]{256}$ = 4
41. $\sqrt{625}$ = 25
42. $\sqrt[5]{243}$ = 3
43. $\sqrt{2,500}$ = 50
44. $\sqrt[9]{512}$ = 2
45. $\sqrt[3]{125}$ = 5
46. $\sqrt{256}$ = 16
47. $\sqrt{484}$ = 22
48. $\sqrt[8]{256}$ = 2

Page 18

Page 19

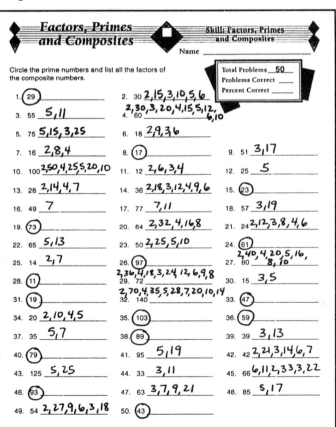

Factors, Primes and Composites
Skill: Factors, Primes and Composites

Name _____

Circle the prime numbers and list all the factors of the composite numbers.

Total Problems __50__
Problems Correct ____
Percent Correct ____

1. (29)
2. 30 2,15,3,10,5,6
3. 55 5,11
4. 60 2,30,3,20,4,15,5,12, 6,10
5. 75 5,15,3,25
6. 18 2,9,3,6
7. 16 2,8,4
8. (17)
9. 51 3,17
10. 100 2,50,4,25,5,20,10
11. 12 2,6,3,4
12. 25 5
13. 28 2,14,4,7
14. 36 2,18,3,12,4,9,6
15. (23)
16. 49 7
17. 77 7,11
18. 57 3,19
19. (73)
20. 64 2,32,4,16,8
21. 24 2,12,3,8,4,6
22. 65 5,13
23. 50 2,25,5,10
24. (61)
25. 14 2,7
26. (97)
27. 80 2,40,4,20,5,16, 8,10
28. (11)
29. 72 2,36,4,18,3,24,12,6,9,8
30. 15 3,5
31. (19)
32. 140 2,70,4,35,5,28,7,20,10,14
33. (47)
34. 20 2,10,4,5
35. (103)
36. (59)
37. 35 5,7
38. (89)
39. 39 3,13
40. (79)
41. 95 5,19
42. 42 2,21,3,14,6,7
43. 125 5,25
44. 33 3,11
45. 66 6,11,2,33,3,22
46. (93)
47. 63 3,7,9,21
48. 85 5,17
49. 54 2,27,9,6,3,18
50. (43)

Page 19

Page 20

Prime Factorization
Skill: Prime Factorization

Name _____

Find the prime factorization of the following numbers.

Total Problems __40__
Problems Correct ____
Percent Correct ____

1. 325 $5^2 \times 13$
2. 420 $2^2 \times 3 \times 5 \times 7$
3. 200 $2^3 \times 5^2$
4. 564 $2^2 \times 3 \times 47$
5. 616 $2^3 \times 7 \times 11$
6. 240 $2^4 \times 3 \times 5$
7. 286 $2 \times 11 \times 13$
8. 270 $2 \times 3^3 \times 5$
9. 150 $2 \times 3 \times 5^2$
10. 476 $2^2 \times 7 \times 17$
11. 1,323 $3^3 \times 7^2$
12. 264 $2^3 \times 3 \times 11$
13. 320 $2^6 \times 5$
14. 500 $2^2 \times 5^3$
15. 432 $3^3 \times 2^4$
16. 104 $2^3 \times 13$
17. 352 $2^5 \times 11$
18. 1,539 $3^4 \times 19$
19. 1,000 $2^3 \times 5^3$
20. 1,372 $2^2 \times 7^3$
21. 224 $2^5 \times 7$
22. 792 $2^3 \times 3^2 \times 11$
23. 858 $2 \times 3 \times 11 \times 13$
24. 1,020 $2^2 \times 3 \times 5 \times 17$
25. 1,125 $3^2 \times 5^3$
26. 8,624 $2^4 \times 7^2 \times 11$
27. 30,030 $2 \times 3 \times 5 \times 7 \times 11 \times 13$
28. 3,036 $2^2 \times 3 \times 11 \times 23$
29. 900 $2^2 \times 3^2 \times 5^2$
30. 3,971 11×19^2
31. 3,375 $3^3 \times 5^3$
32. 6,732 $2^2 \times 3^2 \times 11 \times 17$
33. 296 $2^3 \times 37$
34. 1,435 $5 \times 7 \times 41$
35. 5,824 $2^6 \times 17 \times 13$
36. 10,404 $2^2 \times 3^2 \times 17^2$
37. 5,929 $7^2 \times 11^2$
38. 16,170 $2 \times 3 \times 5 \times 7^2 \times 11$
39. 18,711 $3^5 \times 7 \times 11$
40. 120,050 $2 \times 5^2 \times 7^4$

Page 20

Math IF8771

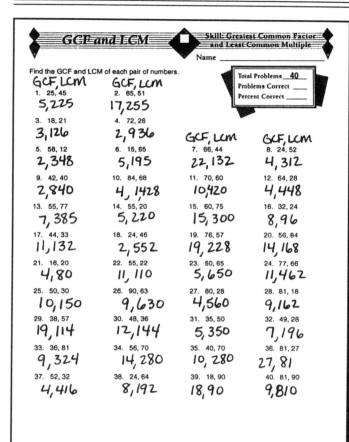

GCF and LCM
Skill: Greatest Common Factor and Least Common Multiple

Name _____

Find the GCF and LCM of each pair of numbers.

Total Problems __40__
Problems Correct _____
Percent Correct _____

GCF, LCM

1. 25, 45   **5, 225**
2. 85, 51   **17, 255**
3. 18, 21   **3, 126**
4. 72, 26   **2, 936**

GCF, LCM   GCF, LCM

5. 58, 12   **2, 348**
6. 15, 65   **5, 195**
7. 66, 44   **22, 132**
8. 24, 52   **4, 312**
9. 42, 40   **2, 840**
10. 84, 68   **4, 1428**
11. 70, 60   **10, 420**
12. 64, 28   **4, 448**
13. 55, 77   **7, 385**
14. 55, 20   **5, 220**
15. 60, 75   **15, 300**
16. 32, 24   **8, 96**
17. 44, 33   **11, 132**
18. 24, 46   **2, 552**
19. 76, 57   **19, 228**
20. 56, 84   **14, 168**
21. 16, 20   **4, 80**
22. 55, 22   **11, 110**
23. 50, 65   **5, 650**
24. 77, 66   **11, 462**
25. 50, 30   **10, 150**
26. 90, 63   **9, 630**
27. 80, 28   **4, 560**
28. 81, 18   **9, 162**
29. 38, 57   **19, 114**
30. 48, 36   **12, 144**
31. 35, 50   **5, 350**
32. 49, 28   **7, 196**
33. 36, 81   **9, 324**
34. 56, 70   **14, 280**
35. 40, 70   **10, 280**
36. 81, 27   **27, 81**
37. 52, 32   **4, 416**
38. 24, 64   **8, 192**
39. 18, 90   **18, 90**
40. 81, 90   **9, 810**

Page 21

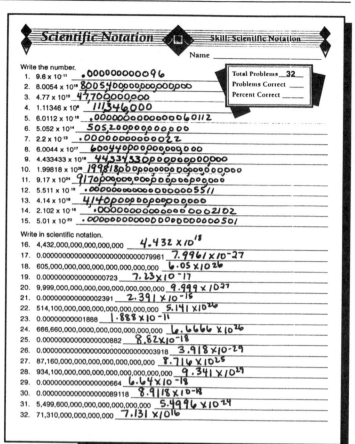

Scientific Notation
Skill: Scientific Notation

Name _____

Write the number.

Total Problems __32__
Problems Correct _____
Percent Correct _____

1. 9.6×10^{-11} **.00000000000 96**
2. 8.0054×10^{18} **8005400000000000000**
3. 4.77×10^{10} **47700000000**
4. 1.11346×10^{8} **111346000**
5. 6.0112×10^{-18} **.000000000000006 0112**
6. 5.052×10^{14} **505200000000000**
7. 2.2×10^{-13} **.00000000000 22**
8. 6.0044×10^{17} **600440000000000000**
9. 4.433433×10^{19} **44334330000000000000**
10. 1.99818×10^{26} **199818000000000000000000000**
11. 9.17×10^{24} **9170000000,000000000000000**
12. 5.511×10^{-19} **.00000000000000005511**
13. 4.14×10^{16} **41400000000000000**
14. 2.102×10^{-18} **.000000000000002102**
15. 5.01×10^{-23} **.0000000000000000000000501**

Write in scientific notation.

16. 4,432,000,000,000,000,000   **4.432×10^{18}**
17. 0.0000000000000000000000079961   **7.9961×10^{-27}**
18. 605,000,000,000,000,000,000,000,000   **6.05×10^{26}**
19. 0.00000000000000000723   **7.23×10^{-17}**
20. 9,999,000,000,000,000,000,000,000,000   **9.999×10^{27}**
21. 0.000000000000002391   **2.391×10^{-15}**
22. 514,100,000,000,000,000,000,000,000   **5.141×10^{26}**
23. 0.00000000001888   **1.888×10^{-11}**
24. 666,660,000,000,000,000,000,000,000   **6.6666×10^{26}**
25. 0.0000000000000000882   **8.82×10^{-18}**
26. 0.00000000000000000000000003918   **3.918×10^{-29}**
27. 87,160,000,000,000,000,000,000,000   **8.716×10^{25}**
28. 934,100,000,000,000,000,000,000   **9.341×10^{24}**
29. 0.00000000000000000664   **6.64×10^{-18}**
30. 0.000000000000000089118   **8.9118×10^{-8}**
31. 5,499,600,000,000,000,000,000,000   **5.4996×10^{24}**
32. 71,310,000,000,000,000   **7.131×10^{16}**

Page 22

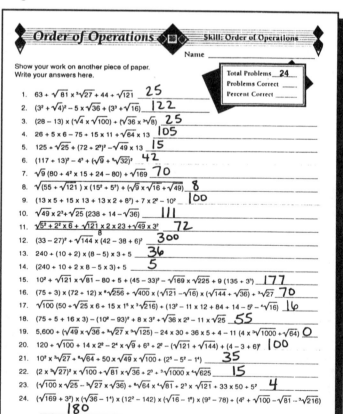

Order of Operations
Skill: Order of Operations

Name _____

Show your work on another piece of paper.
Write your answers here.

Total Problems __24__
Problems Correct _____
Percent Correct _____

1. $63 \div \sqrt{81} \times \sqrt[3]{27} + 44 + \sqrt{121}$ **25**
2. $(3^2 + \sqrt{4})^2 - 5 \times \sqrt{36} + (3^3 + \sqrt{16})$ **122**
3. $(28 - 13) \times (\sqrt{4} \times \sqrt{100}) + (\sqrt{36} \times \sqrt[3]{8})$ **25**
4. $26 + 5 \times 6 - 75 + 15 \times 11 + \sqrt{64} \times 13$ **105**
5. $125 + \sqrt{25} + (72 + 2^3)^2 - \sqrt{49} \times 13$ **15**
6. $(117 + 13)^2 - 4^5 + (\sqrt{9} + \sqrt[5]{32})^3$ **42**
7. $\sqrt{9} (80 + 4^2 \times 15 + 24 - 80) + \sqrt{169}$ **70**
8. $\sqrt{(55 + \sqrt{121})} \times (15^2 + 5^3) + (\sqrt{9} \times \sqrt{16} + \sqrt{49})$ **8**
9. $(13 \times 5 + 15 \times 13 + 13 \times 2 + 8^2) + 7 \times 2^2 - 10^2$ **100**
10. $\sqrt{49} \times 2^3 + \sqrt{25} (238 + 14 - \sqrt{36})$ **111**
11. $\dfrac{\sqrt{5^2 + 2^2} \times 6 + \sqrt{121} \times 2 \times 23 + \sqrt{49} \times 3^2}{8}$ **72**
12. $(33 - 27)^2 + \sqrt{144} \times (42 - 38 + 6)^2$ **300**
13. $240 \div (10 + 2) \times (8 - 5) \times 3 + 5$ **36**
14. $(240 + 10 + 2 \times 8 - 5 \times 3) + 5$ **5**
15. $10^2 + \sqrt{121} \times \sqrt{81} - 80 + 5 + (45 - 33)^2 - \sqrt{169} \times \sqrt{225} + 9 (135 + 3^3)$ **177**
16. $(75 + 3) \times (72 + 12) \times 6 \times \sqrt[8]{256} + \sqrt{400} \times (\sqrt{144} - \sqrt{36}) + \sqrt[3]{27}$ **70**
17. $\sqrt{100} (50 + \sqrt{25} \times 6 + 15 \times 1^5 \times \sqrt[3]{216}) + (13^2 - 11 \times 12 + 84 + 14 - 5 - \sqrt[4]{16})$ **16**
18. $(75 + 5 + 16 \times 3) - (10^2 - 93)^2 + 8 \times 3^2 + \sqrt{36} \times 2^3 - 11 \times \sqrt{25}$ **55**
19. $5,600 + (\sqrt{49} \times \sqrt{36} + \sqrt[3]{27} \times \sqrt[3]{125}) - 24 \times 30 + 36 \times 5 + 4 - 11 (4 \times \sqrt[3]{1000} + \sqrt{64})$ **0**
20. $120 + \sqrt{100} + 14 \times 2^2 - 2^4 \times \sqrt{9} + 6^3 + 2^5 - (\sqrt{121} + \sqrt{144}) + (4 - 3 + 6)^2$ **100**
21. $10^2 \times \sqrt[3]{27} + \sqrt[6]{64} + 50 \times \sqrt{49} \times \sqrt{100} + (2^5 - 5^2 - 1^4)$ **35**
22. $(2 \times \sqrt[3]{27})^2 \times \sqrt{100} + \sqrt{81} \times \sqrt{36} + 2^3 + \sqrt[3]{1000} \times \sqrt[4]{625}$ **15**
23. $(\sqrt{100} \times \sqrt{25} - \sqrt[3]{27} \times \sqrt{36}) + \sqrt[6]{64} \times \sqrt[4]{81} + 2^3 \times \sqrt{121} + 33 \times 50 + 5^2$ **4**
24. $(\sqrt{169} + 3^2) \times (\sqrt{36} - 1^4) \times (12^2 - 142) \times (\sqrt{16} - 1^8) \times (9^2 - 78) + (4^2 + \sqrt{100} - \sqrt{81} - \sqrt[3]{216})$ **180**

Page 23

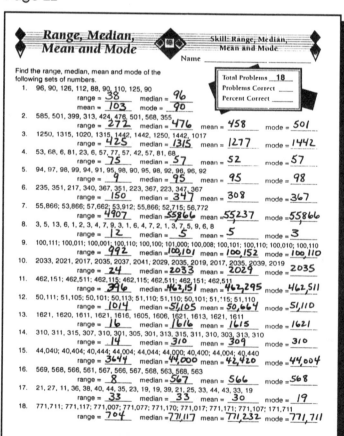

Range, Median, Mean and Mode
Skill: Range, Median, Mean and Mode

Name _____

Find the range, median, mean and mode of the following sets of numbers.

Total Problems __18__
Problems Correct _____
Percent Correct _____

1. 96, 90, 126, 112, 88, 90, 110, 125, 90
   range = **38** median = **96** mean = **103** mode = **90**
2. 585, 501, 399, 313, 424, 476, 501, 568, 355
   range = **272** median = **476** mean = **458** mode = **501**
3. 1250, 1315, 1020, 1315, 1442, 1442, 1250, 1442, 1017
   range = **425** median = **1315** mean = **1277** mode = **1442**
4. 53, 68, 6, 81, 23, 6, 57, 77, 57, 42, 57, 81, 68
   range = **75** median = **57** mean = **52** mode = **57**
5. 94, 97, 98, 99, 94, 91, 95, 98, 90, 95, 98, 92, 96, 96, 92
   range = **9** median = **95** mean = **95** mode = **98**
6. 235, 351, 217, 340, 367, 351, 223, 367, 223, 347, 367
   range = **150** median = **347** mean = 308 mode = **367**
7. 55,866; 53,866; 57,662; 53,912; 55,866; 52,715; 56,772
   range = **4907** median = **55866** mean = **55237** mode = **55866**
8. 3, 5, 13, 6, 1, 2, 3, 4, 7, 9, 3, 1, 6, 4, 7, 2, 1, 3, 7, 5, 9, 6, 8
   range = **12** median = **5** mean = 5 mode = **3**
9. 100,111; 100,011; 100,001; 100,110; 100,100; 101,000; 100,008; 100,101; 100,110; 100,010; 100,110
   range = **992** median = **100,101** mean = **100,152** mode = **100,110**
10. 2033, 2021, 2017, 2035, 2037, 2041; 2029, 2035, 2019, 2017, 2035, 2039, 2019
    range = **24** median = **2033** mean = 2029 mode = **2035**
11. 462,151; 462,511; 462,115; 462,115; 462,511; 462,151; 462,511
    range = **396** median = **462,151** mean = **462,295** mode = **462,511**
12. 50,111; 51,105; 50,101; 50,113; 51,110; 51,110; 50,101; 51,115; 51,110
    range = **1014** median = **51,105** mean = **50,664** mode = **51,110**
13. 1621, 1620, 1611, 1621, 1616, 1605, 1606, 1621, 1613, 1621, 1611
    range = **16** median = **1616** mean = **1615** mode = 1621
14. 310, 311, 315, 307, 310, 301, 305, 301, 315, 311, 310, 303, 313, 310
    range = **14** median = **310** mean = 309 mode = 310
15. 44,040; 40,404; 40,444; 44,004; 44,044; 44,000; 40,400; 44,004; 40,440
    range = **3644** median = **44,000** mean = **42,420** mode = **44,004**
16. 569, 568, 566, 561, 567, 566, 567, 568, 563, 568, 563
    range = **8** median = **567** mean = 566 mode = **568**
17. 21, 27, 11, 36, 38, 40, 44, 35, 23, 19, 19, 39, 21, 25, 33, 44, 43, 33, 19
    range = **33** median = **33** mean = 30 mode = **19**
18. 771,711; 771,117; 771,007; 771,077; 771,170; 771,017; 771,171; 771,107; 171,711
    range = **704** median = **771,117** mean = **771,232** mode = **771,711**

Page 24

Math IF8771

Page 25 — GPE — Skill: Precision and Greatest Possible Error

Name _____

Total Problems __30__
Problems Correct ____
Percent Correct ____

Complete the chart.

	Measurement	Precision to the Nearest	GPE	Actual Length
1.	82 hm	hm	0.5 hm	82 hm ± 0.5 hm
2.	9 dg	decigram	0.5 dg	9 dg ± 0.5 dg
3.	247 L	liter	0.5 L	247 L ± 0.5 L
4.	35 cm	centimeter	0.5 cm	35 cm ± 0.5 cm
5.	49 kg	Kg	0.5 kg	49 kg ± 0.5 kg
6.	112 mL	milliliter	0.5 mL	112 mL ± 0.5 mL
7.	6 dam	dekameter	.5 dam	6 dam ± 0.5 dam
8.	75 kg	kilogram	0.5 kg	75 kg ± 0.5 kg
9.	86 cL	cL	0.5 cL	86 cL ± 0.5 cL
10.	14 hm	hectometer	0.5 hm	14 hm ± 0.5 hm
11.	647 mm	millimeter	0.5 mm	647 mm ± 0.5 mm
12.	51 mg	milligram	0.5 mg	51 mg ± 0.5 mg
13.	33 dL	dL	0.5 dL	33 dL ± 0.5 dL
14.	240 Km	kilometer	0.5 km	240 km ± 0.5 km
15.	467 cg	centigram	0.5 cg	467 cg ± 0.5 cg
16.	21.3 cm	0.1 centimeter	0.05 cm	21.3 cm ± 0.05 cm
17.	346.09 L	.01 L	0.005 L	346.09 L ± 0.005 L
18.	3.7 cm	0.1 centimeter	0.05 cm	3.7 cm ± 0.05 cm
19.	29.88 g	0.01 gram	0.005 g	29.88 g ± 0.005 g
20.	9.2 hL	0.1 hectoliter	0.05 hL	9.2 hL ± 0.05 hL
21.	10.17 dam	.01 dam	0.005 dam	10.17 dam ± 0.005 dam
22.	200 mm	millimeter	0.5 mm	200 mm ± 0.5 mm
23.	918.01 cm	0.01 centimeter	0.005 cm	918.01 cm ± 0.005 cm
24.	63.9 L	0.1 liter	0.05 L	63.9 L ± 0.05 L
25.	4.003 g	.001 g	0.0005 g	4.003 g ± 0.0005 g
26.	26.4 Kg	0.1 kilogram	0.05 kg	26.4 kg ± 0.05 kg
27.	30.7 m	0.1 meter	0.05 m	30.7 m ± 0.05 m
28.	16.42 kg	0.01 kilogram	0.005 kg	16.42 kg ± 0.005 kg
29.	1.111 kL	.001 kL	0.0005 kL	1.111 kL ± 0.0005 kL
30.	114.14 dm	0.01 decimeter	0.005 dm	114.14 dm ± 0.005 dm

Page 25

Page 26 — Rational Numbers — Skill: Rational Numbers

Name _____

Total Problems __50__
Problems Correct ____
Percent Correct ____

Write as a rational number in the form $\frac{a}{b}$.

1. 0.6 → $\frac{6}{10}$
2. $3\frac{4}{7}$ → $\frac{25}{7}$
3. -10 → $\frac{-10}{1}$
4. -0.82 → $\frac{-82}{100}$
5. -3.33 → $\frac{-333}{100}$
6. $-5\frac{5}{6}$ → $\frac{-35}{6}$
7. 2.12 → $\frac{212}{100}$
8. 0.85 → $\frac{85}{100}$
9. 27 → $\frac{27}{1}$
10. -0.68 → $\frac{-68}{100}$
11. -9 → $\frac{-9}{1}$
12. -8.36 → $\frac{-836}{100}$
13. -4.87 → $\frac{-487}{100}$
14. $-8\frac{4}{7}$ → $\frac{-60}{7}$
15. $12\frac{1}{2}$ → $\frac{25}{2}$
16. 0.44 → $\frac{44}{100}$
17. -0.16 → $\frac{-16}{100}$
18. 10.3 → $\frac{103}{10}$
19. -2.99 → $\frac{-299}{100}$
20. -0.24 → $\frac{-24}{100}$
21. 5.25 → $\frac{525}{100}$
22. 72 → $\frac{72}{1}$
23. $7\frac{3}{10}$ → $\frac{73}{10}$
24. 0.28 → $\frac{28}{100}$
25. $-6\frac{4}{5}$ → $\frac{-34}{5}$

Compare. Write >, < or =.

26. $-\frac{3}{5}$ > -0.65
27. $-9\frac{1}{2}$ < $-9\frac{1}{3}$
28. 3.42 > $3\frac{2}{5}$
29. 4.16 = $4\frac{1}{6}$
30. -0.23 < $-0.22\overline{3}$
31. 0.46 > $\frac{7}{16}$
32. $-\frac{2}{9}$ = $-0.\overline{2}$
33. $-\frac{3}{11}$ > $-0.\overline{3}$
34. -2.2 > -2.22
35. $-\frac{13}{14}$ < $-\frac{13}{16}$
36. $-1\frac{3}{11}$ > -1.27
37. $-2\frac{5}{8}$ < -2.5
38. 6.625 = $6\frac{5}{8}$
39. -21 > -21.01
40. $-\frac{3}{7}$ < 0.42857

Put in increasing order.

41. $12\frac{3}{4}$, -12.74, 12.73, $12\frac{11}{15}$ → -12.74, 12.73, $12\frac{11}{15}$, $12\frac{3}{4}$
42. -4.19, -4.201, $-4\frac{2}{5}$, $-4\frac{1}{5}$ → $-4\frac{2}{5}$, -4.201, $-4\frac{1}{5}$, -4.19
43. $\frac{6}{25}$, $\frac{3}{11}$, $\frac{4}{15}$, 0.252 → $\frac{6}{25}$, .252, $\frac{4}{15}$, $\frac{6}{25}$
44. $-1\frac{2}{5}$, -1.401, $-1\frac{3}{8}$, 1.389 → -1.401, $-1\frac{2}{5}$, $-1\frac{3}{8}$, 1.389
45. 15.151, $15\frac{3}{16}$, $15\frac{3}{20}$, 15.185 → $15\frac{3}{20}$, 15.151, 15.185, $15\frac{3}{16}$
46. $-\frac{2}{3}$, -0.66, $-\frac{5}{8}$, $\frac{7}{11}$ → $-\frac{2}{3}$, -.66, $-\frac{7}{11}$, $-\frac{5}{8}$
47. 11.551, $11.\overline{15}$, $11\frac{11}{20}$, $11.\overline{5}$ → $11.\overline{15}$, $11\frac{11}{20}$, 11.551, $11.\overline{5}$
48. $\frac{3}{40}$, 0.0778, 0.081, $\frac{2}{25}$ → $\frac{3}{40}$, .0778, $\frac{2}{25}$, .081
49. $-6\frac{9}{60}$, $-6.\overline{15}$, -6.145, $-6\frac{7}{50}$ → $-6.\overline{15}$, $-6\frac{9}{60}$, -6.145, $-6\frac{7}{50}$
50. $-0.7\overline{3}$, -0.777, $-\frac{11}{15}$, $\frac{7}{9}$ → $-\frac{7}{9}$, -.777, $-.7\overline{3}$, $-\frac{11}{15}$

Page 26

Page 27 — Real Numbers — Skill: Real Numbers

Name _____

Total Problems __46__
Problems Correct ____
Percent Correct ____

Circle the irrational numbers, express fractions as decimals, and write the repeating decimals with a bar over the repetend.

1. $-6\frac{14}{15}$ → $-6.9\overline{3}$
2. (circled) 0.06627827927...
3. -3.024555555... → $-3.024\overline{5}$
4. 27.138138138 → $27.\overline{138}$
5. $20\frac{3}{32}$ → 20.09375
6. $-11\frac{19}{40}$ → -11.475
7. (circled) 0.941941194111...
8. $\frac{7}{8}$ → .875
9. -0.1110626262... → $.11106\overline{2}$
10. $\frac{1}{13}$ → $.\overline{076923}$
11. (circled) -0.424424442...
12. 0.699999999... → $.6\overline{9}$
13. -0.01723723723... → $.0\overline{1723}$
14. (circled) 1.112311231111...
15. $-5\frac{2}{45}$ → $-5.0\overline{4}$
16. $-\frac{7}{60}$ → $-.11\overline{6}$
17. $-\frac{2}{3}$ → $-.\overline{6}$
18. -0.488248824882... → $.\overline{4882}$
19. 0.56071560715... → $.\overline{56071}$
20. (circled) -3.0624106242...
21. 11.1172172172... → $11.1\overline{172}$
22. $-8\frac{15}{16}$ → -8.9375
23. $-14\frac{2}{55}$ → $-14.0\overline{36}$
24. $-\frac{16}{125}$ → -.128
25. $-\frac{3}{110}$ → $-.0\overline{27}$
26. 28.09510995109951... → $28.\overline{0951}$
27. (circled) -0.0563206532...
28. (circled) -33.0044556678...
29. $3\frac{5}{18}$ → $3.2\overline{7}$
30. $1\frac{25}{160}$ → 1.15625

Compare. Write >, < or =.

31. $-0.\overline{126}$ > -0.126126216217
32. -0.233323323... < $\frac{7}{30}$
33. -1.714285823... > $1\frac{5}{7}$
34. -4.003248... < -4.0032480328...
35. 0.8134792601... > 0.81347
36. $-33.\overline{83}$ < $-33\frac{5}{6}$
37. $-\frac{10}{11}$ > -0.90919293...
38. 11.904760915... < $11\frac{19}{21}$
39. -0.0364 < -0.0364363362...
40. $\frac{7}{60}$ < 0.1166678029...

Put in increasing order.

41. $0.\overline{818}$, 0.818283..., $\frac{9}{11}$, $0.\overline{8182}$ → $\frac{9}{11}$, $.\overline{8182}$, .818283..., $.\overline{818}$
42. $-3\frac{19}{40}$, -3.475, -3.47, -3.47491682... → -3.475, $-3\frac{19}{40}$, -3.47491682..., -3.47
43. $0.\overline{316}$, 0.136135134..., $0.\overline{1361}$, $\frac{3}{22}$ → $.\overline{1361}$, .136135134..., $\frac{3}{22}$, $.\overline{316}$
44. $-0.28\overline{1}$, $\frac{9}{32}$, $-0.\overline{28125}$, -0.281259783 → $-.28\overline{1}$, -.281259783, $-.\overline{28125}$, $\frac{9}{32}$
45. -11.035038687..., $-11\frac{7}{200}$, $-11.0\overline{35}$, -11.035 → -11.035, -11.035038687..., $-11.0\overline{35}$, $-11\frac{7}{200}$
46. 0.088789809..., $\frac{4}{45}$, $0.0\overline{8}$, 0.088 → $.0\overline{8}$, .088, .088789809..., $\frac{4}{45}$

Page 27

Page 28 — Irrational Numbers — Skill: Irrational Numbers

Name _____

Total Problems __45__
Problems Correct ____
Percent Correct ____

Circle the irrational numbers.

1. (circled) -3.4556173289985...
2. 6.123737373737...
3. (circled) -0.443655574433665...
4. 0.005680056800...
5. -3.973973973
6. (circled) 85.1436779981268...
7. (circled) 11.131114111151111116...
8. 88.888882573...
9. (circled) -92.989796959493...
10. 0.0587663663663...
11. (circled) -0.15115111511115...
12. -142.42917917917...
13. -0.865486548654
14. -3.965477320115
15. (circled) 488.93100672581...
16. 3.5136851368...
17. (circled) 149.650112762...
18. (circled) -0.431431143111...
19. -62.448931313131...
20. (circled) -5.623623624...
21. 0.882288228822...
22. -0.9817598175...
23. 0.8113662662...
24. (circled) -31.9545645632...
25. (circled) 59.006007008...
26. 0.9538753875...
27. 0.767515151...
28. (circled) 599.623625624...
29. (circled) -0.832883278326...
30. -18.143764376...

Compare. Write >, < or =.

31. -0.4366789967... < -0.4366789867...
32. -13.551038974... > -13.515038974...
33. 0.63009467221... > 0.6309467221...
34. 0.0412411241112... < 0.0412411124112...
35. -8.87543375462... < -8.87534375462...
36. 74.4000399625... < 74.4000399655...
37. -0.6645302684... > -0.6645320684...
38. -56.724724472444... = -56.724724472444...
39. 915.15033150033... < 915.15033315023...
40. 38.00578057857... < 38.00578058758...

Put in increasing order.

41. -0.0673573473..., -0.0673573373..., -0.0673573483..., -0.0673574483... → 3 4 2 1
42. -4.1143111431111..., -4.1143111341111..., -4.143111431111..., -4.114311431111... → 3 4 1 2
43. 62.88787887..., 6.88787887..., 62.887787887..., 62.887878788... → 4 1 2 3
44. 0.7373536272..., 0.7733536272..., 0.7337536272..., 0.7733356272... → 1 4 2 3
45. -12.00000399824..., -12.0000399824..., -12.0000039824..., -12.0000398824... → 3 1 4 2

Page 28

Factorials
Skill: Factorial Notation

Name _____

Find the value of each of the following. Show your work on another piece of paper. Write your answers here.

Total Problems __50__
Problems Correct ____
Percent Correct ____

1. 3! **6**
2. 5! **120**
3. (12 – 8)! **24**
4. 7! – 2! **5038**
5. 6! – 4! **696**
6. (16 – 9)! **5040**
7. (3!) (2!) **12**
8. 6! **720**
9. (4!) (6!) **17,280**
10. 8! **40,320**
11. (18 – 12)! **720**
12. 5! – 3! **114**
13. $\frac{10!}{7!}$ **3,628,800**
14. $\frac{11!}{9!}$ **110**
15. 9! **362,880**
16. $\frac{12!}{8!}$ **11,880**
17. $\frac{9!}{7!}$ **72**
18. (5!) (4!) **2880**
19. $\frac{8! - 4!}{}$ **40,296**
20. (3!) (4!) **144**
21. $\frac{15!}{11!}$ **32,760**
22. $\frac{11!}{20 - 15}$ **332,640**
23. $\frac{12!}{5!}$ **3,991,680**
24. $\frac{8!}{(12 - 9)!}$ **6720**

How many ways can the letters of each of these words be arranged?
(Hint: The letters do not have to spell words.)

25. WORM **24**
26. HORSE **120**
27. FLOWER **720**
28. DRAGONS **5040**

Evaluate. Show your work on another piece of paper. Write your answers here.

29. $_5P_2$ **20**
30. $_7P_3$ **210**
31. $_6P_2$ **30**
32. $_7P_4$ **840**
33. $_8P_1$ **8**
34. $_9P_4$ **3024**
35. $_5P_1$ **5**
36. $_8P_5$ **6720**
37. $_9P_6$ **60,480**
38. $_8P_3$ **336**
39. $_{10}P_3$ **720**
40. $_9P_2$ **72**
41. $_6P_4$ **360**
42. $_7P_5$ **2520**
43. $_{10}P_7$ **604,800**
44. $_9P_?$ **3024**
45. $_{11}P_3 + _8P_?$ **182,430**
46. $_8P_5 + _{12}P_?$ **19,958,420**
47. $_{13}P_2 - _2P_?$ **100**
48. $_9P_6 - _9P_5$ **53,760**
49. $\frac{_9P_4}{_4P_1}$ **756**
50. $\frac{_{10}P_3}{_6P_3}$ **6**

Relatively Prime Numbers
Skill: Relatively Prime Numbers

Name _____

Circle the pairs of numbers that are relatively prime.

Total Problems __50__
Problems Correct ____
Percent Correct ____

1. 14, 112
2. (106, 9)
3. (40, 43)
4. (107, 66)
5. 111, 37
6. 46, 49
7. 10, 35
8. 78, 13
9. 95, 38
10. 133, 76
11. 77, 44
12. (85, 26)
13. 33, 129
14. 64, 16
15. (38, 49)
16. 115 46
17. (26, 125)
18. 75, 6
19. (87, 118)
20. 12, 51
21. 18, 21
22. 52, 39
23. (81, 74)
24. 129, 18
25. (40, 57)
26. 81, 54
27. (92, 15)
28. (63, 20)
29. 26, 91
30. (69, 32)
31. (34, 129)
32. (99, 70)
33. (128, 21)
34. 28, 49
35. (114, 55)
36. 63, 84
37. (123, 26)
38. 125, 20
39. 36, 117
40. 58, 87
41. (88, 17)
42. (47, 7)
43. (29, 129)
44. 48, 15
45. (68, 9)
46. (33, 35)
47. 82, 123
48. (102, 55)
49. 27, 81
50. (63, 8)

Decimals
Skill: Reading and Writing Decimals

Name _____

Write the word form of each decimal.

Total Problems __25__
Problems Correct ____
Percent Correct ____

1. two and six hundred thousand, eight hundred thirty-six millionths
2. four thousand, six hundred sixty-nine and three thousand four hundred fifty-five ten-thousandths
3. one millionth
4. eleven and twenty-three thousand four hundred six hundred-thousandths
5. eight hundred seven and five thousandths
6. ninety-four thousand, one hundred three hundred-thousandths
7. six hundred eighty-two and fifty-nine thousandths
8. five and five thousand, five hundred fifty-five ten-thousandths
9. three thousand, six hundred three millionths
10. nine thousand, one hundred sixty-seven and twenty-two hundredths

Write the correct numeral for each number.

11. 118.00497
12. 39,074.87
13. 5,011.009
14. 900.632
15. 0.890001
16. 0.040602
17. 14.068421
18. 50.1093
19. 0.00003
20. 0.33413
21. 9,056.0048
22. 9.0152
23. 542.688
24. 17.019
25. 1.871018

Decimals
Skill: Decimal Place Value

Name _____

On the following number:

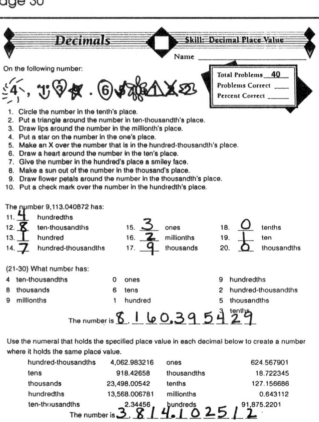

1. Circle the number in the tenth's place.
2. Put a triangle around the number in ten-thousandth's place.
3. Draw lips around the number in the millionth's place.
4. Put a star on the number in the one's place.
5. Make an X over the number that is in the hundred-thousandth's place.
6. Draw a heart around the number in the ten's place.
7. Give the number in the hundred's place a smiley face.
8. Make a sun out of the number in the thousand's place.
9. Draw flower petals around the number in the thousandth's place.
10. Put a check mark over the number in the hundredth's place.

The number 9,113.040872 has:

11. **4** hundredths
12. **8** ten-thousandths
13. **1** hundred
14. **7** hundred-thousandths
15. **3** ones
16. **2** millionths
17. **9** thousands
18. **0** tenths
19. **1** ten
20. **0** thousandths

(21-30) What number has:

4 ten-thousandths	0 ones	9 hundredths
8 thousands	6 tens	2 hundred-thousandths
9 millionths	1 hundred	5 thousandths

The number is **8,160.395429**

Use the numeral that holds the specified place value in each decimal below to create a number where it holds the same place value.

hundred-thousandths	4,062.983216	ones	624.567901
tens	918.42658	thousandths	18.722345
thousands	23,498.00542	tenths	127.156686
hundredths	13,568.006781	millionths	0.643112
ten-thousandths	2.34456	hundreds	91,875.2201

The number is **3,814.102512**

Math IF8771

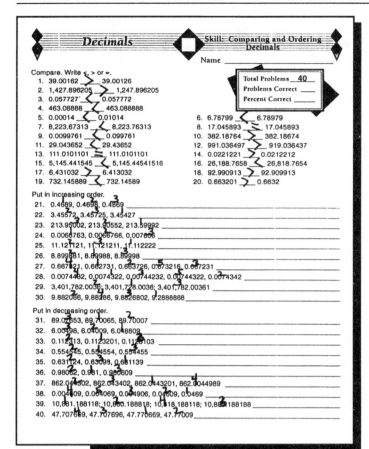

Decimals — Skill: Comparing and Ordering Decimals

Name _____

Total Problems __40__
Problems Correct ____
Percent Correct ____

Compare. Write <, > or =.

1. 39.00162 > 39.00126
2. 1,427.896205 > 1,247.896205
3. 0.057727 < 0.057772
4. 463.08888 < 463.088888
5. 0.00014 < 0.01014
6. 6.78799 < 6.78979
7. 8,223.67313 < 8,223.76313
8. 17.045893 = 17.045893
9. 0.0099761 < 0.099761
10. 382.18764 > 382.18674
11. 29.043652 < 29.43652
12. 991.036497 > 919.036437
13. 111.0101101 = 111.0101101
14. 0.0221221 > 0.0212212
15. 5,145.441545 < 5,145.44541516
16. 26,188.7658 < 26,818.7654
17. 6.431032 > 6.413032
18. 92.990913 > 92.909913
19. 732.145889 > 732.14589
20. 0.663201 > 0.6632

Put in increasing order.

21. 0.4689, 0.4698, 0.4869
22. 3.45572, 3.45725, 3.4547
23. 213.95002, 213.90552, 213.59992
24. 0.0066763, 0.0066766, 0.007606
25. 11.121721, 11.121211, 11.112222
26. 8.899581, 8.89988, 8.89998
27. 0.667121, 0.662731, 0.663726, 0.673216, 0.667231
28. 0.0074462, 0.0074522, 0.00744232, 0.0074322, 0.0074342
29. 3,401,782.0036; 3,401,728.0036; 3,401,782.00361
30. 9.882086, 9.88286, 9.8826802, 9.2888888

Put in decreasing order.

31. 89.07653, 89.70065, 89.70007
32. 6.00498, 6.04009, 6.048809
33. 0.112313, 0.1123201, 0.113103
34. 0.554545, 0.554554, 0.554455
35. 0.631124, 0.63098, 0.681139
36. 0.98062, 0.981, 0.980609
37. 862.044302, 862.043402, 862.0443201, 862.0044989
38. 0.004609, 0.064069, 0.04906, 0.04609, 0.0469
39. 10,881.188118; 10,880.188818; 10,818.188118; 10,882.188188
40. 47.707669, 47.707696, 47.770669, 47.77009

Page 33

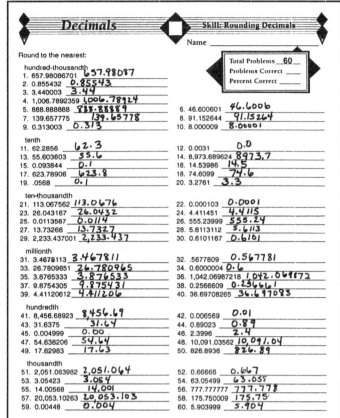

Decimals — Skill: Rounding Decimals

Name _____

Total Problems __60__
Problems Correct ____
Percent Correct ____

Round to the nearest:

hundred-thousandth
1. 657.98086701   657.98087
2. 0.855432   0.85543
3. 3.440003   3.44
4. 1,006.7892359   1006.78924
5. 888.888888   888.88889
6. 46.600601   46.6006
7. 139.657775   139.65778
8. 91.152644   91.15264
9. 0.313003   0.313
10. 8.000009   8.00001

tenth
11. 62.2856   62.3
12. 0.0031   0.0
13. 55.603603   55.6
14. 8,973.689624   8973.7
15. 0.093844   0.1
16. 14.53986   14.5
17. 623.78906   623.8
18. 74.6099   74.6
19. .0568   0.1
20. 3.2761   3.3

ten-thousandth
21. 113.067562   113.0676
22. 0.000103   0.0001
23. 26.043167   26.0432
24. 4.411451   4.4115
25. 0.0113567   0.0114
26. 555.23999   555.24
27. 13.73266   13.7327
28. 5.6113112   5.6113
29. 2,233.437001   2,233.437
30. 0.6101167   0.6101

millionth
31. 3.4678113   3.467811
32. .5677809   0.567781
33. 26.7809651   26.780965
34. 0.6000004   0.6
35. 3.8765333   3.876533
36. 1,042.06987218   1,042.069872
37. 9.8754305   9.875431
38. 0.2566609   0.256661
39. 4.41120612   4.411206
40. 36.69708265   36.697083

hundredth
41. 8,456.68923   8,456.69
42. 0.006569   0.01
43. 31.6375   31.64
44. 0.89023   0.89
45. 0.004999   0.00
46. 2.3996   2.4
47. 54.638206   54.64
48. 10,091.03562   10,091.04
49. 17.62983   17.63
50. 826.8936   826.89

thousandth
51. 2,051.063982   2,051.064
52. 0.66666   0.667
53. 3.05423   3.054
54. 63.05499   63.055
55. 14.00568   14.001
56. 777.777777   777.778
57. 20,053.10263   20,053.103
58. 175.750009   175.75
59. 0.00448   0.004
60. 5.903999   5.904

Page 34

Decimals — Skill: Adding Decimals

Name _____

Total Problems __30__
Problems Correct ____
Percent Correct ____

Add.

1. 31.62394 + 43.49863 = 75.12257
2. 0.046893 + 0.988706 = 1.035599
3. 612.05466 + 80.98802 = 693.04268
4. 132.0638 + 99.542 = 231.6058
5. 1.39876 + 26.8238 + 0.666895 = 28.889455
6. 236.7842 + 8.99999 + 5,689.803 = 5,935.58719
7. 626.887762 + .000903 + 44.44444 = 671.333105
8. 89.0006 + 4.55 + 0.368 = 93.9186
9. 638.421 + 9.99808 + 76.0039 = 724.42298
10. 6.890033 + 2.689763 + 5.589922 = 15.169718
11. 86.982683 + 0.4036 + 9.90032 = 97.294603
12. 46.325 + 29.888 + 98.634 = 174.847
13. 638.26 + 39.84 + 119.08 = 797.18
14. 162.894 + 334.55 + 712.203 = 1209.647
15. 9.0468 + 0.3201 + 14.5066 = 23.8735
16. 63.8907 + 0.0655 + 111.347 = 175.3032
17. 2.368 + 1.114 + 3.226 = 6.708
18. 891.05637 + 673.998 + 1,487.009834 = 3052.064204
19. 33.8912 + 0.7436 + 0.044 = 34.6788
20. 0.368811 + 0.045332 + 0.585657 = 1.0
21. 47.0883 + 681.119956 + 700.8876 = 1429.095856
22. 1,211.426789 + 5,781.330042 + 6,666.000455 = 13,658.757286
23. 565.889 + 404.011 + 300.979 = 1270.879
24. 0.663988 + 0.700707 + 0.301122 = 1.665817
25. 4.327 + 0.689 + 15.901 = 20.917
26. 0.1111 + 0.2222 + 0.3333 + 0.3334 = 1.0
27. 28.43765 + 0.002 + 1.0934 + 3.0 = 32.53305
28. 18 + 0.00976 + 5.703 + 1,426.0008 = 1449.71356
29. 162.009 + 38.468 + 89.001 + 3,277.698 = 3567.176
30. 0.003486 + 0.915541 + 0.2389 + 0.00687 = 1.164797

Page 35

Decimals — Skill: Subtracting Decimals

Name _____

Total Problems __38__
Problems Correct ____
Percent Correct ____

Subtract.

1. 92.6873 − 89.0099 = 3.6774
2. 0.90082 − 0.89726 = 0.00356
3. 3,427.67 − 563.008 = 2864.662
4. 0.99365 − 0.112 = 0.88165
5. 588.1188 − 29.5979 = 558.5209
6. 36.04 − 0.9765 = 35.0635
7. 11.111111 − 10.101010 = 1.010101
8. 3.98902 − 1.19399 = 2.79503
9. 6.537 − 0.9688 = 5.5682
10. 52.5 − 50.75 = 1.75
11. 7.00006 − 5.12349 = 1.87657
12. 0.43683 − 0.09817 = 0.33866
13. 3.066666 − 2.578899 = 0.487767
14. 14.73402 − 8.65211 = 6.08191
15. 891.04 − 763.57 = 127.47
16. 3.467 − 2.00892 = 1.45808
17. 2,657.8532 − 1,748.9104 = 908.9428
18. 666.78918 − 423.88009 = 242.90909
19. 99.123 − 18.0566 = 81.0664
20. 0.773286 − 0.004499 = 0.768787
21. 918.5 − 2.665 = 915.835
22. 4,881.633 − 9.808 = 4871.825
23. 0.116102 − 0.059333 = 0.056769
24. 87.7654 − 69.88888 = 17.87652
25. 4.877681 − 0.119991 = 4.75769
26. 33.45688 − 18.92111 = 14.53577
27. 8.0076 − 1.116542 = 6.891058
28. 0.201 − 0.11998 = 0.08102
29. 386.44444 − 189.98765 = 196.45679
30. 1,100.88 − 26.999 = 1073.881
31. 3.87004 − 1.98112 = 1.88892
32. 19.6389 − 0.9999 = 18.639
33. 0.661132 − 0.450987 = 0.210145
34. 63.00913 − 58.11119 = 4.89794
35. 4.59 − 0.39986 = 4.19014
36. 61.84344 − 18.996 = 42.84744
37. 1.6893 − 0.9109 = 0.7784
38. 419.00461 − 98.74296 = 320.26567

Page 36

Math IF8771

Subtract. Show your work on another piece of paper. Write your answers here.

Total Problems __40__
Problems Correct ____
Percent Correct ____

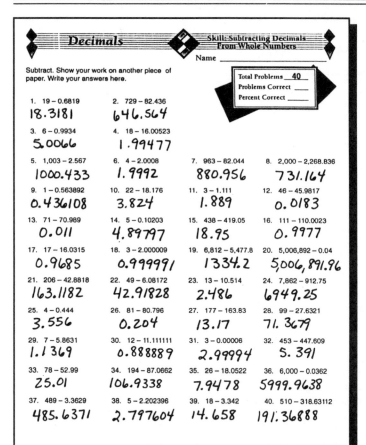

1. 19 − 0.6819 = **18.3181**
2. 729 − 82.436 = **646.564**
3. 6 − 0.9934 = **5.0066**
4. 18 − 16.00523 = **1.99477**
5. 1,003 − 2.567 = **1000.433**
6. 4 − 2.0008 = **1.9992**
7. 963 − 82.044 = **880.956**
8. 2,000 − 2,268.836 = **731.164**
9. 1 − 0.563892 = **0.436108**
10. 22 − 18.176 = **3.824**
11. 3 − 1.111 = **1.889**
12. 46 − 45.9817 = **0.0183**
13. 71 − 70.989 = **0.011**
14. 5 − 0.10203 = **4.89797**
15. 438 − 419.05 = **18.95**
16. 111 − 110.0023 = **0.9977**
17. 17 − 16.0315 = **0.9685**
18. 3 − 2.000009 = **0.999991**
19. 6,812 − 5,477.8 = **1334.2**
20. 5,006,892 − 0.04 = **5,006,891.96**
21. 206 − 42.8818 = **163.1182**
22. 49 − 6.08172 = **42.91828**
23. 13 − 10.514 = **2.486**
24. 7,862 − 912.75 = **6949.25**
25. 4 − 0.444 = **3.556**
26. 81 − 80.796 = **0.204**
27. 177 − 163.83 = **13.17**
28. 99 − 27.6321 = **71.3679**
29. 7 − 5.8631 = **1.1369**
30. 12 − 11.111111 = **0.888889**
31. 3 − 0.00006 = **2.99994**
32. 453 − 447.609 = **5.391**
33. 78 − 52.99 = **25.01**
34. 194 − 87.0662 = **106.9338**
35. 26 − 18.0522 = **7.9478**
36. 6,000 − 0.0362 = **5999.9638**
37. 489 − 3.3629 = **485.6371**
38. 5 − 2.202396 = **2.797604**
39. 18 − 3.342 = **14.658**
40. 510 − 318.63112 = **191.36888**

Solve.

Total Problems __37__
Problems Correct ____
Percent Correct ____

1. 6,183.62 − 5,812.897 = **370.723**
2. 0.883621 + 9.116379 = **10**
3. 818 − 807.66321 = **10.33679**
4. 6.891236 − 5.723445 = **1.167791**
5. 214.68893 + 98.51773 = **313.20666**
6. 26.8 − 0.98712 = **25.81288**
7. 0.86102 − 0.39445 = **0.46657**
8. 118 − 106.0043 = **11.9957**
9. 53.0004 − 19.5567 = **33.4437**
10. 82.065791 + 29.554 = **111.619791**
11. 1,042.9896 + 9,751.003654 = **10,793.993254**
12. 400.68033 + 563.77141 = **964.45174**
13. 9,568 − 8,711.5 = **856.5**
14. 4.68623 + 89.632 = **94.31823**
15. 666,387.491632 + 301,444.516339 = **967,832.007971**
16. 874.00689 + 719.53654 = **1593.54343**
17. 69.7864 + 11.8913 = **81.6777**
18. 68.4388 − 29.5595 = **38.8793**
19. 95 − 1.000041 = **93.999959**
20. 4,689 + 93.684 = **4782.684**
21. 568.007 − 491.63321 = **76.37379**
22. 0.798633 − 0.509752 = **0.288881**
23. 36.81104 + 13.18896 = **50**
24. 5.06073 + 93.684 = **98.74473**
25. 417 − 0.88 = **416.12**
26. 91.66002 − 72.65816 = **19.00186**
27. 388.36259 − 163.445 = **224.91759**
28. 8 − 7.9562 = **0.0438**
29. 3.86214 + 3.60023 + 9.51669 = **16.97906**
30. 189.653 + 445.22222 + 208.303 = **843.17822**
31. 0.606312 + 0.944561 + 0.009999 = **1.560872**
32. 21.68102 + 18.01334 + 73.30564 = **113**
33. 6,183.005 − 5,317.72 = **865.285**
34. 111.11111 + 222.22222 + 33.33333 = **366.66666**
35. 16 − 11.863415 = **4.136585**
36. 2,968 − 871.89 = **2096.11**
37. 348.632 − 192.78 = **155.852**

Answers will vary.

Estimate. Show your work on another piece of paper. Write your answers here.

Total Problems __38__
Problems Correct ____
Percent Correct ____

1. 5.863 + 6.4918 = **12**
2. 364.980662 − 1.06315 = **399**
3. 34.68119 − 14.98772 = **20**
4. 46.0098 + 73.9776 = **120**
5. 3,192.5689 − 814.6108 = **2,200**
6. 443.0261 + 459.3095 = **900**
7. 16,867.086 − 11,309.99 = **10,000**
8. 55,068.7274 + 38,942.3388 = **100,000**
9. 28.000014 + 93.998762 = **120**
10. 9.04399 + 4.5623 = **14**
11. 18.40462 − 14.66 = **10**
12. 3,298.4 − 765.3375 = **2,200**
13. 4,569.0443 − 1,800.99 = **3,000**
14. 245.602 + 918.55634 = **1,100**
15. 7.9892346 + 22.023 = **28**
16. 5,368.77 − 439.646 = **5,400**
17. 327.0963 − 183.8 = **500**
18. 57,620.9187 − 19,412.0006 = **80,000**
19. 113,601.8543 + 47,788.9001 = **150,000**
20. 1,230.976 + 7,681.005 = **9000**
21. 9.48 − 3.76321 = **5**
22. 639.404 + 54.555 = **650**
23. 3,872.6004 − 987.75 = **3,000**
24. 10,475.5 + 12,609.8 = **20,000**
25. 33.98876 + 7.566 = **38**
26. 4,114.4114 + 3,533.5533 = **8,000**
27. 138.006 − 132.98 = **0**
28. 55.78 − 42.00631 = **20**
29. 678.005 − 7.99 = **692**
30. 93.5556 − 18.6611 = **70**
31. 42.818 + 31.44 = **70**
32. 51,412.77 + 3,899.001 = **54,000**
33. 1,920.03 − 1,212.66 = **1,000**
34. 498.0072 − 155.9 = **300**
35. 10,730.201 + 48,666.444 = **60,000**
36. 2,740.63 + 9,112.87 = **12,000**
37. 917.246 + 874.3 = **1,800**
38. 9,870.777 + 1,562.606 = **12,000**

Multiply. Show your work on another piece of paper. Write your answers here.

Total Problems __38__
Problems Correct ____
Percent Correct ____

1. 84.63 × 7.64 = **646.5732**
2. 19.75 × 4.3 = **84.925**
3. 0.876 × 0.54 = **0.47304**
4. 5.33 × 46.7 = **248.911**
5. 0.718 × 9.2 = **6.6056**
6. 312.9 × 0.63 = **197.127**
7. 0.3443 × 5.7 = **1.96251**
8. 99.6 × 0.42 = **41.832**
9. 1.115 × 55.1 = **61.4365**
10. 2.04 × 1.99 = **4.0596**
11. 713.26 × 4.8 = **3423.648**
12. 88.3 × 0.462 = **40.7946**
13. 264.3 × 0.57 = **150.651**
14. 340.22 × 7.7 = **2619.694**
15. 2.005 × 0.97 = **1.94485**
16. 631.8 × 3.4 = **2148.12**
17. 0.698 × 54.7 = **38.1806**
18. 802.6 × 0.479 = **384.4454**
19. 66.5 × 23.3 = **1549.45**
20. 84.11 × 0.76 = **63.9236**
21. 0.981 × 0.23 = **0.22563**
22. 4.468 × 0.392 = **1.751456**
23. 0.688 × 0.499 = **0.343312**
24. 0.5987 × 0.83 = **0.496921**
25. 43.12 × 98.7 = **4255.944**
26. 6.0083 × 7.9 = **47.46557**
27. 0.4458 × 0.81 = **0.361098**
28. 28.9 × 0.103 = **2.9767**
29. 210.23 × 0.654 = **137.49042**
30. 0.988 × 0.99 = **0.97812**
31. 16.05 × 35.6 = **571.38**
32. 67.031 × 0.52 = **34.85612**
33. 5.661 × 1.03 = **5.83083**
34. 0.609 × 0.732 = **0.445788**
35. 4.8912 × 3.3 = **16.14096**
36. 65.7 × 0.104 = **6.8328**
37. 0.70221 × 0.66 = **0.4634586**
38. 0.777 × 34.6 = **26.8842**

Math IF8771

Decimals — Skill: Multiplying Decimals With Zeros in the Product

Total Problems 38
Problems Correct ____
Percent Correct ____

Multiply. Show your work on another piece of paper. Write your answers here.

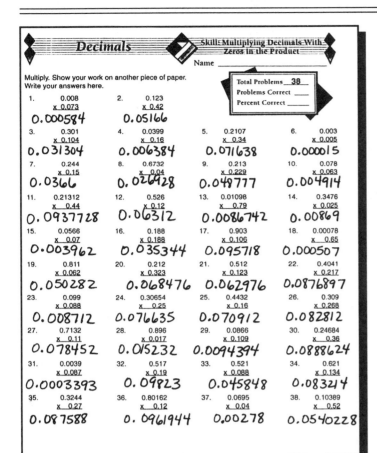

1. 0.008 × 0.073 = 0.000584
2. 0.123 × 0.42 = 0.05166
3. 0.301 × 0.104 = 0.031304
4. 0.0399 × 0.16 = 0.006384
5. 0.2107 × 0.34 = 0.071638
6. 0.003 × 0.005 = 0.000015
7. 0.244 × 0.15 = 0.0366
8. 0.6732 × 0.04 = 0.026928
9. 0.213 × 0.229 = 0.048777
10. 0.078 × 0.063 = 0.004914
11. 0.21312 × 0.44 = 0.0937728
12. 0.526 × 0.12 = 0.06312
13. 0.01098 × 0.79 = 0.0086742
14. 0.3476 × 0.025 = 0.00869
15. 0.0566 × 0.07 = 0.003962
16. 0.188 × 0.188 = 0.035344
17. 0.903 × 0.106 = 0.095718
18. 0.00078 × 0.65 = 0.000507
19. 0.811 × 0.062 = 0.050282
20. 0.212 × 0.323 = 0.068476
21. 0.512 × 0.123 = 0.062976
22. 0.4041 × 0.217 = 0.0876897
23. 0.099 × 0.088 = 0.008712
24. 0.30654 × 0.25 = 0.076635
25. 0.4432 × 0.16 = 0.070912
26. 0.309 × 0.268 = 0.082812
27. 0.7132 × 0.11 = 0.078452
28. 0.896 × 0.017 = 0.015232
29. 0.0866 × 0.109 = 0.0094394
30. 0.24684 × 0.36 = 0.0888624
31. 0.0039 × 0.087 = 0.0003393
32. 0.517 × 0.19 = 0.09823
33. 0.521 × 0.088 = 0.045848
34. 0.621 × 0.134 = 0.083214
35. 0.3244 × 0.27 = 0.087588
36. 0.80162 × 0.12 = 0.0961944
37. 0.0695 × 0.04 = 0.00278
38. 0.10389 × 0.52 = 0.0540228

Decimals — Skill: Multiplying Decimals by Powers of 10

Total Problems 25
Problems Correct ____
Percent Correct ____

Fill in the graph.

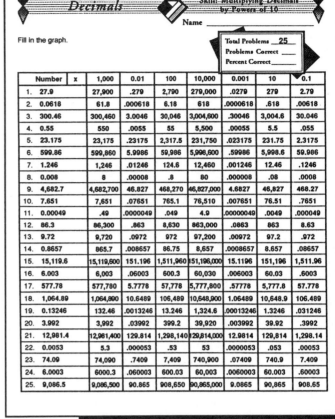

	Number	x	1,000	0.01	100	10,000	0.001	10	0.1
1.	27.9		27,900	.279	2,790	279,000	.0279	279	2.79
2.	0.0618		61.8	.000618	6.18	618	.0000618	.618	.00618
3.	300.46		300,460	3.0046	30,046	3,004,600	.30046	3,004.6	30.046
4.	0.55		550	.0055	55	5,500	.00055	5.5	.055
5.	23.175		23,175	.23175	2,317.5	231,750	.023175	231.75	2.3175
6.	599.86		599,860	5.9986	59,986	5,998,600	.59986	5,998.6	59.986
7.	1.246		1,246	.01246	124.6	12,460	.001246	12.46	.1246
8.	0.008		8	.00008	.8	80	.000008	.08	.0008
9.	4,682.7		4,682,700	46.827	468,270	46,827,000	4.6827	46,827	468.27
10.	7.651		7,651	.07651	765.1	76,510	.007651	76.51	.7651
11.	0.00049		.49	.0000049	.049	4.9	.00000049	.0049	.000049
12.	86.3		86,300	.863	8,630	863,000	.0863	863	8.63
13.	9.72		9,720	.0972	972	97,200	.00972	97.2	.972
14.	0.8657		865.7	.008657	86.75	8,657	.0008657	8.657	.08657
15.	15,119.6		15,119,600	151.196	1,511,960	151,196,000	15.1196	151,196	1,511.96
16.	6.003		6,003	.06003	600.3	60,030	.006003	60.03	.6003
17.	577.78		577,780	5.7778	57,778	5,777,800	.57778	5,777.8	57.778
18.	1,064.89		1,064,890	10.6489	106,489	10,648,900	1.06489	10,648.9	106.489
19.	0.13246		132.46	.0013246	13.246	1,324.6	.00013246	1.3246	.031246
20.	3.992		3,992	.03992	399.2	39,920	.003992	39.92	.3992
21.	12,981.4		12,981,400	129.814	1,298,140	129,814,000	12.9814	129,814	1,298.14
22.	0.0053		5.3	.000053	.53	53	.0000053	.053	.00053
23.	74.09		74,090	.7409	7,409	740,900	.07409	740.9	7.409
24.	6.0003		6000.3	.060003	600.03	60,003	.0060003	60.003	.60003
25.	9,086.5		9,086,500	90.865	908,650	90,865,000	9.0865	90,865	908.65

Decimals — Skill: Dividing Decimals by Whole Numbers

Total Problems 40
Problems Correct ____
Percent Correct ____

Divide. Show your work on another piece of paper. Write your answers here.

1. 12)0.894 = 0.0745
2. 34)2,318.8 = 68.2
3. 76)446.956 = 5.881
4. 42)294.84 = 7.02
5. 9)366.3 = 40.7
6. 55)39,119.3 = 711.26
7. 64)34.688 = 0.542
8. 29)99.789 = 3.441
9. 47)0.01034 = 0.00022
10. 18)3.654 = 0.203
11. 81)530.55 = 6.55
12. 37)37.296 = 1.008
13. 52)10.4364 = 0.2007
14. 26)256.62 = 9.87
15. 71)4.473 = 0.063
16. 90)636.3 = 7.07
17. 15)520.5 = 34.7
18. 44)4.3956 = 0.0999
19. 57)4400.97 = 77.21
20. 70)11.711 = 0.1673
21. 68)115.464 = 1.698
22. 31)6888.2 = 222.2
23. 86)410.22 = 4.77
24. 14)42.0658 = 3.0047
25. 28)0.252 = 0.009
26. 95)134.045 = 1.411
27. 17)1,121.711 = 65.983
28. 22)0.0143 = 0.00065
29. 50)875.2 = 17.504
30. 78)14.469 = 0.1855
31. 65)50.193 = 0.7722
32. 41)0.8282 = 0.0202
33. 88)5.632 = 0.064
34. 13)0.3198 = 0.0246
35. 91)778.05 = 8.55
36. 21)63.9366 = 3.0446
37. 75)5783.325 = 77.111
38. 53)0.07102 = 0.00134
39. 35)194.425 = 5.555
40. 61)195.2061 = 3.2001

Decimals — Skill: Dividing Decimals by Decimals

Total Problems 40
Problems Correct ____
Percent Correct ____

Divide. Show your work on another piece of paper. Write your answers here.

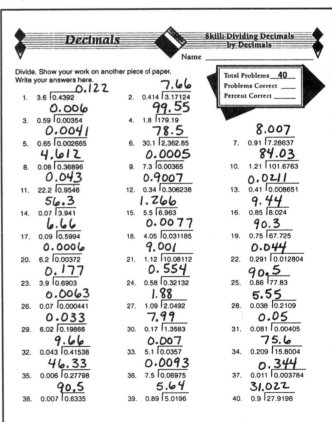

1. 3.6)0.4392 = 0.122
2. 0.414)3.17124 = 7.66
3. 0.59)0.00354 = 0.006
4. 1.8)179.19 = 99.55
5. 0.65)0.002665 = 0.0041
6. 30.1)2,362.85 = 78.5
7. 0.91)7.28637 = 8.007
8. 0.08)0.36896 = 4.612
9. 7.3)0.00365 = 0.0005
10. 1.21)101.6763 = 84.03
11. 22.2)0.9546 = 0.043
12. 0.34)0.306238 = 0.9007
13. 0.41)0.008651 = 0.0211
14. 0.07)3.941 = 56.3
15. 5.5)6.963 = 1.266
16. 0.85)8.024 = 9.44
17. 0.09)0.5994 = 6.66
18. 4.05)0.031185 = 0.0077
19. 0.75)67.725 = 90.3
20. 6.2)0.00372 = 0.0006
21. 1.12)10.08112 = 9.001
22. 0.291)0.012804 = 0.044
23. 3.9)0.6903 = 0.177
24. 0.58)0.32132 = 0.554
25. 0.86)77.83 = 90.5
26. 0.07)0.000441 = 0.0063
27. 1.09)2.0492 = 1.88
28. 0.038)0.2109 = 5.55
29. 6.02)0.19866 = 0.033
30. 0.17)1.3583 = 7.99
31. 0.081)0.00405 = 0.05
32. 0.043)0.41538 = 9.66
33. 5.1)0.0357 = 0.007
34. 0.209)15.8004 = 75.6
35. 0.006)0.27798 = 46.33
36. 7.5)0.06975 = 0.0093
37. 0.011)0.003784 = 0.344
38. 0.007)0.6335 = 90.5
39. 0.89)5.0196 = 5.64
40. 0.9)27.9198 = 31.022

Math IF8771

Name _____

Total Problems 25
Problems Correct ____
Percent Correct ____

Fill in the graph.

Number	÷	0.01	10,000	100	0.0001	0.1	1,000	0.001
1. 63.8		6,380	.00638	.638	638,000	638	.0638	63,800
2. 0.0092		.92	.00000092	.000092	92	.092	.0000092	9.2
3. 718.4		71,840	.07184	7.184	7,184,000	7,184	.7184	718,400
4. 9.663		966.3	.0009663	.09663	96,630	96.63	.009663	9,663
5. 500.6		50,060	.05006	5.006	5,006,000	5,006	.5006	500,600
6. 0.00081		.081	.000000081	.0000081	8.1	.0081	.00000081	.81
7. 8.005		800.5	.0008005	.08005	80,050	80.05	.008005	8,005
8. 40.067		4,006.7	.0040067	.40067	400,670	400.67	.040067	40,067
9. 7,100.5		710,050	.71005	71.005	71,005,000	71,005	7.1005	7,100,500
10. 0.06123		6.123	.000006123	.0006123	612.3	.6123	.00006123	61.23
11. 19.63		1,963	.001963	.1963	196,300	196.3	.01963	19,630
12. 44.441		4,444.1	.0044441	.44441	444,410	444.41	.044441	44,441
13. 1,003.6		100,360	.10036	10.036	10,036,000	10,036	1.0036	1,003,600
14. 6.022		602.2	.0006022	.06022	60,220	60.22	.006022	6,022
15. 0.00055		.055	.000000055	.0000055	5.5	.0055	.00000055	.55
16. 21,560.3		2,156,030	2.15603	215.603	215,603,000	215,603	21.5603	21,560,300
17. 0.1399		13.99	.00001399	.001399	1,399	1.399	.0001399	139.9
18. 20.441		2,044.1	.0020441	.20441	204,410	204.41	.020441	20,441
19. 7,115.8		711,580	.71158	71.158	71,158,000	71,158	7.1158	7,115,800
20. 6.8897		688.97	.00068897	.068897	68,897	68.897	.0068897	6,889.7
21. 17.099		1,709.9	.0017099	.17099	170,990	170.99	.017099	17,099
22. 321.05		32,105	.032105	3.2105	3,210,500	3,210.5	.32105	32,105
23. 69.4003		6,940.03	.00694003	.694003	694,003	694.003	.0694003	69,400.3
24. 1.0008		100.08	.00010008	.010008	10,008	10.008	.0010008	1,000.8
25. 555.11		55,511	.055511	5.5511	5,551,100	5,551.1	.55511	555,110

Page 45

Name _____

Total Problems 40
Problems Correct ____
Percent Correct ____

Estimate. Show your work on another piece of paper. Write your answers here.

1. 6.324 x 82.099 = 480
2. 70.862 x 67.934 = 4900
3. 41,078.6211 ÷ 82.3678 = 500
4. 13,815.621 ÷ 7,456.008 = 2
5. 53,872.563 ÷ 609.717 = 90
6. 497.18 x 38.88 = 20,000
7. 310,814.366 ÷ 299.0063 = 1000
8. 87.651 x 62.453 = 5400
9. 27,900.6544 ÷ 38.9881 = 700
10. 24,319.066 ÷ 5,894.57 = 4
11. 2,099.06 x 3.246 = 6000
12. 1.9123 x 48,072.004 = 100,000
13. 381.786 x 8,132.704 = 3,200,000
14. 51,433.276 ÷ 10,387.655 = 5
15. 1,799,446.8 ÷ 8,777.0654 = 200
16. 9.4632 x 3,118.766 = 27,000
17. 8,888.888 ÷ 29.6354 = 300
18. 491.005 x 572.909 = 300,000
19. 98.0732 x 69.5621 = 7000
20. 3,197.6042 ÷ 7.78063 = 400
21. 28.7119 x 7,232.604 = 210,000
22. 354.6328 ÷ 68.0435 = 5
23. 12,406.77112 ÷ 58.6337 = 200
24. 628.541 x 63.454 = 36,000
25. 1,759.6369 ÷ 8.8832 = 200
26. 53.276 x 676.543 = 35,000
27. 55,763.0032 ÷ 72.3009 = 800
28. 8.2478 x 8642.987 = 72,000
29. 442.102 x 278.865 = 120,000
30. 63.0041 x 6,009.872 = 360,000
31. 2,460.31477 ÷ 45.78913 = 50
32. 7,218.044 x 93.43006 = 80
33. 325.5678 x 5,411.8227 = 1,500,000
34. 6,018.405 ÷ 1.8976 = 3000
35. 677.8045 x 760.554321 = 560,000
36. 1,587.4311 ÷ 57.6005 = 40
37. 41,890.6332 ÷ 68.552 = 600
38. 809.5563 ÷ 9.23877 = 90
39. 77.666 x 8,349.08667 = 640,000
40. 3,567.9982 x 14.7664 = 40,000

Page 46

Name _____

Total Problems 25
Problems Correct ____
Percent Correct ____

Fill in the chart.

	kilometer (km)	hectometer (hm)	dekameter (dam)	meter (m)	decimeter (dm)	centimeter (cm)	millimeter (mm)
1.	.0052	.052	.52	5.2	52	520	5,200
2.	.00367	.0367	.367	3.67	36.7	367	3,670
3.	.000103	.00103	.0103	.103	1.03	10.3	103
4.	.61	6.1	61	610	6,100	61,000	610,000
5.	.008856	.08856	.8856	8.856	88.56	885.6	8,856
6.	.00032	.0032	.032	.32	3.2	32	320
7.	.73	7.3	73	730	7,300	73,000	730,000
8.	.04069	.4069	4.069	40.69	406.9	4,069	40.690
9.	.0000038	.000038	.00038	.0038	.038	.38	3.8
10.	4.4	44	440	4,400	44,000	440,000	4,400,000
11.	.016	.16	1.6	16	160	1,600	16,000
12.	.916	9.16	91.6	916	9,160	91,600	916,000
13.	.0000005	.000005	.00005	.0005	.005	.05	.5
14.	.01007	.1007	1.007	10.07	100.7	1,007	10,070
15.	.142	1.42	14.2	142	1,420	14,200	142,000
16.	.0000082	.000082	.00082	.0082	.082	.82	8.2
17.	.000111	.00111	.0111	.111	1.11	11.11	111.1
18.	.000194	.00194	.0194	.194	1.94	19.4	194
19.	.3	3	30	300	3,000	30,000	300,000
20.	.00007641	.0007641	.007641	.07641	.7641	7.641	76.41
21.	90	900	9,000	90,000	900,000	9,000,000	90,000,000
22.	.00703	.0703	.703	7.03	70.3	703	7,030
23.	.000118	.00118	.0118	.118	1.18	11.8	118
24.	.005	.05	.5	5	50	500	5,000
25.	.0000645	.000645	.00645	.0645	.645	6.45	64.5

Page 47

Name _____

Total Problems 50
Problems Correct ____
Percent Correct ____

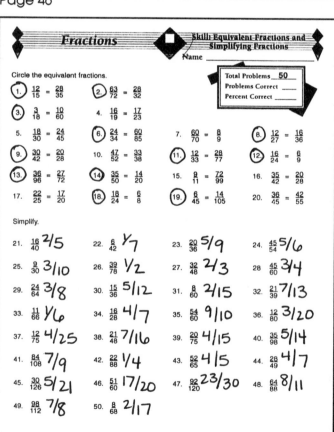

Circle the equivalent fractions.

1. (circled) $\frac{12}{15} = \frac{28}{35}$
2. (circled) $\frac{63}{72} = \frac{28}{32}$
3. (circled) $\frac{3}{18} = \frac{10}{60}$
4. $\frac{16}{19} = \frac{17}{23}$
5. $\frac{18}{30} = \frac{24}{45}$
6. (circled) $\frac{24}{34} = \frac{60}{85}$
7. $\frac{60}{70} = \frac{8}{9}$
8. (circled) $\frac{12}{27} = \frac{16}{36}$
9. (circled) $\frac{30}{42} = \frac{20}{28}$
10. $\frac{47}{52} = \frac{33}{28}$
11. (circled) $\frac{12}{33} = \frac{28}{77}$
12. (circled) $\frac{16}{24} = \frac{6}{9}$
13. (circled) $\frac{36}{96} = \frac{27}{72}$
14. $\frac{35}{50} = \frac{14}{20}$
15. $\frac{9}{11} = \frac{72}{99}$
16. $\frac{35}{42} = \frac{20}{28}$
17. $\frac{22}{25} = \frac{17}{20}$
18. (circled) $\frac{18}{24} = \frac{6}{8}$
19. (circled) $\frac{6}{45} = \frac{14}{105}$
20. $\frac{36}{45} = \frac{42}{55}$

Simplify.

21. $\frac{16}{40}$ = 2/5
22. $\frac{6}{42}$ = 1/7
23. $\frac{20}{36}$ = 5/9
24. $\frac{45}{54}$ = 5/6
25. $\frac{9}{30}$ = 3/10
26. $\frac{39}{78}$ = 1/2
27. $\frac{32}{48}$ = 2/3
28. $\frac{45}{60}$ = 3/4
29. $\frac{24}{64}$ = 3/8
30. $\frac{15}{36}$ = 5/12
31. $\frac{8}{60}$ = 2/15
32. $\frac{21}{39}$ = 7/13
33. $\frac{11}{66}$ = 1/6
34. $\frac{16}{28}$ = 4/7
35. $\frac{54}{60}$ = 9/10
36. $\frac{12}{80}$ = 3/20
37. $\frac{12}{75}$ = 4/25
38. $\frac{21}{48}$ = 7/16
39. $\frac{20}{75}$ = 4/15
40. $\frac{35}{98}$ = 5/14
41. $\frac{84}{108}$ = 7/9
42. $\frac{22}{88}$ = 1/4
43. $\frac{52}{65}$ = 4/5
44. $\frac{28}{49}$ = 4/7
45. $\frac{30}{126}$ = 5/21
46. $\frac{51}{60}$ = 17/20
47. $\frac{92}{120}$ = 23/30
48. $\frac{64}{88}$ = 8/11
49. $\frac{98}{112}$ = 7/8
50. $\frac{8}{68}$ = 2/17

Page 48

Fractions
Skill: Comparing and Ordering Fractions
Name _____

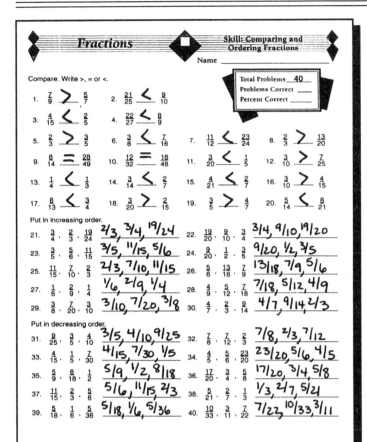

Total Problems __40__
Problems Correct ____
Percent Correct ____

Compare. Write >, =, or <.

1. $\frac{7}{9}$ > $\frac{5}{7}$
2. $\frac{21}{25}$ < $\frac{9}{10}$
3. $\frac{4}{15}$ < $\frac{2}{4}$
4. $\frac{22}{27}$ < $\frac{8}{9}$
5. $\frac{2}{3}$ > $\frac{3}{5}$
6. $\frac{3}{8}$ < $\frac{7}{16}$
7. $\frac{11}{12}$ < $\frac{23}{24}$
8. $\frac{2}{3}$ > $\frac{13}{20}$
9. $\frac{8}{14}$ = $\frac{28}{49}$
10. $\frac{12}{32}$ = $\frac{18}{48}$
11. $\frac{3}{20}$ < $\frac{1}{5}$
12. $\frac{3}{10}$ > $\frac{7}{25}$
13. $\frac{1}{4}$ < $\frac{1}{3}$
14. $\frac{3}{14}$ < $\frac{2}{7}$
15. $\frac{4}{21}$ < $\frac{2}{7}$
16. $\frac{2}{3}$ > $\frac{4}{15}$
17. $\frac{8}{13}$ < $\frac{3}{4}$
18. $\frac{3}{20}$ < $\frac{2}{15}$
19. $\frac{3}{5}$ > $\frac{1}{4}$
20. $\frac{5}{14}$ < $\frac{8}{21}$

Put in increasing order.

21. $\frac{3}{4}, \frac{2}{3}, \frac{19}{24}$ → 2/3, 3/4, 19/24
22. $\frac{19}{20}, \frac{9}{10}, \frac{3}{4}$ → 3/4, 9/10, 19/20
23. $\frac{3}{5}, \frac{5}{6}, \frac{11}{15}$ → 3/5, 11/15, 5/6
24. $\frac{9}{20}, \frac{1}{2}, \frac{3}{5}$ → 9/20, 1/2, 3/5
25. $\frac{11}{15}, \frac{7}{10}, \frac{2}{3}$ → 2/3, 7/10, 11/15
26. $\frac{5}{6}, \frac{13}{18}, \frac{7}{9}$ → 13/18, 7/9, 5/6
27. $\frac{1}{6}, \frac{2}{9}, \frac{1}{4}$ → 1/6, 2/9, 1/4
28. $\frac{4}{9}, \frac{5}{12}, \frac{7}{18}$ → 7/18, 5/12, 4/9
29. $\frac{3}{8}, \frac{7}{20}, \frac{3}{10}$ → 3/10, 7/20, 3/8
30. $\frac{4}{7}, \frac{2}{3}, \frac{9}{14}$ → 4/7, 9/14, 2/3

Put in decreasing order.

31. $\frac{9}{25}, \frac{3}{5}, \frac{4}{10}$ → 3/5, 4/10, 9/25
32. $\frac{7}{8}, \frac{7}{12}, \frac{2}{3}$ → 7/8, 2/3, 7/12
33. $\frac{4}{15}, \frac{1}{5}, \frac{7}{30}$ → 4/15, 7/30, 1/5
34. $\frac{4}{5}, \frac{5}{6}, \frac{23}{20}$ → 23/20, 5/6, 4/5
35. $\frac{5}{9}, \frac{8}{18}, \frac{1}{2}$ → 5/9, 1/2, 8/18
36. $\frac{17}{20}, \frac{3}{4}, \frac{5}{8}$ → 17/20, 3/4, 5/8
37. $\frac{11}{15}, \frac{2}{3}, \frac{5}{6}$ → 5/6, 11/15, 2/3
38. $\frac{1}{3}, \frac{5}{21}, \frac{2}{7}$ → 1/3, 2/7, 5/21
39. $\frac{5}{18}, \frac{1}{6}, \frac{5}{36}$ → 5/18, 1/6, 5/36
40. $\frac{10}{33}, \frac{3}{11}, \frac{7}{22}$ → 7/22, 10/33, 3/11

Fractions and Mixed Numbers
Skill: Mixed Numbers and Improper Fractions
Name _____

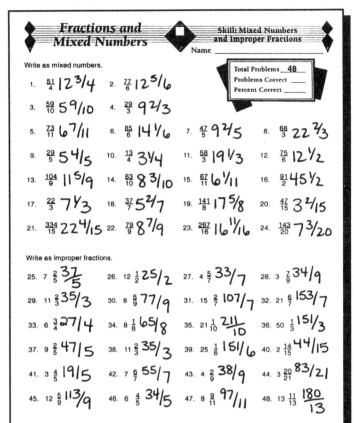

Total Problems __48__
Problems Correct ____
Percent Correct ____

Write as mixed numbers.

1. $\frac{51}{4}$ = 12 3/4
2. $\frac{77}{6}$ = 12 5/6
3. $\frac{59}{10}$ = 5 9/10
4. $\frac{29}{3}$ = 9 2/3
5. $\frac{73}{11}$ = 6 7/11
6. $\frac{85}{6}$ = 14 1/6
7. $\frac{47}{5}$ = 9 2/5
8. $\frac{68}{3}$ = 22 2/3
9. $\frac{29}{5}$ = 5 4/5
10. $\frac{13}{4}$ = 3 1/4
11. $\frac{58}{3}$ = 19 1/3
12. $\frac{75}{6}$ = 12 1/2
13. $\frac{104}{9}$ = 11 5/9
14. $\frac{83}{10}$ = 8 3/10
15. $\frac{67}{11}$ = 6 1/11
16. $\frac{91}{2}$ = 45 1/2
17. $\frac{22}{3}$ = 7 1/3
18. $\frac{37}{7}$ = 5 2/7
19. $\frac{141}{8}$ = 17 5/8
20. $\frac{47}{15}$ = 3 2/15
21. $\frac{334}{15}$ = 22 4/15
22. $\frac{79}{9}$ = 8 7/9
23. $\frac{267}{16}$ = 16 11/16
24. $\frac{143}{20}$ = 7 3/20

Write as improper fractions.

25. 7 $\frac{2}{5}$ = 37/5
26. 12 $\frac{1}{2}$ = 25/2
27. 4 $\frac{5}{7}$ = 33/7
28. 3 $\frac{7}{9}$ = 34/9
29. 11 $\frac{2}{3}$ = 35/3
30. 8 $\frac{5}{9}$ = 77/9
31. 15 $\frac{2}{7}$ = 107/7
32. 21 $\frac{6}{7}$ = 153/7
33. 6 $\frac{3}{4}$ = 27/4
34. 8 $\frac{1}{8}$ = 65/8
35. 21 $\frac{1}{10}$ = 211/10
36. 50 $\frac{1}{3}$ = 151/3
37. 9 $\frac{2}{5}$ = 47/5
38. 11 $\frac{2}{3}$ = 35/3
39. 25 $\frac{1}{6}$ = 151/6
40. 2 $\frac{14}{15}$ = 44/15
41. 3 $\frac{4}{5}$ = 19/5
42. 7 $\frac{6}{7}$ = 55/7
43. 4 $\frac{2}{9}$ = 38/9
44. 3 $\frac{20}{21}$ = 83/21
45. 12 $\frac{5}{9}$ = 113/9
46. 6 $\frac{4}{5}$ = 34/5
47. 8 $\frac{9}{11}$ = 97/11
48. 13 $\frac{11}{13}$ = 180/13

Fractions
Skill: Relating Fractions and Decimals
Name _____

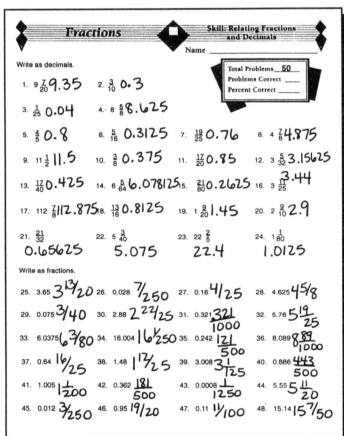

Total Problems __50__
Problems Correct ____
Percent Correct ____

Write as decimals.

1. 9 $\frac{7}{20}$ = 9.35
2. $\frac{3}{10}$ = 0.3
3. $\frac{1}{25}$ = 0.04
4. 8 $\frac{5}{8}$ = 8.625
5. $\frac{4}{5}$ = 0.8
6. $\frac{5}{16}$ = 0.3125
7. $\frac{19}{25}$ = 0.76
8. 4 $\frac{7}{8}$ = 4.875
9. 11 $\frac{1}{2}$ = 11.5
10. $\frac{3}{8}$ = 0.375
11. $\frac{17}{20}$ = 0.85
12. 3 $\frac{5}{32}$ = 3.15625
13. $\frac{17}{40}$ = 0.425
14. 6 $\frac{5}{64}$ = 6.078125
15. $\frac{21}{80}$ = 0.2625
16. 3 $\frac{11}{25}$ = 3.44
17. 112 $\frac{7}{8}$ = 112.875
18. $\frac{13}{16}$ = 0.8125
19. 1 $\frac{9}{20}$ = 1.45
20. 2 $\frac{9}{10}$ = 2.9
21. $\frac{21}{32}$ = 0.65625
22. 5 $\frac{3}{40}$ = 5.075
23. 22 $\frac{2}{5}$ = 22.4
24. 1 $\frac{1}{80}$ = 1.0125

Write as fractions.

25. 3.65 = 3 13/20
26. 0.028 = 7/250
27. 0.16 = 4/25
28. 4.625 = 4 5/8
29. 0.075 = 3/40
30. 2.88 = 2 22/25
31. 0.321 = 321/1000
32. 5.76 = 5 19/25
33. 6.0375 = 6 3/80
34. 16.004 = 16 1/250
35. 0.242 = 121/500
36. 8.089 = 8 89/1000
37. 0.64 = 16/25
38. 1.48 = 1 12/25
39. 3.008 = 3 1/125
40. 0.886 = 443/500
41. 1.005 = 1 1/200
42. 0.362 = 181/500
43. 0.0008 = 1/1250
44. 5.55 = 5 11/20
45. 0.012 = 3/250
46. 0.95 = 19/20
47. 0.11 = 11/100
48. 15.14 = 15 7/50

Fractions
Skill: Fractions as Repeating Decimals
Name _____

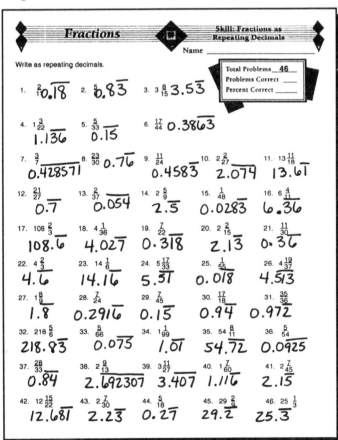

Total Problems __46__
Problems Correct ____
Percent Correct ____

Write as repeating decimals.

1. $\frac{2}{11}$ = 0.$\overline{18}$
2. $\frac{5}{6}$ = 0.8$\overline{3}$
3. 3 $\frac{8}{15}$ = 3.5$\overline{3}$
4. 1 $\frac{3}{22}$ = 1.13$\overline{6}$
5. $\frac{5}{33}$ = 0.$\overline{15}$
6. $\frac{17}{44}$ = 0.386$\overline{3}$
7. $\frac{3}{7}$ = 0.$\overline{428571}$
8. $\frac{23}{30}$ = 0.7$\overline{6}$
9. $\frac{11}{24}$ = 0.458$\overline{3}$
10. 2 $\frac{2}{27}$ = 2.0$\overline{74}$
11. 13 $\frac{11}{18}$ = 13.6$\overline{1}$
12. $\frac{21}{27}$ = 0.$\overline{7}$
13. $\frac{2}{37}$ = 0.$\overline{054}$
14. 2 $\frac{5}{?}$ = 2.5$\overline{}$
15. $\frac{1}{48}$ = 0.0283$\overline{}$
16. 6 $\frac{4}{11}$ = 6.$\overline{36}$
17. 108 $\frac{2}{3}$ = 108.$\overline{6}$
18. 4 $\frac{1}{36}$ = 4.02$\overline{7}$
19. $\frac{7}{22}$ = 0.3$\overline{18}$
20. 2 $\frac{2}{15}$ = 2.1$\overline{3}$
21. $\frac{11}{30}$ = 0.3$\overline{6}$
22. 4 $\frac{2}{3}$ = 4.$\overline{6}$
23. 14 $\frac{1}{6}$ = 14.1$\overline{6}$
24. 5 $\frac{17}{33}$ = 5.5$\overline{51}$
25. $\frac{1}{?}$ = 0.01$\overline{8}$
26. 4 $\frac{19}{37}$ = 4.$\overline{513}$
27. 1 $\frac{8}{9}$ = 1.$\overline{8}$
28. $\frac{7}{24}$ = 0.291$\overline{6}$
29. $\frac{7}{45}$ = 0.1$\overline{5}$
30. $\frac{17}{18}$ = 0.9$\overline{4}$
31. $\frac{35}{36}$ = 0.97$\overline{2}$
32. 218 $\frac{5}{6}$ = 218.8$\overline{3}$
33. $\frac{5}{66}$ = 0.07$\overline{5}$
34. 1 $\frac{9}{?}$ = 1.0$\overline{1}$
35. 54 $\frac{8}{11}$ = 54.$\overline{72}$
36. $\frac{5}{54}$ = 0.0$\overline{925}$
37. $\frac{28}{33}$ = 0.$\overline{84}$
38. 2 $\frac{9}{13}$ = 2.$\overline{692307}$
39. 3 $\frac{11}{27}$ = 3.$\overline{407}$
40. 1 $\frac{7}{60}$ = 1.11$\overline{6}$
41. 2 $\frac{4}{45}$ = 2.1$\overline{5}$
42. 12 $\frac{15}{?}$ = 12.68$\overline{1}$
43. 2 $\frac{7}{30}$ = 2.2$\overline{3}$
44. $\frac{5}{18}$ = 0.2$\overline{7}$
45. 29 $\frac{2}{9}$ = 29.$\overline{2}$
46. 25 $\frac{1}{3}$ = 25.$\overline{3}$

Math IF8771

Fractions — Skill: Fractions and Exponents

Name _____

Solve. Show your work on another piece of paper. Write your answers here.

Total Problems __40__
Problems Correct ____
Percent Correct ____

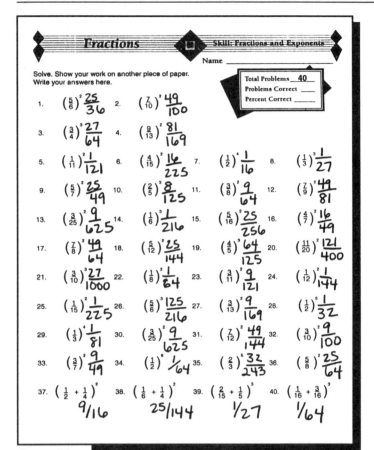

1. $(\frac{5}{6})^2$ $\frac{25}{36}$
2. $(\frac{7}{10})^2$ $\frac{49}{100}$
3. $(\frac{3}{4})^3$ $\frac{27}{64}$
4. $(\frac{9}{13})^2$ $\frac{81}{169}$
5. $(\frac{1}{11})^2$ $\frac{1}{121}$
6. $(\frac{4}{15})^2$ $\frac{16}{225}$
7. $(\frac{1}{2})^4$ $\frac{1}{16}$
8. $(\frac{1}{3})^3$ $\frac{1}{27}$
9. $(\frac{5}{7})^2$ $\frac{25}{49}$
10. $(\frac{2}{5})^3$ $\frac{8}{125}$
11. $(\frac{3}{8})^2$ $\frac{9}{64}$
12. $(\frac{7}{9})^2$ $\frac{49}{81}$
13. $(\frac{3}{25})^2$ $\frac{9}{625}$
14. $(\frac{1}{6})^3$ $\frac{1}{216}$
15. $(\frac{5}{16})^2$ $\frac{25}{256}$
16. $(\frac{4}{7})^2$ $\frac{16}{49}$
17. $(\frac{7}{8})^2$ $\frac{49}{64}$
18. $(\frac{5}{12})^2$ $\frac{25}{144}$
19. $(\frac{4}{5})^3$ $\frac{64}{125}$
20. $(\frac{11}{20})^2$ $\frac{121}{400}$
21. $(\frac{3}{10})^3$ $\frac{27}{1000}$
22. $(\frac{1}{8})^2$ $\frac{1}{64}$
23. $(\frac{3}{11})^2$ $\frac{9}{121}$
24. $(\frac{1}{12})^2$ $\frac{1}{144}$
25. $(\frac{1}{15})^2$ $\frac{1}{225}$
26. $(\frac{5}{6})^3$ $\frac{125}{216}$
27. $(\frac{3}{13})^2$ $\frac{9}{169}$
28. $(\frac{1}{2})^5$ $\frac{1}{32}$
29. $(\frac{1}{3})^4$ $\frac{1}{81}$
30. $(\frac{3}{25})^2$ $\frac{9}{625}$
31. $(\frac{7}{12})^2$ $\frac{49}{144}$
32. $(\frac{3}{10})^2$ $\frac{9}{100}$
33. $(\frac{3}{7})^2$ $\frac{9}{49}$
34. $(\frac{1}{2})^6$ $\frac{1}{64}$
35. $(\frac{2}{3})^5$ $\frac{32}{243}$
36. $(\frac{5}{8})^2$ $\frac{25}{64}$
37. $(\frac{1}{2}+\frac{1}{4})^2$ $\frac{9}{16}$
38. $(\frac{1}{6}+\frac{1}{4})^2$ $\frac{25}{144}$
39. $(\frac{2}{15}+\frac{1}{5})^3$ $\frac{1}{27}$
40. $(\frac{1}{16}+\frac{3}{16})^3$ $\frac{1}{64}$

Fractions — Skill: Adding Fractions With Unlike Denominators

Name _____

Add. Show your work on another piece of paper. Write your answer here.

Total Problems __40__
Problems Correct ____
Percent Correct ____

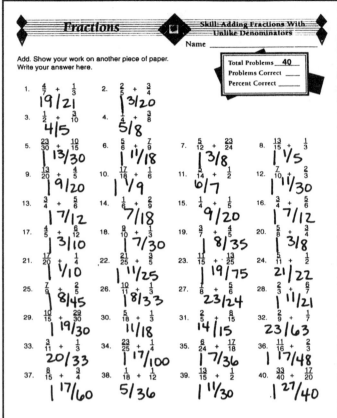

1. $\frac{4}{7}+\frac{1}{3}$ $19/21$
2. $\frac{2}{5}+\frac{3}{4}$ $1\ 3/20$
3. $\frac{1}{2}+\frac{3}{10}$ $4/5$
4. $\frac{1}{2}+\frac{1}{8}$ $5/8$
5. $\frac{23}{30}+\frac{10}{15}$ $1\ 13/30$
6. $\frac{1}{2}+\frac{7}{9}$ $1\ 11/18$
7. $\frac{5}{12}+\frac{23}{24}$ $1\ 3/8$
8. $\frac{13}{15}+\frac{1}{3}$ $1\ 1/5$
9. $\frac{13}{20}+\frac{4}{20}$ $9/20$
10. $\frac{17}{18}+\frac{1}{9}$ $1\ 1/9$
11. $\frac{1}{14}+\frac{1}{2}$ $6/7$
12. $\frac{7}{10}+\frac{2}{3}$ $1\ 11/30$
13. $\frac{3}{4}+\frac{2}{3}$ $1\ 7/12$
14. $\frac{9}{18}+\frac{2}{9}$ $7/18$
15. $\frac{1}{4}+\frac{2}{5}$ $9/20$
16. $\frac{3}{4}+\frac{1}{3}$ $1\ 7/12$
17. $\frac{4}{5}+\frac{1}{2}$ $3/10$
18. $\frac{9}{10}+\frac{2}{3}$ $1\ 7/30$
19. $\frac{3}{5}+\frac{4}{7}$ $8/35$
20. $\frac{5}{8}+\frac{3}{4}$ $1\ 3/8$
21. $\frac{17}{20}+\frac{1}{4}$ $1\ 1/10$
22. $\frac{21}{25}+\frac{4}{5}$ $1\ 11/25$
23. $\frac{11}{15}+\frac{13}{25}$ $19/75$
24. $\frac{21}{22}+\frac{1}{11}$ $21/22$
25. $\frac{7}{9}+\frac{1}{5}$ $8/45$
26. $\frac{10}{18}+\frac{4}{33}$ $18/33$
27. $\frac{23}{24}$ $23/24$
28. $\frac{2}{3}+\frac{2}{7}$ $1\ 11/21$
29. $\frac{10}{15}+\frac{29}{30}$ $1\ 19/30$
30. $\frac{5}{18}+\frac{4}{9}$ $11/18$
31. $\frac{2}{5}+\frac{1}{3}$ $14/15$
32. $\frac{13}{16}+\frac{2}{3}$ $23/63$
33. $\frac{3}{11}+\frac{1}{3}$ $20/33$
34. $\frac{23}{25}+\frac{4}{4}$ $1\ 17/100$
35. $\frac{6}{24}+\frac{17}{16}$ $1\ 7/36$
36. $\frac{11}{16}+\frac{2}{3}$ $1\ 17/48$
37. $\frac{8}{15}+\frac{3}{4}$ $1\ 17/60$
38. $\frac{1}{18}+\frac{1}{12}$ $5/36$
39. $\frac{13}{15}+\frac{2}{3}$ $1\ 11/30$
40. $\frac{33}{40}+\frac{17}{20}$ $1\ 27/40$

Mixed Numbers — Skill: Adding Mixed Numbers With Unlike Denominators

Name _____

Add. Show your work on another piece of paper. Write your answers here.

Total Problems __40__
Problems Correct ____
Percent Correct ____

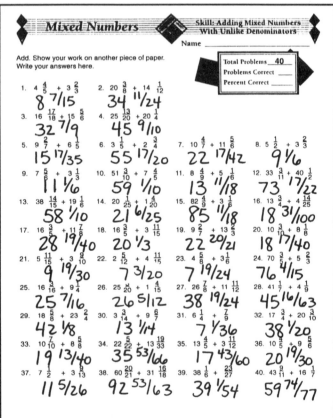

1. $4\frac{4}{5}+3\frac{2}{3}$ $8\ 7/15$
2. $20\frac{3}{8}+14\frac{1}{12}$ $34\ 11/24$
3. $16\frac{17}{18}+15\frac{5}{6}$ $32\ 7/9$
4. $25\frac{13}{20}+20\frac{1}{4}$ $45\ 9/10$
5. $7\frac{3}{5}+7\frac{4}{7}$ $15\ 17/35$
6. $3\frac{5}{12}+5\frac{2}{5}$ $55\ 17/20$
7. $10\frac{4}{7}+11\frac{5}{6}$ $22\ 17/42$
8. $5\frac{1}{2}+3\frac{2}{3}$ $9\ 1/6$
9. $7\frac{5}{6}+3\frac{1}{3}$ $11\ 1/6$
10. $51\frac{3}{5}+7\frac{1}{2}$ $59\ 1/10$
11. $8\frac{4}{9}+5\frac{2}{6}$ $13\ 11/18$
12. $33\frac{3}{11}+40\frac{1}{2}$ $73\ 17/22$
13. $38\frac{14}{15}+19\frac{1}{6}$ $58\ 1/10$
14. $20\frac{3}{25}+3\frac{1}{20}$ $21\ 6/25$
15. $82\frac{2}{3}+3\frac{1}{6}$ $85\ 11/18$
16. $13\frac{3}{4}+4\frac{14}{25}$ $18\ 31/100$
17. $16\frac{3}{8}+11\frac{1}{2}$ $28\ 19/40$
18. $16\frac{1}{3}+4\frac{13}{15}$ $20\ 1/3$
19. $9\frac{2}{3}+13\frac{2}{7}$ $22\ 20/21$
20. $10\frac{3}{8}+8\frac{1}{8}$ $18\ 17/40$
21. $5\frac{11}{15}+4\frac{1}{6}$ $9\ 19/30$
22. $2\frac{5}{12}+4\frac{11}{15}$ $7\ 3/20$
23. $4\frac{5}{8}+3\frac{1}{6}$ $7\ 19/24$
24. $70\frac{3}{5}+5\frac{8}{15}$ $76\ 4/15$
25. $16\frac{11}{16}+9\frac{1}{4}$ $25\ 7/16$
26. $25\frac{3}{20}+4\frac{1}{15}$ $26\ 5/12$
27. $26\frac{7}{8}+11\frac{11}{24}$ $38\ 19/24$
28. $41\frac{1}{7}+4\frac{1}{9}$ $45\ 16/63$
29. $18\frac{5}{8}+23\frac{1}{2}$ $42\ 1/8$
30. $3\frac{1}{14}+1\frac{1}{7}$ $13\ 1/14$
31. $6\frac{1}{4}+1\frac{1}{9}$ $7\ 1/36$
32. $17\frac{3}{4}+20\frac{3}{10}$ $38\ 1/20$
33. $10\frac{7}{10}+8\frac{5}{8}$ $19\ 13/40$
34. $22\frac{22}{33}+13\frac{1}{6}$ $35\ 53/66$
35. $13\frac{3}{5}+4\frac{1}{12}$ $17\ 43/60$
36. $10\frac{5}{6}+9\frac{5}{6}$ $20\ 19/30$
37. $7\frac{1}{2}+3\frac{7}{13}$ $11\ 5/26$
38. $60\frac{5}{21}+31\frac{16}{18}$ $92\ 53/63$
39. $38\frac{1}{6}+1\frac{7}{27}$ $39\ 1/54$
40. $43\frac{5}{11}+16\frac{7}{7}$ $59\ 74/77$

Fractions — Skill: Subtracting Fractions With Unlike Denominators

Name _____

Subtract. Show your work on another piece of paper. Write your answer here.

Total Problems __40__
Problems Correct ____
Percent Correct ____

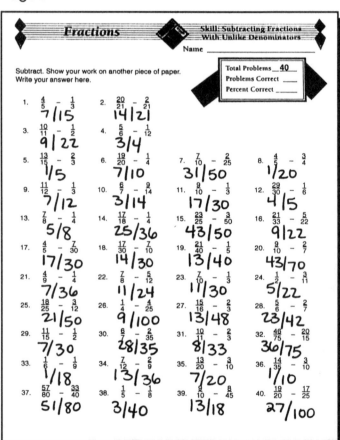

1. $\frac{4}{5}-\frac{1}{3}$ $7/15$
2. $\frac{20}{21}-\frac{2}{21}$ $14/21$
3. $\frac{10}{11}-\frac{1}{2}$ $9/22$
4. $\frac{5}{6}-\frac{1}{12}$ $3/4$
5. $\frac{13}{15}-\frac{2}{3}$ $1/5$
6. $\frac{19}{20}-\frac{1}{4}$ $7/10$
7. $\frac{7}{10}-\frac{1}{25}$ $31/50$
8. $\frac{4}{5}-\frac{3}{4}$ $1/20$
9. $\frac{11}{12}-\frac{1}{3}$ $7/12$
10. $\frac{6}{7}-\frac{9}{14}$ $3/14$
11. $\frac{9}{10}-\frac{1}{3}$ $17/30$
12. $\frac{29}{30}-\frac{1}{6}$ $4/5$
13. $\frac{7}{8}-\frac{1}{4}$ $5/8$
14. $\frac{17}{18}-\frac{1}{4}$ $25/36$
15. $\frac{23}{25}-\frac{1}{50}$ $43/50$
16. $\frac{21}{33}-\frac{5}{22}$ $9/22$
17. $\frac{4}{5}-\frac{7}{30}$ $17/30$
18. $\frac{17}{18}-\frac{2}{3}$ $14/30$
19. $\frac{21}{40}-\frac{1}{5}$ $13/40$
20. $\frac{4}{5}-\frac{3}{7}$ $43/70$
21. $\frac{4}{9}-\frac{1}{12}$ $7/36$
22. $\frac{7}{8}-\frac{5}{12}$ $11/24$
23. $\frac{7}{10}-\frac{1}{3}$ $11/30$
24. $\frac{1}{2}-\frac{3}{11}$ $5/22$
25. $\frac{18}{25}-\frac{1}{10}$ $21/50$
26. $\frac{2}{5}-\frac{3}{100}$ $9/100$
27. $\frac{15}{16}-\frac{2}{3}$ $13/48$
28. $\frac{1}{2}-\frac{3}{21}$ $23/42$
29. $\frac{11}{15}-\frac{1}{3}$ $7/30$
30. $\frac{6}{7}-\frac{2}{35}$ $28/35$
31. $\frac{10}{16}-\frac{2}{3}$ $8/33$
32. $\frac{46}{75}-\frac{20}{15}$ $36/75$
33. $\frac{1}{9}-\frac{1}{18}$ $1/18$
34. $\frac{7}{12}-\frac{2}{7}$ $13/36$
35. $\frac{13}{20}-\frac{1}{10}$ $7/20$
36. $\frac{14}{35}-\frac{1}{4}$ $1/10$
37. $\frac{57}{80}-\frac{33}{40}$ $51/80$
38. $\frac{1}{5}-\frac{1}{8}$ $3/40$
39. $\frac{9}{10}-\frac{8}{45}$ $13/18$
40. $\frac{19}{20}-\frac{17}{25}$ $27/100$

Math IF8771

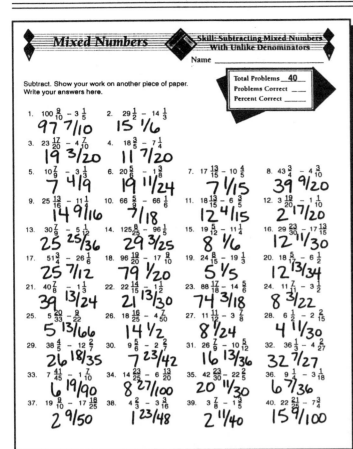

Mixed Numbers — Skill: Subtracting Mixed Numbers With Unlike Denominators

Name _____

Total Problems __40__
Problems Correct ____
Percent Correct ____

Subtract. Show your work on another piece of paper.
Write your answers here.

1. $100\frac{9}{10} - 3\frac{1}{5}$ **97 7/10**
2. $29\frac{2}{3} - 14\frac{1}{3}$ **15 1/6**
3. $23\frac{17}{20} - 4\frac{7}{10}$ **19 3/20**
4. $18\frac{5}{6} - 7\frac{1}{4}$ **11 7/20**
5. $10\frac{7}{9} - 3\frac{1}{3}$ **7 4/9**
6. $20\frac{5}{8} - 1\frac{1}{8}$ **19 11/24**
7. $17\frac{13}{15} - 10\frac{4}{5}$ **7 1/15**
8. $43\frac{3}{4} - 4\frac{3}{5}$ **39 9/20**
9. $25\frac{13}{16} - 11\frac{1}{4}$ **14 9/16**
10. $66\frac{5}{9} - 66\frac{1}{6}$ **7/18**
11. $18\frac{13}{15} - 4\frac{1}{3}$ **12 4/15**
12. $3\frac{19}{20} - 1\frac{1}{10}$ **2 17/20**
13. $30\frac{7}{9} - 5\frac{1}{12}$ **25 25/36**
14. $125\frac{24}{25} - 96\frac{4}{5}$ **29 3/25**
15. $19\frac{2}{3} - 11\frac{1}{4}$ **8 1/6**
16. $29\frac{23}{30} - 17\frac{7}{10}$ **12 11/30**
17. $51\frac{3}{4} - 26\frac{1}{6}$ **25 7/12**
18. $96\frac{19}{20} - 17\frac{9}{10}$ **79 1/20**
19. $24\frac{8}{15} - 19\frac{1}{3}$ **5 1/5**
20. $18\frac{5}{6} - 6\frac{1}{2}$ **12 13/34**
21. $40\frac{7}{8} - 1\frac{1}{3}$ **39 13/24**
22. $22\frac{14}{15} - 1\frac{1}{2}$ **21 13/30**
23. $88\frac{17}{18} - 14\frac{5}{6}$ **74 3/18**
24. $11\frac{7}{11} - 3\frac{1}{2}$ **8 3/22**
25. $5\frac{20}{33} - 9\frac{1}{22}$ **5 13/66**
26. $18\frac{16}{25} - 4\frac{1}{50}$ **14 1/2**
27. $11\frac{5}{12} - 3\frac{1}{4}$ **8 1/24**
28. $6\frac{1}{3} - 2\frac{1}{5}$ **4 11/30**
29. $38\frac{4}{5} - 12\frac{2}{7}$ **26 18/35**
30. $9\frac{5}{6} - 2\frac{2}{7}$ **7 23/42**
31. $26\frac{7}{9} - 10\frac{5}{12}$ **16 13/36**
32. $36\frac{1}{3} - 4\frac{2}{27}$ **32 7/27**
33. $7\frac{41}{45} - 1\frac{7}{10}$ **6 19/90**
34. $14\frac{24}{25} - 6\frac{11}{20}$ **8 27/100**
35. $42\frac{23}{30} - 22\frac{2}{5}$ **20 11/30**
36. $9\frac{1}{4} - 3\frac{1}{18}$ **6 7/36**
37. $19\frac{9}{10} - 17\frac{18}{25}$ **2 9/50**
38. $4\frac{2}{3} - 3\frac{1}{16}$ **1 23/48**
39. $3\frac{7}{8} - 1\frac{4}{5}$ **2 11/40**
40. $22\frac{21}{25} - 7\frac{3}{4}$ **15 9/100**

Page 57

Mixed Numbers — Skill: Subtracting Mixed Numbers With Renaming

Name _____

Total Problems __40__
Problems Correct ____
Percent Correct ____

Subtract. Show your work on another piece of paper.
Write your answers here.

1. $33\frac{3}{16} - 13\frac{7}{16}$ **19 3/4**
2. $16\frac{2}{7} - 3\frac{20}{21}$ **12 1/3**
3. $29\frac{1}{6} - 27\frac{2}{3}$ **1 1/2**
4. $18\frac{1}{3} - 12\frac{3}{7}$ **5 19/21**
5. $17\frac{1}{8} - 12\frac{3}{8}$ **4 3/4**
6. $11\frac{1}{8} - 3\frac{7}{12}$ **7 17/24**
7. $10\frac{1}{9} - 9\frac{7}{45}$ **43/45**
8. $76\frac{1}{2} - 19\frac{7}{9}$ **56 7/18**
9. $38\frac{1}{2} - 35\frac{13}{15}$ **2 19/30**
10. $25\frac{1}{5} - 20\frac{8}{9}$ **4 19/36**
11. $86\frac{3}{5} - 82\frac{7}{10}$ **3 9/20**
12. $36\frac{4}{15} - 14\frac{11}{15}$ **21 13/15**
13. $2\frac{1}{25} - 1\frac{4}{5}$ **6/25**
14. $88\frac{7}{20} - 62\frac{3}{5}$ **25 3/4**
15. $100\frac{1}{4} - 99\frac{7}{10}$ **9/20**
16. $15\frac{4}{9} - 4\frac{3}{4}$ **10 19/36**
17. $4\frac{3}{10} - 3\frac{2}{7}$ **31/70**
18. $30\frac{7}{20} - 11\frac{17}{20}$ **18 3/5**
19. $35\frac{1}{10} - 25\frac{2}{5}$ **9 7/10**
20. $2\frac{3}{22} - 1\frac{7}{11}$ **1/2**
21. $16\frac{5}{28} - 2\frac{19}{28}$ **13 1/2**
22. $20\frac{1}{4} - 13\frac{13}{15}$ **6 23/60**
23. $19\frac{1}{4} - 2\frac{5}{6}$ **16 5/12**
24. $51\frac{3}{10} - 22\frac{1}{10}$ **28 1/5**
25. $93\frac{1}{2} - 77\frac{4}{5}$ **15 7/10**
26. $8\frac{3}{10} - 5\frac{12}{25}$ **2 41/50**
27. $3\frac{1}{2} - 1\frac{8}{15}$ **1 29/30**
28. $7\frac{1}{2} - 3\frac{2}{5}$ **3 29/40**
29. $55\frac{2}{9} - 13\frac{3}{4}$ **41 17/36**
30. $11\frac{1}{6} - 8\frac{3}{10}$ **2 13/15**
31. $14\frac{9}{50} - 11\frac{39}{50}$ **2 2/5**
32. $48\frac{1}{3} - 45\frac{13}{18}$ **2 11/18**
33. $16\frac{2}{21} - 14\frac{2}{7}$ **18/21**
34. $62\frac{23}{50} - 27\frac{29}{50}$ **34 4/5**
35. $6\frac{1}{2} - 2\frac{7}{16}$ **3 43/48**
36. $100\frac{8}{45} - 50\frac{7}{10}$ **49 5/18**
37. $80\frac{19}{75} - 6\frac{26}{75}$ **73 2/3**
38. $2\frac{1}{4} - \frac{24}{25}$ **1 29/100**
39. $40\frac{2}{3} - 39\frac{5}{6}$ **19/60**
40. $13\frac{17}{33} - 10\frac{13}{22}$ **2 61/66**

Page 58

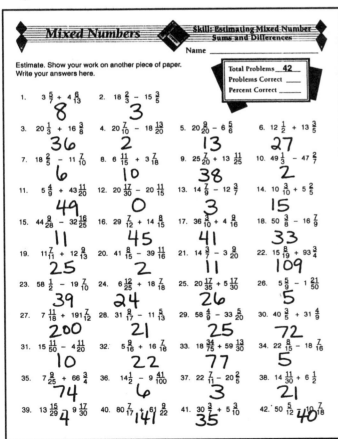

Mixed Numbers — Skill: Estimating Mixed Number Sums and Differences

Name _____

Total Problems __42__
Problems Correct ____
Percent Correct ____

Estimate. Show your work on another piece of paper.
Write your answers here.

1. $3\frac{5}{7} + 4\frac{6}{13}$ **8**
2. $18\frac{2}{3} - 15\frac{3}{5}$ **3**
3. $20\frac{1}{3} + 16\frac{3}{8}$ **36**
4. $20\frac{7}{10} - 18\frac{13}{20}$ **2**
5. $20\frac{9}{20} - 6\frac{6}{9}$ **13**
6. $12\frac{1}{2} + 13\frac{3}{5}$ **27**
7. $18\frac{2}{5} - 11\frac{7}{10}$ **6**
8. $6\frac{11}{15} + 3\frac{1}{4}$ **10**
9. $25\frac{7}{9} + 13\frac{11}{25}$ **38**
10. $49\frac{1}{3} - 47\frac{2}{7}$ **2**
11. $5\frac{4}{9} + 43\frac{11}{20}$ **49**
12. $20\frac{17}{30} - 20\frac{11}{15}$ **0**
13. $14\frac{7}{9} - 12\frac{3}{7}$ **3**
14. $10\frac{3}{10} + 5\frac{2}{9}$ **15**
15. $44\frac{8}{28} - 32\frac{16}{25}$ **11**
16. $29\frac{7}{12} + 14\frac{8}{15}$ **45**
17. $36\frac{9}{10} + 4\frac{1}{16}$ **41**
18. $50\frac{3}{8} - 16\frac{7}{9}$ **33**
19. $11\frac{1}{11} + 12\frac{3}{13}$ **25**
20. $41\frac{1}{4} - 39\frac{7}{16}$ **2**
21. $14\frac{7}{9} - 3\frac{9}{20}$ **11**
22. $15\frac{1}{19} + 93\frac{3}{4}$ **109**
23. $58\frac{1}{2} - 19\frac{7}{10}$ **39**
24. $6\frac{12}{13} + 18\frac{7}{8}$ **24**
25. $20\frac{17}{30} + 5\frac{17}{30}$ **26**
26. $5\frac{5}{9} - 1\frac{21}{22}$ **5**
27. $7\frac{11}{17} + 191\frac{7}{12}$ **200**
28. $31\frac{9}{17} - 11\frac{3}{8}$ **21**
29. $58\frac{4}{9} - 33\frac{2}{9}$ **25**
30. $40\frac{3}{7} + 31\frac{4}{9}$ **72**
31. $15\frac{11}{50} - 4\frac{1}{20}$ **10**
32. $5\frac{8}{16} + 16\frac{7}{18}$ **22**
33. $18\frac{34}{75} + 59\frac{13}{30}$ **77**
34. $22\frac{3}{15} - 18\frac{7}{16}$ **5**
35. $7\frac{4}{25} + 66\frac{3}{4}$ **74**
36. $14\frac{1}{2} - 9\frac{41}{100}$ **6**
37. $22\frac{7}{11} - 20\frac{2}{5}$ **3**
38. $14\frac{11}{30} + 6\frac{1}{2}$ **21**
39. $13\frac{15}{29} + 9\frac{17}{30}$ **4**
40. $80\frac{7}{12} + 61\frac{9}{22}$ **141**
41. $30\frac{3}{7} + 5\frac{1}{3}$ **35**
42. $50\frac{5}{12} + 10\frac{7}{22}$ **40**

Page 59

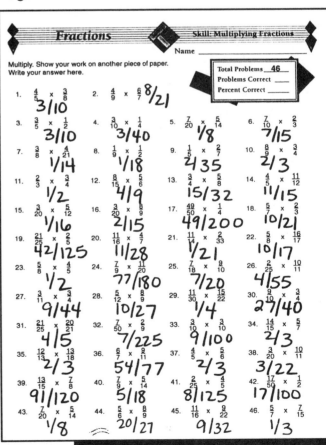

Fractions — Skill: Multiplying Fractions

Name _____

Total Problems __46__
Problems Correct ____
Percent Correct ____

Multiply. Show your work on another piece of paper.
Write your answer here.

1. $\frac{4}{5} \times \frac{3}{8}$ **3/10**
2. $\frac{4}{9} \times \frac{6}{7}$ **8/21**
3. $\frac{3}{4} \times \frac{2}{5}$ **3/10**
4. $\frac{3}{10} \times \frac{1}{4}$ **3/40**
5. $\frac{7}{20} \times \frac{5}{14}$ **1/8**
6. $\frac{7}{10} \times \frac{2}{3}$ **7/15**
7. $\frac{3}{8} \times \frac{4}{21}$ **1/14**
8. $\frac{1}{6} \times \frac{1}{3}$ **1/18**
9. $\frac{5}{7} \times \frac{1}{5}$ **4/35**
10. $\frac{8}{9} \times \frac{3}{4}$ **2/3**
11. $\frac{2}{3} \times \frac{3}{4}$ **1/2**
12. $\frac{8}{15} \times \frac{5}{6}$ **4/9**
13. $\frac{4}{5} \times \frac{8}{5}$ **15/32**
14. $\frac{4}{5} \times \frac{11}{12}$ **11/15**
15. $\frac{3}{20} \times \frac{5}{12}$ **1/16**
16. $\frac{8}{20} \times \frac{1}{3}$ **2/15**
17. $\frac{49}{50} \times \frac{1}{4}$ **49/200**
18. $\frac{5}{7} \times \frac{6}{7}$ **10/21**
19. $\frac{21}{25} \times \frac{4}{5}$ **42/125**
20. $\frac{11}{16} \times \frac{4}{7}$ **11/28**
21. $\frac{1}{14} \times \frac{3}{3}$ **1/21**
22. $\frac{5}{6} \times \frac{16}{7}$ **10/17**
23. $\frac{5}{8} \times \frac{4}{5}$ **1/2**
24. $\frac{7}{18} \times \frac{2}{5}$ **77/180**
25. $\frac{4}{7} \times \frac{3}{10}$ **7/20**
26. $\frac{5}{8} \times \frac{5}{7}$ **4/55**
27. $\frac{3}{11} \times \frac{2}{4}$ **9/44**
28. $\frac{5}{12} \times \frac{4}{5}$ **10/27**
29. $\frac{1}{30} \times \frac{5}{22}$ **1/4**
30. $\frac{5}{9} \times \frac{10}{11}$ **27/40**
31. $\frac{25}{7} \times \frac{20}{21}$ **4/5**
32. $\frac{7}{50} \times \frac{2}{9}$ **7/225**
33. $\frac{3}{10} \times \frac{3}{10}$ **9/100**
34. $\frac{14}{15} \times \frac{1}{7}$ **2/3**
35. $\frac{12}{13} \times \frac{13}{18}$ **2/3**
36. $\frac{6}{7} \times \frac{9}{11}$ **54/77**
37. $\frac{4}{5} \times \frac{5}{6}$ **2/3**
38. $\frac{3}{20} \times \frac{9}{11}$ **3/22**
39. $\frac{13}{15} \times \frac{7}{8}$ **91/120**
40. $\frac{5}{9} \times \frac{5}{14}$ **5/18**
41. $\frac{25}{3} \times \frac{3}{5}$ **8/125**
42. $\frac{17}{50} \times \frac{1}{2}$ **17/100**
43. $\frac{7}{20} \times \frac{4}{5}$ **1/8**
44. $\frac{5}{7} \times \frac{4}{9}$ **20/27**
45. $\frac{11}{12} \times \frac{2}{7}$ **9/32**
46. $\frac{5}{7} \times \frac{7}{15}$ **1/3**

Page 60

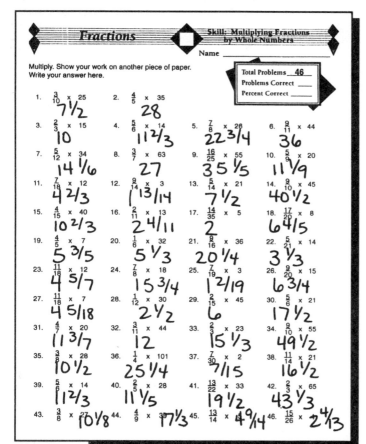

Fractions — Skill: Multiplying Fractions by Whole Numbers

Name ____________

Multiply. Show your work on another piece of paper. Write your answer here.

Total Problems 46
Problems Correct ____
Percent Correct ____

1. $\frac{3}{10} \times 25$ — $7\frac{1}{2}$
2. $\frac{4}{5} \times 35$ — 28
3. $\frac{2}{3} \times 15$ — 10
4. $\frac{5}{6} \times 14$ — $11\frac{2}{3}$
5. $\frac{7}{8} \times 26$ — $22\frac{3}{4}$
6. $\frac{9}{11} \times 44$ — 36
7. $\frac{5}{12} \times 34$ — $14\frac{1}{6}$
8. $\frac{3}{7} \times 63$ — 27
9. $\frac{16}{25} \times 55$ — $35\frac{1}{5}$
10. $\frac{5}{9} \times 20$ — $11\frac{1}{9}$
11. $\frac{7}{18} \times 12$ — $4\frac{2}{3}$
12. $\frac{9}{14} \times 3$ — $1\frac{13}{14}$
13. $\frac{5}{14} \times 21$ — $7\frac{1}{2}$
14. $\frac{9}{10} \times 45$ — $40\frac{1}{2}$
15. $\frac{4}{15} \times 40$ — $10\frac{2}{3}$
16. $\frac{2}{11} \times 13$ — $2\frac{4}{11}$
17. $\frac{14}{35} \times 5$ — 2
18. $\frac{17}{20} \times 8$ — $6\frac{4}{5}$
19. $\frac{4}{5} \times 7$ — $5\frac{3}{5}$
20. $\frac{1}{6} \times 32$ — $5\frac{1}{3}$
21. $\frac{9}{16} \times 36$ — $20\frac{1}{4}$
22. $\frac{5}{21} \times 14$ — $3\frac{1}{3}$
23. $\frac{11}{18} \times 12$ — $4\frac{5}{7}$
24. $\frac{7}{8} \times 18$ — $15\frac{3}{4}$
25. $\frac{7}{19} \times 3$ — $1\frac{2}{19}$
26. $\frac{9}{20} \times 15$ — $6\frac{3}{4}$
27. $\frac{11}{18} \times 7$ — $4\frac{5}{18}$
28. $\frac{1}{12} \times 30$ — $2\frac{1}{2}$
29. $\frac{2}{15} \times 45$ — 6
30. $\frac{5}{6} \times 21$ — $17\frac{1}{2}$
31. $\frac{4}{7} \times 20$ — $11\frac{3}{7}$
32. $\frac{3}{11} \times 44$ — 12
33. $\frac{2}{3} \times 23$ — $15\frac{1}{3}$
34. $\frac{9}{10} \times 55$ — $49\frac{1}{2}$
35. $\frac{3}{8} \times 28$ — $10\frac{1}{2}$
36. $\frac{1}{4} \times 101$ — $25\frac{1}{4}$
37. $\frac{7}{30} \times 2$ — $\frac{7}{15}$
38. $\frac{11}{14} \times 21$ — $16\frac{1}{2}$
39. $\frac{5}{6} \times 14$ — $11\frac{2}{3}$
40. $\frac{2}{5} \times 28$ — $11\frac{1}{5}$
41. $\frac{13}{22} \times 33$ — $19\frac{1}{2}$
42. $\frac{2}{3} \times 65$ — $43\frac{1}{3}$
43. $\frac{3}{8} \times 27$ — $10\frac{1}{8}$
44. $\frac{4}{9} \times 39$ — $17\frac{1}{3}$
45. $\frac{13}{14} \times$ [illegible] — $4\frac{9}{14}$
46. $\frac{15}{26} \times$ [illegible] — $2\frac{4}{13}$

Page 61

Mixed Numbers — Skill: Multiplying Mixed Numbers

Name ____________

Multiply. Show your work on another piece of paper. Write your answers here.

Total Problems 40
Problems Correct ____
Percent Correct ____

1. $3\frac{3}{4} \times 5\frac{1}{3}$ — 20
2. $2\frac{6}{7} \times 1\frac{4}{15}$ — $3\frac{13}{21}$
3. $1\frac{7}{10} \times 5\frac{5}{6}$ — $9\frac{11}{12}$
4. $1\frac{3}{10} \times 1\frac{1}{20}$ — $1\frac{73}{200}$
5. $2\frac{5}{6} \times 1\frac{2}{9}$ — $3\frac{25}{54}$
6. $13\frac{1}{2} \times 1\frac{5}{12}$ — $19\frac{1}{8}$
7. $3\frac{2}{3} \times 2\frac{4}{5}$ — $10\frac{4}{15}$
8. $1\frac{7}{18} \times 1\frac{1}{15}$ — $1\frac{13}{27}$
9. $2\frac{16}{25} \times 3\frac{2}{11}$ — $8\frac{2}{3}$
10. $11\frac{3}{7} \times 2\frac{1}{5}$ — $25\frac{1}{7}$
11. $5\frac{5}{9} \times 2\frac{1}{20}$ — $11\frac{7}{18}$
12. $1\frac{7}{11} \times 2\frac{1}{2}$ — $4\frac{1}{11}$
13. $5\frac{3}{4} \times 3\frac{3}{5}$ — $20\frac{7}{10}$
14. $3\frac{1}{2} \times 2\frac{1}{7}$ — $7\frac{1}{2}$
15. $1\frac{13}{50} \times 1\frac{11}{14}$ — $2\frac{1}{4}$
16. $1\frac{13}{20} \times 5\frac{5}{9}$ — $9\frac{1}{6}$
17. $2\frac{3}{16} \times 1\frac{5}{14}$ — $2\frac{31}{32}$
18. $2\frac{4}{7} \times 1\frac{5}{16}$ — $3\frac{3}{8}$
19. $7\frac{1}{2} \times 1\frac{23}{25}$ — $14\frac{2}{5}$
20. $1\frac{5}{13} \times 2\frac{1}{4}$ — $3\frac{3}{26}$
21. $2\frac{2}{15} \times 2\frac{5}{8}$ — $5\frac{3}{5}$
22. $2\frac{1}{4} \times 4\frac{1}{3}$ — $9\frac{3}{4}$
23. $1\frac{1}{6} \times 4\frac{4}{5}$ — $5\frac{3}{5}$
24. $2\frac{8}{21} \times 4\frac{9}{10}$ — $11\frac{2}{3}$
25. $1\frac{4}{5} \times 13\frac{1}{3}$ — 24
26. $2\frac{2}{5} \times 10\frac{1}{2}$ — $25\frac{1}{5}$
27. $2\frac{8}{11} \times 2\frac{5}{14}$ — $6\frac{3}{7}$
28. $2\frac{2}{3} \times 7\frac{1}{2}$ — 20
29. $4\frac{1}{6} \times 4\frac{1}{20}$ — $16\frac{7}{8}$
30. $9\frac{1}{3} \times 4\frac{2}{7}$ — 40
31. $1\frac{4}{31} \times 20\frac{2}{3}$ — $23\frac{1}{3}$
32. $1\frac{1}{5} \times 1\frac{17}{18}$ — $2\frac{1}{3}$
33. $1\frac{1}{12} \times 5\frac{5}{7}$ — $6\frac{4}{21}$
34. $2\frac{8}{9} \times 5\frac{1}{4}$ — $15\frac{1}{6}$
35. $3\frac{3}{4} \times 7\frac{1}{5}$ — 27
36. $2\frac{14}{25} \times 4\frac{3}{8}$ — $11\frac{1}{5}$
37. $1\frac{1}{6} \times 4\frac{1}{5}$ — $4\frac{9}{10}$
38. $2\frac{13}{25} \times 4\frac{2}{7}$ — $10\frac{4}{5}$
39. $11\frac{1}{13} \times 14\frac{1}{12}$ — 156
40. $2\frac{2}{11} \times 2\frac{14}{15}$ — $6\frac{2}{5}$

Page 62

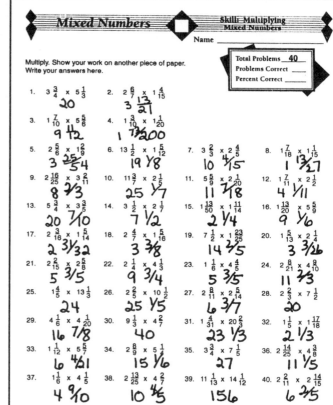

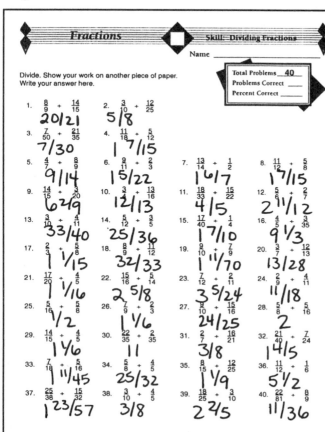

Fractions — Skill: Dividing Fractions

Name ____________

Divide. Show your work on another piece of paper. Write your answer here.

Total Problems 40
Problems Correct ____
Percent Correct ____

1. $\frac{8}{9} \div \frac{14}{15}$ — $\frac{20}{21}$
2. $\frac{3}{10} \div \frac{12}{25}$ — $\frac{5}{8}$
3. $\frac{7}{50} \div \frac{21}{35}$ — $\frac{7}{30}$
4. $\frac{11}{18} \div \frac{5}{12}$ — $1\frac{7}{15}$
5. $\frac{4}{7} \div \frac{8}{9}$ — $\frac{9}{14}$
6. $\frac{9}{11} \div \frac{2}{3}$ — $1\frac{5}{22}$
7. $\frac{13}{14} \div \frac{1}{2}$ — $1\frac{6}{7}$
8. $\frac{11}{12} \div \frac{5}{8}$ — $1\frac{7}{15}$
9. $\frac{14}{15} \div \frac{3}{20}$ — $6\frac{2}{9}$
10. $\frac{3}{4} \div \frac{13}{16}$ — $\frac{12}{13}$
11. $\frac{18}{33} \div \frac{15}{22}$ — $\frac{4}{5}$
12. $\frac{5}{6} \div \frac{2}{7}$ — $2\frac{11}{12}$
13. $\frac{3}{10} \div \frac{4}{11}$ — $\frac{33}{40}$
14. $\frac{5}{12} \div \frac{3}{5}$ — $\frac{25}{36}$
15. $\frac{17}{40} \div \frac{1}{4}$ — $1\frac{7}{10}$
16. $\frac{4}{5} \div \frac{3}{35}$ — $9\frac{1}{3}$
17. $\frac{2}{3} \div \frac{5}{8}$ — $1\frac{1}{15}$
18. $\frac{8}{9} \div \frac{11}{12}$ — $\frac{32}{33}$
19. $\frac{9}{10} \div \frac{7}{9}$ — $1\frac{11}{70}$
20. $\frac{3}{7} \div \frac{12}{13}$ — $\frac{13}{28}$
21. $\frac{17}{20} \div \frac{4}{5}$ — $1\frac{1}{16}$
22. $\frac{15}{16} \div \frac{5}{14}$ — $2\frac{5}{8}$
23. $\frac{7}{12} \div \frac{2}{11}$ — $3\frac{5}{24}$
24. $\frac{2}{9} \div \frac{4}{11}$ — $\frac{11}{18}$
25. $\frac{5}{16} \div \frac{5}{8}$ — $\frac{1}{2}$
26. $\frac{7}{9} \div \frac{2}{3}$ — $1\frac{1}{6}$
27. $\frac{9}{10} \div \frac{15}{16}$ — $\frac{24}{25}$
28. $\frac{5}{8} \div \frac{5}{16}$ — 2
29. $\frac{14}{15} \div \frac{4}{5}$ — $1\frac{1}{6}$
30. $\frac{22}{35} \div \frac{2}{35}$ — 11
31. $\frac{2}{7} \div \frac{16}{21}$ — $\frac{3}{8}$
32. $\frac{21}{40} \div \frac{7}{24}$ — $1\frac{4}{5}$
33. $\frac{7}{18} \div \frac{5}{16}$ — $1\frac{11}{45}$
34. $\frac{5}{8} \div \frac{4}{5}$ — $\frac{25}{32}$
35. $\frac{8}{15} \div \frac{12}{25}$ — $1\frac{1}{9}$
36. $\frac{11}{12} \div \frac{1}{6}$ — $5\frac{1}{2}$
37. $\frac{25}{38} \div \frac{15}{32}$ — $1\frac{23}{57}$
38. $\frac{3}{10} \div \frac{4}{5}$ — $\frac{3}{8}$
39. $\frac{18}{25} \div \frac{3}{10}$ — $2\frac{2}{5}$
40. $\frac{22}{81} \div \frac{8}{9}$ — $\frac{11}{36}$

Page 63

Mixed Numbers — Skill: Dividing Mixed Numbers

Name ____________

Divide. Show your work on another piece of paper. Write your answers here.

Total Problems 40
Problems Correct ____
Percent Correct ____

1. $4\frac{2}{7} \div 5\frac{1}{4}$ — $\frac{40}{49}$
2. $3\frac{1}{5} \div 1\frac{7}{15}$ — $2\frac{2}{11}$
3. $1\frac{13}{20} \div 6\frac{7}{8}$ — $\frac{4}{5}$
4. $12\frac{1}{2} \div 13\frac{1}{3}$ — $\frac{15}{16}$
5. $1\frac{3}{16} \div 1\frac{1}{6}$ — $1\frac{1}{56}$
6. $1\frac{19}{25} \div 1\frac{1}{10}$ — $1\frac{3}{5}$
7. $2\frac{1}{12} \div 2\frac{2}{9}$ — $\frac{15}{16}$
8. $3\frac{6}{7} \div 7\frac{1}{5}$ — $\frac{15}{28}$
9. $2\frac{14}{15} \div 4\frac{7}{12}$ — $\frac{16}{25}$
10. $3\frac{1}{8} \div 16\frac{2}{3}$ — $\frac{3}{16}$
11. $4\frac{4}{9} \div 6\frac{2}{3}$ — $\frac{2}{3}$
12. $5\frac{1}{5} \div 7\frac{3}{5}$ — $\frac{13}{19}$
13. $4\frac{1}{6} \div 18\frac{1}{3}$ — $\frac{5}{22}$
14. $7\frac{1}{3} \div 1\frac{5}{6}$ — 4
15. $3\frac{2}{3} \div 1\frac{1}{4}$ — $2\frac{14}{15}$
16. $22\frac{1}{2} \div 4\frac{4}{9}$ — $5\frac{1}{16}$
17. $2\frac{1}{7} \div 8\frac{4}{7}$ — $\frac{1}{4}$
18. $11\frac{3}{5} \div 3\frac{1}{15}$ — $3\frac{18}{23}$
19. $15\frac{3}{4} \div 5\frac{1}{7}$ — $3\frac{1}{16}$
20. $6\frac{2}{9} \div 2\frac{1}{12}$ — $2\frac{74}{75}$
21. $9\frac{1}{6} \div 8\frac{1}{4}$ — $1\frac{1}{9}$
22. $4\frac{7}{12} \div 2\frac{14}{15}$ — $1\frac{9}{16}$
23. $4\frac{2}{3} \div 1\frac{7}{9}$ — $2\frac{5}{8}$
24. $9\frac{3}{5} \div 4\frac{4}{15}$ — $2\frac{1}{4}$
25. $2\frac{11}{12} \div 7\frac{7}{8}$ — $\frac{10}{27}$
26. $7\frac{7}{10} \div 8\frac{1}{6}$ — $\frac{33}{35}$
27. $4\frac{6}{7} \div 1\frac{19}{21}$ — $2\frac{11}{20}$
28. $5\frac{5}{11} \div 6\frac{2}{3}$ — $\frac{9}{11}$
29. $3\frac{3}{5} \div 1\frac{3}{25}$ — $3\frac{3}{14}$
30. $5\frac{1}{7} \div 5\frac{1}{3}$ — $\frac{27}{28}$
31. $23\frac{1}{3} \div 5\frac{5}{9}$ — $4\frac{1}{5}$
32. $8\frac{4}{5} \div 4\frac{1}{8}$ — $2\frac{2}{15}$
33. $2\frac{11}{20} \div 3\frac{2}{5}$ — $\frac{3}{4}$
34. $28\frac{2}{3} \div 2\frac{14}{15}$ — $9\frac{17}{22}$
35. $1\frac{11}{14} \div 1\frac{19}{21}$ — $\frac{15}{16}$
36. $5\frac{5}{6} \div 6\frac{1}{8}$ — $\frac{20}{21}$
37. $3\frac{7}{8} \div 1\frac{2}{3}$ — $2\frac{13}{40}$
38. $1\frac{37}{40} \div 1\frac{7}{15}$ — $1\frac{5}{16}$
39. $3\frac{9}{10} \div 2\frac{1}{6}$ — $1\frac{4}{5}$
40. $1\frac{3}{7} \div 18\frac{1}{3}$ — $\frac{6}{77}$

Page 64

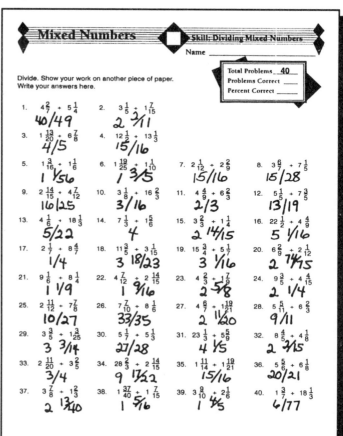

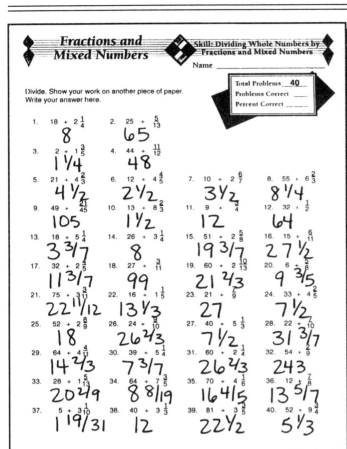

Fractions and Mixed Numbers
Skill: Dividing Whole Numbers by Fractions and Mixed Numbers

Name _____

Total Problems __40__
Problems Correct _____
Percent Correct _____

Divide. Show your work on another piece of paper. Write your answer here.

1. $18 \div 2\frac{1}{4}$ **8**
2. $25 \div \frac{5}{13}$ **65**
3. $2 \div 1\frac{3}{5}$ **1¼**
4. $44 \div \frac{11}{12}$ **48**
5. $21 \div 4\frac{3}{5}$ **4½**
6. $12 \div 4\frac{4}{5}$ **2½**
7. $10 \div 2\frac{6}{7}$ **3½**
8. $55 \div 6\frac{2}{3}$ **8¼**
9. $49 \div \frac{21}{45}$ **105**
10. $13 \div 8\frac{2}{3}$ **1½**
11. $9 \div \frac{3}{4}$ **12**
12. $32 \div \frac{1}{2}$ **64**
13. $18 \div 5\frac{1}{4}$ **3 3/7**
14. $26 \div 3\frac{1}{4}$ **8**
15. $51 \div 2\frac{5}{8}$ **19 3/7**
16. $15 \div \frac{6}{11}$ **27½**
17. $32 \div 2\frac{4}{5}$ **11 3/7**
18. $27 \div \frac{3}{11}$ **99**
19. $60 \div 2\frac{10}{13}$ **21 4/3**
20. $6 \div \frac{5}{3}$ **9 3/5**
21. $75 \div 3\frac{3}{11}$ **22 11/12**
22. $16 \div 1\frac{1}{5}$ **13 1/3**
23. $21 \div \frac{7}{9}$ **27**
24. $33 \div 4\frac{2}{5}$ **7½**
25. $52 \div 2\frac{8}{9}$ **18**
26. $24 \div \frac{9}{10}$ **26 2/3**
27. $40 \div 5\frac{1}{3}$ **7½**
28. $22 \div \frac{7}{10}$ **31 3/7**
29. $64 \div 4\frac{4}{11}$ **14 2/3**
30. $39 \div 5\frac{1}{4}$ **7 3/7**
31. $60 \div 2\frac{1}{4}$ **26 2/3**
32. $54 \div \frac{2}{9}$ **243**
33. $28 \div 1\frac{5}{13}$ **20 2/9**
34. $64 \div 7\frac{3}{5}$ **8 8/19**
35. $70 \div 4\frac{1}{3}$ **16 4/5**
36. $12 \div \frac{7}{8}$ **13 5/7**
37. $5 \div 3\frac{1}{3}$ **1 19/31**
38. $40 \div 4\frac{1}{3}$ **12**
39. $81 \div 3\frac{3}{5}$ **22½**
40. $52 \div 9\frac{3}{4}$ **5 1/3**

Page 65

Mixed Numbers
Skill: Estimating Mixed Number Products and Quotients

Name _____

Total Problems __42__
Problems Correct _____
Percent Correct _____

Estimate. Show your work on another piece of paper. Write your answers here.

1. $47\frac{3}{5} \div 5\frac{5}{8}$ **8**
2. $7\frac{7}{13} \times 4\frac{4}{7}$ **40**
3. $26\frac{7}{10} \div 9\frac{1}{3}$ **3**
4. $6\frac{2}{3} \times 6\frac{5}{8}$ **42**
5. $18\frac{5}{11} \div 1\frac{4}{7}$ **9**
6. $10\frac{9}{16} \times 5\frac{7}{15}$ **55**
7. $41\frac{8}{15} \div 13\frac{7}{16}$ **3**
8. $1\frac{7}{16} \times 7\frac{7}{12}$ **16**
9. $12\frac{1}{6} \div 2\frac{4}{5}$ **4**
10. $3\frac{9}{10} \times 9\frac{12}{25}$ **27**
11. $71\frac{8}{15} \div 7\frac{11}{20}$ **9**
12. $6\frac{6}{11} \times 6\frac{3}{8}$ **49**
13. $90\frac{5}{12} \div 2\frac{3}{5}$ **30**
14. $21\frac{4}{9} \times 4\frac{1}{9}$ **88**
15. $36\frac{7}{16} \div 9\frac{10}{21}$ **4**
16. $3\frac{5}{8} \times 25\frac{5}{12}$ **75**
17. $76\frac{13}{25} \div 7\frac{10}{21}$ **11**
18. $9\frac{23}{45} \times 9\frac{21}{50}$ **90**
19. $79\frac{19}{30} \div 9\frac{5}{28}$ **8**
20. $8\frac{4}{15} \times 6\frac{3}{8}$ **54**
21. $42\frac{3}{8} \div 6\frac{3}{5}$ **6**
22. $20\frac{4}{9} \times 4\frac{11}{18}$ **100**
23. $31\frac{5}{6} \div 16\frac{3}{8}$ **2**
24. $1\frac{5}{8} \times 10\frac{7}{10}$ **22**
25. $44\frac{6}{11} \div 2\frac{7}{10}$ **15**
26. $24\frac{7}{9} \times 2\frac{1}{3}$ **50**
27. $55\frac{17}{30} \div 8\frac{7}{20}$ **7**
28. $14\frac{7}{12} \times 3\frac{8}{15}$ **60**
29. $36\frac{5}{9} \div 6\frac{5}{14}$ **6**
30. $13\frac{7}{20} \times 3\frac{9}{25}$ **39**
31. $49\frac{7}{15} \div 6\frac{11}{18}$ **7**
32. $2\frac{11}{15} \times 13\frac{11}{14}$ **28**
33. $60\frac{2}{21} \div 6\frac{13}{30}$ **10**
34. $9\frac{21}{40} \times 9\frac{18}{35}$ **100**
35. $48\frac{9}{19} \div 7\frac{11}{17}$ **6**
36. $9\frac{7}{30} \times 8\frac{7}{20}$ **72**
37. $61\frac{7}{10} \div 2\frac{2}{5}$ **31**
38. $5\frac{33}{50} \times 3\frac{6}{7}$ **24**
39. $99\frac{4}{7} \div 19\frac{6}{11}$ **5**
40. $5\frac{2}{6} \times 7\frac{4}{5}$ **35**
41. $25\frac{1}{6} \div 4\frac{8}{9}$ **5**
42. $19\frac{3}{5} \times 3\frac{5}{10}$ **60**

Page 66

Ratios
Skill: Equality of Ratios

Name _____

Total Problems __15__
Problems Correct _____
Percent Correct _____

Decide if the two ratios are equal. If you check the "equal" box, finish the rest of the chart by writing the ratios in lowest terms three different ways. Follow the example.

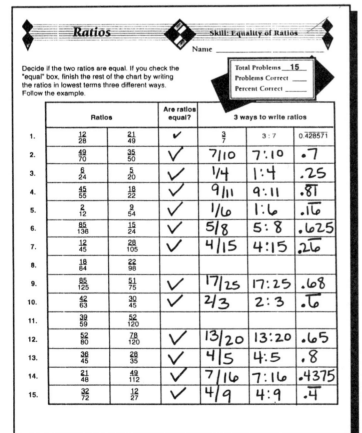

	Ratios		Are ratios equal?	3 ways to write ratios		
1.	$\frac{12}{28}$	$\frac{21}{49}$	✔	$\frac{3}{7}$	3 : 7	0.428571
2.	$\frac{49}{70}$	$\frac{35}{50}$	✔	7/10	7:10	.7
3.	$\frac{6}{24}$	$\frac{5}{20}$	✔	1/4	1:4	.25
4.	$\frac{45}{55}$	$\frac{18}{22}$	✔	9/11	9:11	.81̄
5.	$\frac{2}{12}$	$\frac{9}{54}$	✔	1/6	1:6	.16̄
6.	$\frac{85}{136}$	$\frac{15}{24}$	✔	5/8	5:8	.625
7.	$\frac{12}{45}$	$\frac{28}{105}$	✔	4/15	4:15	.26̄
8.	$\frac{18}{84}$	$\frac{22}{98}$				
9.	$\frac{85}{125}$	$\frac{51}{75}$	✔	17/25	17:25	.68
10.	$\frac{42}{63}$	$\frac{30}{45}$	✔	2/3	2:3	.6̄
11.	$\frac{39}{59}$	$\frac{52}{120}$				
12.	$\frac{52}{80}$	$\frac{78}{120}$	✔	13/20	13:20	.65
13.	$\frac{36}{45}$	$\frac{28}{35}$	✔	4/5	4:5	.8
14.	$\frac{21}{48}$	$\frac{49}{112}$	✔	7/16	7:16	.4375
15.	$\frac{32}{72}$	$\frac{12}{27}$	✔	4/9	4:9	.4̄

Page 67

Rate
Skill: Rate

Name _____

Total Problems __40__
Problems Correct _____
Percent Correct _____

What is the unit rate? Show your work on another piece of paper. Write your answers here.

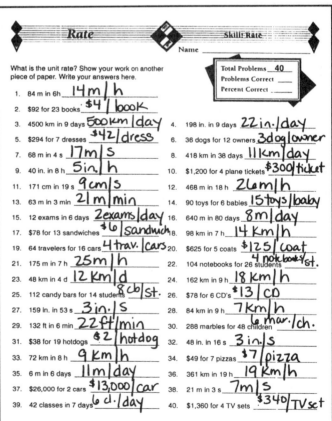

1. 84 m in 6h **14 m/h**
2. $92 for 23 books **$4/book**
3. 4500 km in 9 days **500 km/day**
4. 198 in. in 9 days **22 in./day**
5. $294 for 7 dresses **$42/dress**
6. 36 dogs for 12 owners **3 dog/owner**
7. 68 m in 4 s **17 m/s**
8. 418 km in 38 days **11 km/day**
9. 40 in. in 8 h **5 in./h**
10. $1,200 for 4 plane tickets **$300/ticket**
11. 171 cm in 19 s **9 cm/s**
12. 468 m in 18 h **26 m/h**
13. 63 m in 3 min **21 m/min**
14. 90 toys for 6 babies **15 toys/baby**
15. 12 exams in 6 days **2 exams/day**
16. 640 m in 80 days **8 m/day**
17. $78 for 13 sandwiches **$6/sandwich**
18. 98 km in 7 h **14 km/h**
19. 64 travelers for 16 cars **4 trav./cars**
20. $625 for 5 coats **$125/coat**
21. 175 m in 7 h **25 m/h**
22. 104 notebooks for 26 students **4 notebooks/st.**
23. 48 km in 4 d **12 km/d**
24. 162 km in 9 h **18 km/h**
25. 112 candy bars for 14 students **8 cb/st.**
26. $78 for 6 CD's **$13/CD**
27. 159 in. in 53 s **3 in./s**
28. 84 km in 9 h **7 km/h**
29. 132 ft in 6 min **22 ft/min**
30. 288 marbles for 48 children **6 mar./ch.**
31. $38 for 19 hotdogs **$2/hotdog**
32. 48 in. in 16 s **3 in./s**
33. 72 km in 8 h **9 km/h**
34. $49 for 7 pizzas **$7/pizza**
35. 6 m in 6 days **1 m/day**
36. 361 km in 19 h **19 km/h**
37. $26,000 for 2 cars **$13,000/car**
38. 21 m in 3 s **7 m/s**
39. 42 classes in 7 days **6 cl./day**
40. $1,360 for 4 TV sets **$340/TV set**

Page 68

Page 69

Proportions — Skill: Proportions

Name _____

Total Problems __40__
Problems Correct ____
Percent Correct ____

Solve the proportions. Show your work on another piece of paper. Write your answer here.

1. $\frac{15}{n} = \frac{24}{128}$ **80**
2. $\frac{n}{200} = \frac{28}{80}$ **70**
3. $\frac{15}{110} = \frac{24}{n}$ **176**
4. $\frac{4}{5} = \frac{n}{20}$ **16**
5. $\frac{54}{63} = \frac{n}{49}$ **42**
6. $\frac{5}{n} = \frac{2}{38}$ **95**
7. $\frac{n}{12} = \frac{45}{108}$ **5**
8. $\frac{42}{n} = \frac{8}{12}$ **63**
9. $\frac{8}{30} = \frac{28}{n}$ **105**
10. $\frac{n}{108} = \frac{20}{72}$ **30**
11. $\frac{7}{13} = \frac{n}{78}$ **42**
12. $\frac{56}{n} = \frac{7}{31}$ **248**
13. $\frac{n}{22} = \frac{63}{154}$ **9**
14. $\frac{120}{n} = \frac{40}{55}$ **165**
15. $\frac{95}{110} = \frac{n}{22}$ **19**
16. $\frac{33}{44} = \frac{132}{n}$ **176**
17. $\frac{9}{27} = \frac{n}{21}$ **7**
18. $\frac{10}{22} = \frac{30}{n}$ **66**
19. $\frac{n}{120} = \frac{15}{100}$ **18**
20. $\frac{68}{n} = \frac{102}{108}$ **72**
21. $\frac{3}{n} = \frac{12}{76}$ **19**
22. $\frac{15}{18} = \frac{n}{12}$ **10**
23. $\frac{44}{77} = \frac{24}{n}$ **42**
24. $\frac{n}{70} = \frac{36}{63}$ **63**
25. $\frac{84}{96} = \frac{35}{n}$ **40**
26. $\frac{n}{27} = \frac{14}{63}$ **6**
27. $\frac{32}{n} = \frac{28}{40}$ **40**
28. $\frac{11}{12} = \frac{n}{60}$ **55**
29. $\frac{17}{20} = \frac{n}{120}$ **102**
30. $\frac{30}{54} = \frac{20}{n}$ **36**
31. $\frac{n}{24} = \frac{56}{64}$ **21**
32. $\frac{11}{n} = \frac{44}{60}$ **15**
33. $\frac{18}{150} = \frac{15}{n}$ **125**
34. $\frac{45}{72} = \frac{n}{56}$ **35**
35. $\frac{77}{n} = \frac{42}{54}$ **99**
36. $\frac{n}{56} = \frac{42}{49}$ **48**
37. $\frac{n}{41} = \frac{9}{123}$ **3**
38. $\frac{35}{n} = \frac{5}{28}$ **196**
39. $\frac{12}{52} = \frac{n}{39}$ **9**
40. $\frac{40}{70} = \frac{32}{n}$ **56**

Page 69

Page 70

Percents — Skill: Percents and Proportions

Name _____

Total Problems __40__
Problems Correct ____
Percent Correct ____

Write as a proportion and solve. Show your work on another piece of paper. Write your answers here.

1. What number is 17% of 200? **34**
2. 16 is what percent of 80? **20%**
3. 25% of what number is 35? **140**
4. What percent of 90 is 27? **30%**
5. 112 is what percent of 400? **28%**
6. What number is 140% of 280? **392**
7. 12% of what number is 66? **550**
8. What percent of 30 is 54? **180%**
9. What number is 15% of 40? **6**
10. What percent of 90 is 72? **80%**
11. 495 is what percent of 500? **99%**
12. 125% of what number is 85? **68**
13. 70% of what number is 42? **60**
14. What number is 20% of 95? **19**
15. 216 is what percent of 600? **36%**
16. What number is 230% of 40? **92**
17. What percent of 900 is 792? **88%**
18. 27 is what percent of 90? **30%**
19. What number is 175% of 220? **385**
20. 18% of what number is 117? **650**
21. 42 is what percent of 120? **35%**
22. What percent of 260 is 247? **95%**
23. What percent of 315 is 63? **20%**
24. 40% of what number is 16? **40**
25. 16 is what percent of 50? **32%**
26. What number is 65% of 80? **52**
27. 325% of what number is 143? **44**
28. What percent of 225 is 207? **92%**
29. 136 is what percent of 80? **170%**
30. What number is 55% of 420? **231**
31. What percent of 30 is 21? **70%**
32. 60% of what number is 72? **120**
33. What number is 35% of 440? **154**
34. 121 is what percent of 550? **22%**
35. What percent of 150 is 114? **76%**
36. 130% of what number is 78? **60**
37. 12 is what percent of 80? **15%**
38. What number is 85% of 60? **51**
39. 45% of what number is 54? **120**
40. What percent of 165 is 198? **120%**

Page 70

Page 71

Percents — Skill: Ratios as Percents

Name _____

Total Problems __40__
Problems Correct ____
Percent Correct ____

Write the following ratios as percents. Show your work on another piece of paper. Write your answers here.

1. $\frac{2}{5}$ **40%**
2. 15 : 16 **93.75%**
3. $\frac{12}{25}$ **48%**
4. 0.125 **12.5%**
5. 17 : 20 **85%**
6. $\frac{9}{10}$ **90%**
7. 0.525 **52.5%**
8. $\frac{3}{4}$ **75%**
9. $\frac{11}{32}$ **34.375%**
10. 7 : 50 **14%**
11. 5 : 8 **62.5%**
12. 0.8 **80%**
13. 23 : 250 **9.2%**
14. $\frac{137}{200}$ **68.5%**
15. $\frac{17}{25}$ **68%**
16. 17 : 80 **21.25%**
17. 0.6875 **68.75%**
18. 0.3 **30%**
19. $\frac{7}{8}$ **87.5%**
20. 9 : 40 **22.5%**
21. $\frac{3}{5}$ **60%**
22. 5 : 32 **15.625%**
23. $\frac{333}{500}$ **66.6%**
24. 3 : 8 **37.5%**
25. 0.04 **4%**
26. $\frac{1}{5}$ **20%**
27. 33 : 40 **82.5%**
28. $\frac{121}{250}$ **48.4%**
29. 7 : 16 **43.75%**
30. $\frac{19}{20}$ **95%**
31. $\frac{23}{50}$ **46%**
32. 0.748 **74.8%**
33. 0.5625 **56.25%**
34. 111 : 400 **27.75%**
35. $\frac{21}{80}$ **26.25%**
36. $\frac{8}{25}$ **32%**
37. 0.7 **70%**
38. $\frac{211}{500}$ **42.2%**
39. 11 : 200 **5.5%**
40. $\frac{27}{40}$ **67.5%**

Page 71

Page 72

Decimals, Percents and Fractions — Skill: Decimals, Percents and Fractions

Name _____

Total Problems __40__
Problems Correct ____
Percent Correct ____

Complete the charts by converting percents, decimals and fractions.

	Percent	Fraction	Decimal
1.	187.5%	$1\frac{7}{8}$	1.875
2.	18%	$\frac{9}{50}$	0.18
3.	2%	$\frac{1}{50}$	.02
4.	85%	$\frac{17}{20}$	.85
5.	120%	$1\frac{1}{5}$	1.2
6.	135%	$1\frac{7}{20}$	1.35
7.	20.4%	$\frac{51}{250}$	0.204
8.	44.5%	$\frac{89}{200}$	.445
9.	33%	$\frac{33}{100}$	0.33
10.	77%	$\frac{77}{100}$	.77
11.	40%	$\frac{2}{5}$	.4
12.	42.5%	$\frac{17}{40}$	.425
13.	5.5%	$\frac{11}{200}$	.055
14.	195%	$1\frac{19}{20}$	1.95
15.	394%	$3\frac{47}{50}$	3.94
16.	264%	$2\frac{16}{25}$	2.64
17.	88%	$\frac{22}{25}$	0.88
18.	30%	$\frac{3}{10}$	.3
19.	12%	$\frac{3}{25}$	.12
20.	71.75%	$\frac{287}{400}$	0.7175

	Percent	Fraction	Decimal
21.	19%	$\frac{19}{100}$	.19
22.	87.5%	$\frac{7}{8}$	.875
23.	180%	$1\frac{4}{5}$	1.8
24.	128%	$1\frac{7}{25}$	1.28
25.	5%	$\frac{1}{20}$	.05
26.	13.5%	$\frac{27}{200}$	0.135
27.	86.5%	$\frac{173}{200}$	.865
28.	290%	$2\frac{9}{10}$	2.9
29.	352%	$3\frac{13}{25}$	3.52
30.	81.25%	$\frac{13}{16}$	0.8125
31.	72%	$\frac{18}{25}$	.72
32.	144%	$1\frac{11}{25}$	1.44
33.	61%	$\frac{61}{100}$	.61
34.	13.2%	$\frac{33}{250}$	0.132
35.	27.6%	$\frac{69}{250}$	.276
36.	95.5%	$\frac{151}{200}$	.955
37.	45%	$\frac{9}{20}$	0.45
38.	87.5%	$\frac{7}{8}$	.875
39.	27.75%	$\frac{111}{400}$	.2775
40.	85.8%	$\frac{429}{500}$	0.858

Page 72

Math IF8771

Write as a percent rounded to the nearest:

one of a percent

1. $\frac{4}{9}$ 44%
2. $\frac{9}{16}$ 56%
3. $\frac{3}{40}$ 8%

4. $\frac{2}{3}$ 67%
5. $\frac{7}{8}$ 88%
6. $\frac{17}{30}$ 57%
7. $\frac{8}{15}$ 53%
8. $\frac{8}{11}$ 73%

9. $\frac{27}{32}$ 84%
10. $\frac{17}{80}$ 21%

tenth of a percent

11. $\frac{8}{9}$ 88.9%
12. $\frac{22}{45}$ 48.9%
13. $\frac{4}{7}$ 57.1%
14. $\frac{5}{12}$ 41.7%
15. $\frac{77}{80}$ 96.3%

16. $\frac{13}{30}$ 43.3%
17. $\frac{111}{160}$ 69.4%
18. $\frac{5}{16}$ 31.3%
19. $\frac{19}{75}$ 25.3%
20. $\frac{17}{18}$ 94.4%

hundredth of a percent

21. $\frac{7}{15}$ 46.67%
22. $\frac{3}{11}$ 27.27%
23. $\frac{5}{18}$ 27.78%
24. $\frac{81}{160}$ 50.63%
25. $\frac{6}{13}$ 46.15%

26. $\frac{21}{44}$ 47.73%
27. $\frac{2}{9}$ 22.22%
28. $\frac{97}{120}$ 80.83%
29. $\frac{8}{21}$ 38.1%
30. $\frac{6}{7}$ 85.71%

thousandth of a percent

31. $\frac{5}{19}$ 26.316%
32. $\frac{13}{28}$ 46.429%
33. $\frac{5}{26}$ 19.231%
34. $\frac{13}{24}$ 54.167%
35. $\frac{4}{21}$ 19.048%

36. $\frac{11}{12}$ 91.667%
37. $\frac{2}{7}$ 28.571%
38. $\frac{2}{13}$ 15.385%
39. $\frac{1}{3}$ 33.333%
40. $\frac{10}{11}$ 90.909%

Page 73

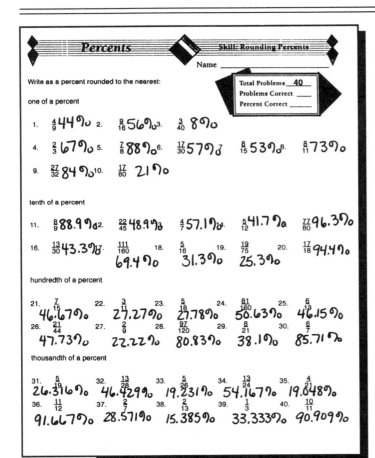

Write the percents with a decimal point instead of a fractional part, rounding to the nearest ten-thousandth of a percent when necessary. Then, write this new percent as a decimal.

1. 1.5% = .015
2. 3.375% = .03375
3. 18.75% = .1875
4. 20.85% = .2085
5. 9.2% = .092
6. 14.6667% = .146667
7. 66.8333% = .668333
8. 40.4167% = .404167
9. 55.42869% = .554286
10. 10.44% = .1044
11. 180.3% = 1.803
12. 75.78% = .7578
13. 14.8% = .148
14. 90.8889% = .908889
15. 33.4667% = .33467
16. 23.25% = .2325
17. 120.625% = 1.20625
18. 220.55% = 2.2055
19. 8.3889% = .083889
20. 2.9% = .029
21. 11.0833% = .110833
22. 28.3% = .283
23. 12.9% = .129
24. 18.875% = .18875
25. 110.5833% = 1.105833
26. 12.25% = .1225
27. 450.96% = 4.5096
28. 90.3333% = .903333
29. 72.5833% = .725833
30. 34.1875% = .341875
31. 17.6% = .176
32. 22.7778% = .227778
33. 8.125% = .08125
34. 200.5% = 2.005
35. 50.36% = .5036
36. 5.1% = .051
37. 88.5% = .885
38. 11.1677 = .111667
39. 99.9899% = .999899
40. 105.1429% = 1.051429
41. 45.44% = .4544
42. 70.7333 = .707333
43. 89.1176% = .891176
44. 125.4% = 1.254
45. 65.15% = .6515
46. 19.9167% = .199167
47. 62.8125% = .628125
48. 95.7% = .957

Page 74

Solve. Show your work on another piece of paper. Write your answers here.

1. How much is 19% of 45? 8.55
2. 88% of 70 is how much? 61.6
3. 3.6% of 40 is how much? 1.44
4. How much is 125% of 72? 90
5. How much is 58% of 95? 55.1
6. 220% of 8 is how much? 17.6
7. 110% of 39 is how much? 42.9
8. How much is 12% of 130? 15.6
9. How much is 90% of 70? 63
10. 0.5% of 400 is how much? 2
11. 45% of 80 is how much? 36
12. How much is 60% of 30? 18
13. How much is 190% of 33? 62.7
14. 70% of 90 is how much? 63
15. 24% of 55 is how much? 13.2
16. How much is 215% of 420? 903
17. How much is 30% of 70? 21
18. 55% of 80 is how much? 44
19. 90% of 130 is how much? 117
20. How much is 4% of 16? 0.64
21. How much is 22% of 66? 14.52
22. 16% of 85 is how much? 13.6
23. 120% of 90 is how much? 108
24. How much is 35% of 44? 15.4
25. How much is 0.2% of 470? 0.94
26. 6% of 20 is how much? 1.2
27. 170% of 3 is how much? 5.1
28. How much is 2.5% of 140? 3.5
29. Huch much is 80% of 210? 168
30. 22% of 20 is how much? 4.4
31. 35% of 17 is how much? 5.95
32. How much is 14.8% of 50? 7.4
33. How much is 60% of 80? 48
34. 92% of 300 is how much? 276
35. 290% of 5 is how much? 14.5
36. How much is 105% of 25? 26.25
37. How much is 40% of 60? 24
38. 35.8% of 190 is how much? 68.02
39. 9% of 200 is how much? 18
40. How much is 150% of 150? 225

Page 75

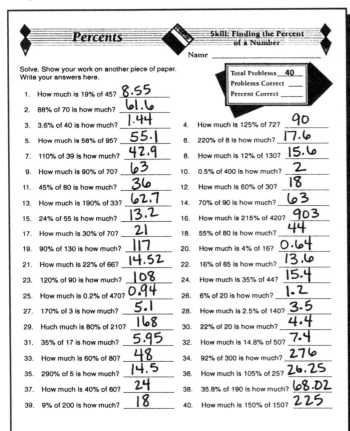

Solve. Show your work on another piece of paper. Write your answers here.

1. What percent of 20 is 8? 40%
2. 50 is what percent of 16? 312.5%
3. 18 is what percent of 120? 15%
4. What percent of 200 is 121? 60.5%
5. What percent of 4 is 5? 125%
6. 3 is what percent of 250? 1.2%
7. 15 is what percent of 80? 18.75%
8. What percent of 24 is 33? 137.5%
9. What percent of 25 is 29? 116%
10. 39 is what percent of 75? 52%
11. 28 is what percent of 40? 70%
12. What percent of 160 is 55? 34.375%
13. What percent of 200 is 111? 55.5%
14. 120 is what percent of 600? 20%
15. 193 is what percent of 80? 241.25%
16. What percent of 24 is 21? 87.5%
17. What percent of 250 is 193? 77.2%
18. 36 is what percent of 96? 37.5%
19. 18 is what percent of 48? 37.5%
20. What percent of 220 is 44? 20%
21. What percent of 8 is 20? 250%
22. 8 is what percent of 128? 6.25%
23. 15 is what percent of 125? 12%
24. What percent of 160 is 88? 55%
25. What percent of 400 is 301? 75.25%
26. 10 is what percent of 64? 15.625%
27. 18 is what percent of 45? 40%
28. What percent of 480 is 198? 41.25%
29. What percent of 120 is 9? 7.5%
30. 38 is what percent of 95? 40%
31. 63 is what percent of 112? 56.25%
32. What percent of 256 is 32? 12.5%
33. What percent of 18 is 45? 250%
34. 12 is what percent of 150? 8%
35. 156 is what percent of 160? 97.5%
36. What percent of 300 is 132? 44%
37. What percent of 72 is 45? 62.5%
38. 180 is what percent of 450? 40%
39. 42 is what percent of 56? 75%
40. What percent of 220 is 77? 35%

Page 76

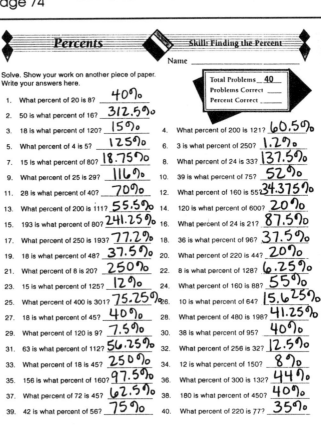

Percents — Skill: Finding the Total Number

Name _____

Solve. Show your work on another piece of paper. Write your answers here.

Total Problems **40**
Problems Correct ____
Percent Correct ____

1. 6.48 is 18% of what number? **36**
2. 360% of what number is 7.2? **2**
3. 135% of what number is 99.9? **74**
4. 3 is 15% of what number? **20**
5. 59.4 is 90% of what number? **66**
6. 38% of what number is 20.9? **55**
7. 80% of what number is 24? **30**
8. 404 is 101% of what number? **400**
9. 192 is 240% of what number? **80**
10. 11% of what number is 13.2? **120**
11. 86% of what number is 184.9? **215**
12. 79.9 is 85% of what number? **94**
13. 28 is 40% of what number? **70**
14. 70% of what number is 133? **190**
15. 22% of what number is 27.5? **125**
16. 10.6 is 256% of what number? **4**
17. 114 is 95% of what number? **120**
18. 325% of what number is 39? **12**
19. 140% of what number is 42? **30**
20. 39 is 20% of what number? **195**
21. 18.2 is 28% of what number? **65**
22. 250% of what number is 15? **6**
23. 25% of what number is 40? **160**
24. 122.1 is 185% of what number? **66**
25. 98 is 35% of what number? **280**
26. 60% of what number is 90? **150**
27. 5% of what number is 9? **180**
28. 105 is 25% of what number? **420**
29. 645 is 215% of what number? **300**
30. 75% of what number is 15? **20**
31. 70% of what number is 56? **80**
32. 76 is 95% of what number? **80**
33. 9.24 is 14% of what number? **66**
34. 120% of what number is 72? **60**
35. 2% of what number is 1.92? **96**
36. 9.2 is 8% of what number? **115**
37. 288 is 144% of what number? **200**
38. 92% of what number is 110.4? **120**
39. 96% of what number is 144? **150**
40. 79.2 is 198% of what number? **40**

Percents — Skill: Percent Increase and Decrease

Name _____

Solve. Show your work on another piece of paper. Write your answers here.

Total Problems **30**
Problems Correct ____
Percent Correct ____

1. What is the percent increase from 12 to 60? **400%**
2. What is 70 decreased by 20%? **56**
3. What is 66 increased by 88%? **124.08**
4. What is the percent decrease from 300 to 12? **96%**
5. What is the percent decrease from 72 to 45? **37.53**
6. What is the percent increase from 120 to 150? **25%**
7. What is the percent increase from 80 to 95? **18.75%**
8. What is 200 increased by 18%? **236**
9. What is 90 increased by 13%? **78.3**
10. What is 480 decreased by 95%? **24**
11. What is the percent decrease from 105 to 42? **60%**
12. What is the percent increase from 16 to 93? **481.25%**
13. What is 120 increased by 13%? **135.6**
14. What is 45 increased by 35%? **60.75**
15. What is the percent increase from 20 to 30? **50%**
16. What is the percent decrease from 25 to 17? **32%**
17. What is 175 decreased by 80%? **35**
18. What is 60 increased by 28%? **76.8**
19. What is the percent decrease from 220 to 33? **85%**
20. What is the percent increase from 40 to 51? **27.5%**
21. What is 94 increased by 30%? **122.2**
22. What is 16 decreased by 60%? **6.4**
23. What is the percent increase from 35 to 56? **60%**
24. What is the percent dcrease from 150 to 108? **28%**
25. What is 212 increased by 11%? **188.68**
26. What is 105 decreased by 15%? **89.25**
27. What is the percent decrease from 168 to 63? **62.5%**
28. What is 90 increased by 95%? **175.5**
29. What is 15 decreased by 4%? **14.4**
30. What is the percent increase from 72 to 81? **12.5%**

Sales Tax — Skill: Sales Tax

Name _____

Complete the chart. Round to the nearest cent.

Total Problems **20**
Problems Correct ____
Percent Correct ____

	Cost of Item	% Sales Tax	Tax Paid	Total Cost
1.	$4.99	$3\frac{1}{4}$%	$ .16	$ 5.15
2.	$12.50	5.65%	.71	13.21
3.	$.58	$6\frac{3}{4}$%	.04	.62
4.	$372.48	12%	44.70	417.18
5.	$111.20	$18\frac{1}{8}$%	20.16	131.36
6.	$13.84	4.3%	.60	14.44
7.	$25.25	7.11%	1.80	27.05
8.	$30.18	$8\frac{5}{8}$%	2.60	32.78
9.	$441.89	9.0625%	40.05	481.94
10.	$580.60	14%	81.28	661.88
11.	$14.12	1.35%	.19	14.31
12.	$8.19	6.8%	.56	8.75
13.	$5.45	$5\frac{1}{4}$%	.29	5.74
14.	$613.20	22%	134.90	748.10
15.	$125.50	$11\frac{3}{8}$%	14.28	139.78
16.	$220.16	$9\frac{1}{2}$%	20.92	241.08
17.	$8.12	2.625%	.21	8.33
18.	$9.00	8.9375%	.80	9.80
19.	$16.85	19%	3.20	20.05
20.	$21.22	5.0375%	1.07	22.29

Simple Interest — Skill: Simple Interest

Name _____

Complete the chart. Round to the nearest cent.

Total Problems **20**
Problems Correct ____
Percent Correct ____

	Principal	Interest Rate Per Year	Time	Interest Earned
1.	$625.00	16%	6 months	$ 50.00
2.	$720.50	$7\frac{1}{2}$%	1 year	54.04
3.	$5,670.80	22%	9 months	935.68
4.	$4,112.20	$11\frac{1}{8}$%	$4\frac{1}{4}$ years	1944.30
5.	$905.60	14%	$5\frac{1}{2}$ years	697.31
6.	$814.75	$5\frac{3}{4}$%	4 years	187.39
7.	$1,100.50	15%	3 months	41.27
8.	$870.20	$8\frac{3}{8}$%	$9\frac{3}{4}$ years	710.57
9.	$415.15	$6\frac{1}{2}$%	5 months	11.24
10.	$6,540.50	11%	$1\frac{1}{4}$ years	899.32
11.	$11,140.25	5.0375%	8 years	4489.52
12.	$26,500.75	8%	6 months	1060.03
13.	$408.50	2.625%	4 months	3.57
14.	$910.80	21%	3 years	573.80
15.	$12,540.00	$14\frac{5}{8}$%	7 months	1069.82
16.	$9,750.50	12.0625%	$11\frac{1}{2}$ years	13,525.77
17.	$810.40	$10\frac{1}{2}$%	6 years	510.55
18.	$4,480.10	4.6875%	3 months	52.50
19.	$33,500.00	33%	$4\frac{1}{4}$ years	46983.75
20.	$18,549.99	9.6%	5 years	8,904.00

Math IF8771

Complete the chart. Round to the nearest cent.

Total Problems __20__
Problems Correct _____
Percent Correct _____

	Principal	Interest Rate	Compounded	Time	Interest
1.	$4,000.00	12.4%	semiannually	1 year	$1053.50
2.	$650.00	8%	quarterly	1 year	234.31
3.	$18,999.99	$7\frac{1}{4}$%	annually	3 years	4439.35
4.	$525.25	$19\frac{3}{4}$%	monthly	2 months	227.96
5.	$27,428.20	21%	annually	2 years	12,729.43
6.	$5,000.00	$8\frac{3}{8}$%	quarterly	1 year	1897.42
7.	$16,888.75	14%	semiannually	18 months	8132.68
8.	$21,050.25	10.6%	semiannually	2 years	10,447.37
9.	$9,420.55	16.2%	monthly	4 months	7754.61
10.	$625.00	$18\frac{1}{8}$%	monthly	2 months	247.09
11.	$718.99	20.5%	annually	2 years	325
12.	$330.20	17.9%	quarterly	6 months	128.79
13.	$890.15	$13\frac{7}{8}$%	annually	2 years	264.15
14.	$10,000.00	8.85%	quarterly	1 year	4038.27
15.	$15,980.00	9.8%	monthly	2 months	3285.55
16.	$25,400.00	12.35%	annually	2 years	6661.21
17.	$29,590.25	$19\frac{5}{8}$%	semiannually	1 year	12,753.82
18.	$18,670.20	$21\frac{1}{4}$%	quarterly	9 months	14,610.63
19.	$6,430.05	22.1%	annually	3 years	5274.68
20.	$780.10	$5\frac{3}{4}$%	annually	4 years	195.50

Page 81

Complete the last two columns of the chart using the discount rate or markup rate. Round to the nearest cent.

Total Problems __20__
Problems Correct _____
Percent Correct _____

	Cost/Price	Discount Rate	Markup Rate	Discount or Markup	Sale Price or Selling Price
1.	$35.00	25%		$ 8.75	$ 26.25
2.	$42.00		18%	7.56	49.56
3.	$68.00		20%	13.60	81.60
4.	$24.99	70%		17.49	7.50
5.	$50.00		65%	32.50	82.50
6.	$20.00	35%		7.00	13.00
7.	$17.50	5%		.88	16.62
8.	$110.90		33%	36.60	147.50
9.	$240.50	60%		144.30	96.20
10.	$89.75		28%	25.13	114.88
11.	$64.25	40%		25.70	38.55
12.	$19.99		88%	17.59	37.58
13.	$595.00		8%	47.60	642.60
14.	$616.80	12%		74.02	542.78
15.	$200.00		15%	30.00	230.00
16.	$450.50	55%		247.78	202.72
17.	$38.90	64%		24.90	14.00
18.	$14.98		70%	10.49	25.47
19.	$5.65	95%		5.37	11.02
20.	$717.20		18%	129.10	846.30

Page 82

Complete the charts. Round to the nearest cent.

Total Problems __40__
Problems Correct _____
Percent Correct _____

	Rate of Commission	Total Sales	Commission		Rate of Commission	Total Sales	Commission
1.	14%	$950.00	$133	21.	$4\frac{7}{8}$%	$412.13	20.09
2.	22%	$412.75	90.81	22.	18%	$5,678.20	1022.08
3.	11%	$1,020.80	112.29	23.	5.6%	$718.65	40.24
4.	25%	$428.66	107.17	24.	28%	$95.25	26.67
5.	15%	$505.15	75.77	25.	$12\frac{1}{2}$%	$648.29	81.04
6.	9%	$3,496.98	314.73	26.	33.3%	$300.50	100.07
7.	$10\frac{1}{2}$%	$54.75	5.75	27.	8.2%	$982.17	80.54
8.	30%	$104.73	31.42	28.	16%	$1,546.70	247.47
9.	$13\frac{1}{4}$%	$64.00	8.48	29.	$15\frac{1}{4}$%	$3,009.75	458.99
10.	16%	$89.11	14.26	30.	18.5%	$818.40	151.40
11.	35%	$715.25	250.34	31.	14%	$335.25	46.94
12.	44%	$300.50	132.22	32.	9.6%	$1,124.55	107.96
13.	$8\frac{3}{8}$%	$2,450.75	205.25	33.	12%	$39,428.00	4731.36
14.	$11\frac{1}{4}$%	$918.75	103.36	34.	28%	$518.95	145.31
15.	13%	$600.00	78	35.	$17\frac{3}{4}$%	$499.99	88.75
16.	24%	$818.95	196.55	36.	31%	$4,000.00	1240
17.	28%	$42.82	11.99	37.	42%	$780.99	328.02
18.	$7\frac{1}{2}$%	$348.60	26.15	38.	14.2%	$395.00	56.09
19.	6%	$659.34	39.56	39.	14%	$488.62	68.41
20.	5%	$205.12	10.26	40.	$8\frac{3}{4}$%	$199.00	17.41

Page 83

Complete the tables. Round to the nearest cent.

Total Problems __40__
Problems Correct _____
Percent Correct _____

	Purchase Price	Down Payment Percentage	Down Payment		Purchase Price	Down Payment Percentage	Down Payment
1.	$5,000.00	15%	$750	21.	$750.00	8%	$60
2.	$1,125.00	20%	225	22.	$990.95	12%	118.91
3.	$890.50	19%	169.20	23.	$4,508.85	20%	901.77
4.	$7,500.00	14%	1050	24.	$1,427.99	15%	214.20
5.	$9,000.00	10%	900	25.	$843.75	$14\frac{1}{2}$%	122.34
6.	$1,546.88	5%	77.34	26.	$6,000.00	12%	720
7.	$2,999.99	25%	750	27.	$7,300.00	20%	1460
8.	$8,500.00	50%	4250	28.	$640.25	25%	160.06
9.	$7,400.00	40%	2960	29.	$900.00	40%	360
10.	$658.75	35%	230.56	30.	$415.50	$11\frac{3}{8}$%	47.26
11.	$400.00	20%	80	31.	$21,750.00	22%	4785
12.	$925.50	15%	138.83	32.	$8,173.25	35%	2860.64
13.	$717.25	18%	129.11	33.	$767.20	$16\frac{3}{4}$%	128.51
14.	$629.84	15%	94.48	34.	$2,480.25	45%	1116.11
15.	$3,985.15	10%	398.52	35.	$960.00	14.2%	136.32
16.	$200.00	$12\frac{1}{2}$%	25	36.	$817.20	20.8%	169.98
17.	$718.99	14%	100.66	37.	$415.10	16%	66.42
18.	$515.20	25%	128.80	38.	$9,000.00	$9\frac{1}{2}$%	855
19.	$7,600.00	40%	3040	39.	$11,400.00	7%	798
20.	$95,000.00	30%	28,500	40.	$880.15	6.8%	59.85

Page 84

©Instructional Fair, Inc.

Page 85

Name _____

Total Problems 50
Problems Correct ____
Percent Correct ____

Is the number positive or negative?
Write positive or negative.

1. -44 neg. 2. 36 pos. 3. 51 pos.
4. -19 neg. 5. 26 pos. 6. 93 pos.
7. -12 neg. 8. -71 neg. 9. 86 pos. 10. -113 neg. 11. 225 pos.
12. -5 neg. 13. -16 neg. 14. 29 pos. 15. -85 neg.

Write the opposite of each number.

16. 42 -42 17. -7 7 18. -12 12 19. -15 15 20. 21 -21
21. 106 -106 22. -230 230 23. -81 81 24. -60 60 25. 75 -75
26. -111 111 27. 525 -525 28. -65 65 29. -33 33 30. -2 2

Each symbol represents a number on the number line. Tell which integer is represented by each symbol.

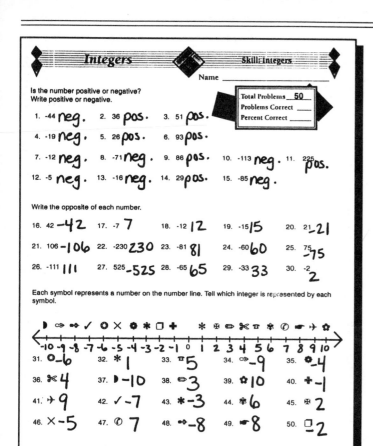

31. ◐ -6 32. ✱ 1 33. π 5 34. ∾ -9 35. ✿ -4
36. ✖ 4 37. ◑ -10 38. ⬭ 3 39. ✿ 10 40. + -1
41. ✦ 9 42. ✓ -7 43. ✱ -3 44. ✳ 6 45. ⊞ 2
46. ✕ -5 47. ∅ 7 48. ⚬ -8 49. 👉 8 50. ▢ 2

Page 86

Name _____

Total Problems 30
Problems Correct ____
Percent Correct ____

Write which property is used.

1. 8 x (3 + 6) = (8 x 3) + (8 x 6) distributive
2. -55 + 0 = -55 identity
3. -14 x -8 = -8 x -14 commutative
4. -18 x (-5 x -7) = (-18 x -5) x -7 associative
5. 8 + (11 + -5) = (8 + 11) + -5 associative
6. -5 x (-2 + 9) = (-5 x -2) + (-5 x 9) distributive
7. 0 + -16 = -16 identity
8. -132 + 114 = 114 + -132 commutative
9. 11 x (-4 + -5) = (11 x -4) + (11 x -5) distributive
10. -46 x 1 = -46 identity
11. (-12 x 4) x -3 = -12 x (4 x -3) associative
12. 28 x -5 = -5 x 28 commutative
13. 66 + -98 = -98 + 66 Commutative
14. (13 + -12) + -39 = 13 + (-12 + -39) associative
15. 1 x -98 = -98 identity
16. -7 x (9 + 7) = (-7 x 9) + (-7 x 7) distributive

Use the properties to solve the equations.

17. -36 + x = -36 0
18. (3 x -7) + (3 x n) = 3 x (-7 + 9) 9
19. n x -11 = -11 x 9 9
20. -5 x (4 x -18) = (-5 x 4) x n -18
21. (-11 x -5) + (-11 x 6) = n x (-5 + 6) -11
22. 19 x (n + -4) = (19 x -5) + (19 x -4) -5
23. 14 + 17 = 17 + n 14
24. 1 x n = -55 -55
25. (6 + -11) + n = 6 + (-11 + -13) -13
26. 36 + -15 = n + 36 -15
27. n x -18 = -18 1
28. 0 + n = -75 -75
29. 8 x (4 + -10) = (8 x n) + (8 x -10) 4
30. n + (-12 + -13) = (-9 + -12) + -13 -9

Page 87

Name _____

Total Problems 52
Problems Correct ____
Percent Correct ____

Add.

1. 18 + 11 29
2. -13 + -11 -24
3. -22 + -5 -27
4. 19 + 5 24
5. -7 + -12 -19
6. -8 + -6 -14
7. -4 + -5 -9
8. -13 + -2 -15
9. -20 + -4 -24
10. 8 + 13 21
11. 22 + 2 24
12. -15 + -1 -16
13. -14 + -6 -20
14. -3 + -9 -12
15. 9 + 9 18
16. 8 + 31 39
17. -20 + -2 -22
18. -9 + -7 -16
19. 15 + 14 29
20. -19 + -8 -27
21. -15 + -6 -21
22. -18 + -3 -21
23. 17 + 7 24
24. -16 + 5 21
25. -6 + -7 -13
26. -34 + -5 -39
27. 28 + 13 41
28. -25 + -1 -26
29. -20 + -13 -33
30. 30 + 30 60
31. 14 + 7 21
32. -17 + -8 -25
33. -18 + -4 -22
34. -50 + -5 -55
35. -27 + -5 -32
36. 16 + 13 29
37. -25 + -16 -41
38. -28 + -9 -37
39. 19 + 12 31
40. -11 + -18 -29
41. -15 + -21 -36
42. -8 + -80 -88
43. -6 + -17 -23
44. 4 + 62 66
45. -2 + -19 -21
46. 35 + 62 97
47. -28 + -31 -59
48. -19 + -23 -42
49. -14 + -9 -23
50. 16 + 24 40
51. -103 + -207 -310
52. -244 + -244 -488

Page 88

Name _____

Total Problems 52
Problems Correct ____
Percent Correct ____

Add.

1. 8 + -10 -2
2. 19 + -20 -1
3. -18 + 6 -12
4. -17 + 7 -10
5. 12 + -18 -6
6. 33 + -12 21
7. -21 + 18 -3
8. -15 + 11 -4
9. 26 + -12 14
10. 34 + -15 19
11. -16 + 18 2
12. -14 + 22 8
13. 15 + -33 -18
14. 17 + -16 1
15. 14 + -20 -6
16. -18 + 22 4
17. -19 + 13 -6
18. 18 + -28 -10
19. 31 + -5 26
20. -42 + 41 -1
21. 11 + -19 -8
22. -4 + 20 16
23. -18 + 11 -7
24. 26 + -29 -3
25. 14 + -8 6
26. -48 + 96 48
27. 81 + -66 15
28. 28 + -90 -62
29. -42 + 100 58
30. 88 + -140 -52
31. -16 + 12 -4
32. -90 + 72 -18
33. 14 + -56 -42
34. 20 + -35 -15
35. -28 + 51 23
36. 17 + -42 -25
37. 28 + -11 17
38. -53 + 62 9
39. -40 + 28 -12
40. -93 + 105 12
41. 42 + -20 22
42. -80 + 64 -16
43. 59 + -84 -25
44. -4 + 89 85
45. -18 + 75 57
46. 71 + -44 27
47. 92 + -200 -108
48. 22 + -63 -41
49. 16 + -59 -43
50. -94 + 163 69
51. -303 + 303 0
52. 422 + -109 313

Integers — Skill: Subtracting Integers

Name _____

Total Problems **52**
Problems Correct ____
Percent Correct ____

Subtract.

1. -70 – 42 = **-112**
2. 18 – -12 = **30**
3. -90 – -26 = **-64**
4. 42 – 86 = **-44**
5. -38 – 14 = **-52**
6. 49 – -58 = **107**
7. -16 – 63 = **-79**
8. 22 – -36 = **58**
9. -33 – -51 = **18**
10. -11 – 72 = **-83**
11. 10 – 46 = **-36**
12. -13 – 48 = **-61**
13. 28 – -94 = **122**
14. -54 – -25 = **-29**
15. -38 – 65 = **-103**
16. -16 – -39 = **23**
17. 75 – 96 = **-21**
18. -81 – 105 = **-186**
19. -95 – -45 = **-50**
20. 60 – -49 = **109**
21. -35 – 20 = **-55**
22. -150 – 390 = **-540**
23. 70 – 246 = **-176**
24. 18 – -94 = **112**
25. -39 – -59 = **20**
26. 50 – 120 = **-70**
27. 9 – -30 = **39**
28. -2 – 45 = **-47**
29. 14 – -27 = **41**
30. -98 – -43 = **-55**
31. -42 – 64 = **-106**
32. 38 – 55 = **-17**
33. 77 – -21 = **98**
34. -60 – 40 = **-100**
35. -181 – -105 = **-76**
36. -10 – 28 = **-38**
37. 8 – -25 = **33**
38. -3 – 64 = **-67**
39. -5 – -38 = **33**
40. 15 – -202 = **217**
41. 21 – -9 = **30**
42. -8 – 37 = **-45**
43. 79 – -14 = **93**
44. -84 – 28 = **-112**
45. -120 – -98 = **-22**
46. 105 – -73 = **178**
47. 1 – -99 = **100**
48. -4 – 86 = **-90**
49. 50 – -43 = **93**
50. -62 – -50 = **-12**
51. -84 – 84 = **-168**
52. 212 – 506 = **-294**

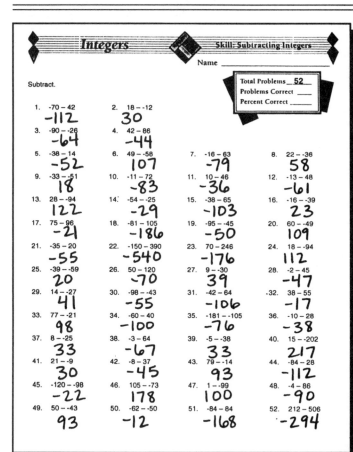

Integers — Skill: Adding and Subtracting Integers

Name _____

Total Problems **24**
Problems Correct ____
Percent Correct ____

Add and subtract. Show your work on another piece of paper. Write your answers here.

1. -9 + -11 – 4 + -8 – 10 = **-22**
2. 8 – 14 + 95 – -105 + -111 – 63 = **20**
3. 111 + -128 – -98 – -74 + 110 = **265**
4. -28 – -43 – 16 – -20 + 89 – -105 = **3**
5. 89 – -62 – 49 + 68 + 3 – -41 = **214**
6. 16 – -21 – 28 + -99 – -54 – -17 = **-19**
7. -400 – 32 – -58 + 63 – -94 – 6 = **-411**
8. 48 – 63 + -11 + 25 – -26 + -21 = **4**
9. 78 – -23 – 49 + 63 + -98 – -19 = **36**
10. -65 + -94 + 68 – 23 – -89 + 63 = **-88**
11. 36 – -42 + 6 – -28 – 43 – -81 – 6 = **144**
12. -4 + 8 – 10 – -11 + -13 + 5 – 11 + 12 – -14 = **12**
13. -90 – -27 + 105 – -230 + -64 = **208**
14. 81 – 104 + 29 – -33 + -56 – 78 = **-95**
15. 42 + 40 + -89 – -64 – 76 + 91 = **72**
16. -50 – -41 – 65 + 205 – 318 + -5 = **-62**
17. -18 – 29 – -60 + 58 + -70 = **1**
18. 39 – -82 – 68 + 95 – 53 – -48 + -18 = **125**
19. -193 – -205 + -68 – 211 – 150 = **-117**
20. 420 – 561 – -502 + 418 + -715 – -42 = **106**
21. -73 – -68 – 52 + 19 + -105 = **-143**
22. 218 + 195 – 75 + -188 – 163 = **313**
23. -50 + 77 – -84 – 93 + -60 – 22 = **-20**
24. 409 + -518 – -210 + -68 – -115 + 96 = **244**

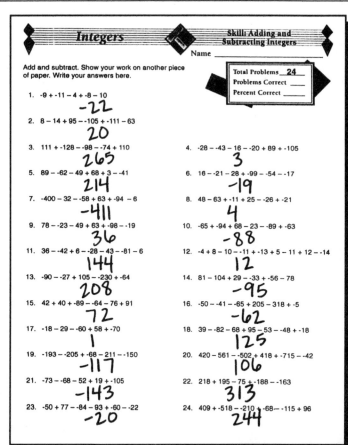

Integers — Skill: Multiplying Integers

Name _____

Total Problems **26**
Problems Correct ____
Percent Correct ____

Multiply. Show your work on another piece of paper. Write your answers here.

1. -628 × 433 = **-271,924**
2. -716 × -87 = **62,292**
3. 914 × -533 = **-487,162**
4. -328 × -319 = **104,632**
5. 52,864 × -96 = **-5,074,944**
6. -7,862 × 99 = **-778,338**
7. -64,515 × -980 = **63,224,700**
8. 70,426 × 88 = **6,197,488**
9. -562 × -198 = **111,276**
10. 516 × -293 = **-151,188**
11. -3,842 × 19 = **-72,998**
12. 51,826 × -77 = **-3,990,602**
13. 8,265 × -444 = **-3,669,660**
14. 54,178 × 328 = **17,770,384**
15. -665 × -313 = **208,145**
16. -908 × 113 = **-102,604**
17. -7,268 × 158 = **-1,148,344**
18. -60,170 × -425 = **25,572,250**
19. 9,119 × 205 = **1,869,395**
20. -516 × -39 = **20,124**
21. 3,009 × -717 = **-2,157,453**
22. -16,412 × -908 = **14,902,096**
23. -28,110 × 91 = **-2,558,010**
24. -5,648 × -99 = **559,152**
25. -2,372 × 71 = **-168,412**
26. -30,194 × -28 = **845,432**

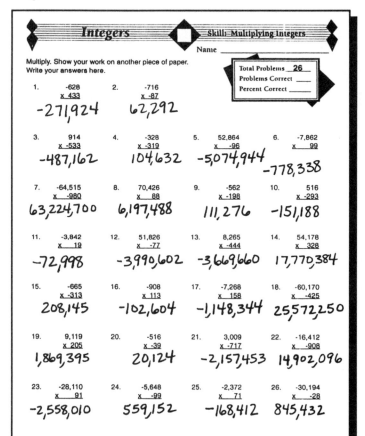

Integers — Skill: Dividing Integers

Name _____

Total Problems **36**
Problems Correct ____
Percent Correct ____

Divide. Show your work on another piece of paper. Write your answers here.

1. -828 ÷ -92 = **9**
2. 308 ÷ -14 = **-22**
3. -608 ÷ 8 = **-76**
4. -612 ÷ -9 = **68**
5. -2,958 ÷ 34 = **-87**
6. 3,234 ÷ -42 = **-77**
7. 2,548 ÷ 26 = **98**
8. -1,504 ÷ -47 = **32**
9. 6,888 ÷ -56 = **-123**
10. 40,572 ÷ 98 = **414**
11. -5,610 ÷ 55 = **-102**
12. -8,892 ÷ -38 = **234**
13. -23,408 ÷ 56 = **-418**
14. 6,480 ÷ -18 = **-360**
15. -9,252 ÷ -12 = **771**
16. -33,048 ÷ 81 = **-408**
17. 37,668 ÷ -73 = **-516**
18. 56,482 ÷ 62 = **911**
19. -6,902 ÷ -58 = **119**
20. 28,576 ÷ -47 = **-608**
21. -6,176 ÷ -32 = **193**
22. 8,236 ÷ -29 = **-284**
23. 13,536 ÷ -94 = **-144**
24. -56,712 ÷ 51 = **-1,112**
25. 13,158 ÷ -43 = **-306**
26. -46,260 ÷ -90 = **514**
27. 33,538 ÷ 82 = **409**
28. -6,150 ÷ -75 = **82**
29. -16,188 ÷ -71 = **228**
30. -9,021 ÷ 93 = **-97**
31. 15,447 ÷ -19 = **-813**
32. -4,624 ÷ 68 = **-68**
33. 6,372 ÷ -59 = **-108**
34. -37,584 ÷ -58 = **648**
35. 35,388 ÷ 36 = **983**
36. -29,232 ÷ -48 = **609**

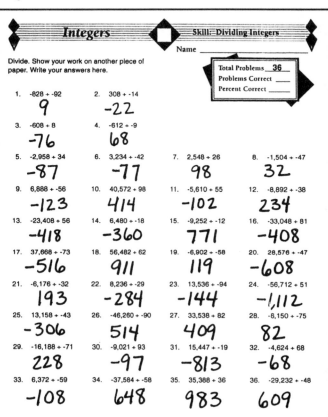

Page 93

Integers — Skill: Multiplying and Dividing Integers

Name _____

Multiply and divide. Show your work on another piece of paper. Write your answers here.

Total Problems __30__
Problems Correct _____
Percent Correct _____

1. $-18 \times -45 + 54 \times -40 \div -30$ — **20**
2. $588 \div 14 \times -6 \div -21 \times 20 \div -8 \times 5$ — **150**
3. $2,400 \div -15 \times -3 \div -60 \times 11$ — **-88**
4. $21 \times -2 \div -14 \times 25 \div -15 \times -9$ — **45**
5. $-85 \times -4 + 17 \times -22 \div 55 \times 8$ — **-64**
6. $-1,584 \div 44 \times -21 \div 6 \times -5 \div -90$ — **7**
7. $-216 \div 18 \times -13 \div 2 \times 5 + 39$ — **10**
8. $90 \times 35 \div 210 \times -8 \div 60 \times 17$ — **-34**
9. $81 \times -15 + 27 \times -4 \div 60 \times -14$ — **-42**
10. $540 \div -18 \times 16 \div 24 \times 11 \div -4 \times 6 \div -33$ — **-10**
11. $-270 \div -18 \times 16 \div -15 \times -22 \div -44$ — **-8**
12. $-81 \times 75 \div -15 \times -4 \div 27 \times -11 \div -4$ — **-165**
13. $22 \times -55 + 10 \times -36 + 33 \times 4$ — **528**
14. $195 \times -2 \div 26 \times -12 \div 9 \times -5 \div -25$ — **4**
15. $-528 \div 24 \times -9 \div -11 \times 50 \div -45$ — **20**
16. $1,000 \div -40 \times 21 \div 15 \times -2 - 7$ — **10**
17. $28 \times -15 \div 21 \times -35 \div 28 \times -6$ — **-150**
18. $-210 \div -14 \times 21 \div -35 \times 16 \div -12 \times -5$ — **-60**
19. $-504 \div -42 \times -33 \div 2 \times -21 + 77$ — **54**
20. $-36 \times 25 \div -4 \times 7 \div -63 \times 3 \div 5$ — **-15**
21. $72 \times 11 \div -12 \times 18 \div 4 \times 5 + 33$ — **-45**
22. $750 \div -5 \times 6 \div 75 \times 12 \div -8 \times 3$ — **54**
23. $156 \div -2 \times -5 \div 13 \times -7 \div -35 \times -6$ — **-36**
24. $18 \times 28 \div 36 \times -110 \div 2 \times 3 + 66$ — **-35**
25. $33 \times -56 \div -77 \times 25 \div -300 \times 27 \div -18$ — **3**
26. $-1,080 \div -54 \times 55 \div -44 \times 12 \div -15$ — **20**
27. $2,640 \div -22 \times 9 \div 24 \times -5 + 15$ — **15**
28. $64 \times -9 \div 24 \times 25 \div -15 \times 11 \div -20$ — **-22**
29. $-26 \times -20 \div 52 \times -9 \div 5 \times -7 \div -6$ — **-21**
30. $-360 \div -15 \times -35 \div -28 \times 40 \div -30$ — **-40**

Page 93

Page 94

Absolute Value — Skill: Absolute Value

Name _____

Evaluate.

Total Problems __52__
Problems Correct _____
Percent Correct _____

1. $|-11|$ — **11**
2. $|28|$ — **28**
3. $|33|$ — **33**
4. $|-110|$ — **110**
5. $|-50|$ — **50**
6. $|35|$ — **35**
7. $|4|$ — **4**
8. $|-18|$ — **18**
9. $|-72|$ — **72**
10. $|-18|$ — **18**
11. $|-25|$ — **25**
12. $|-71|$ — **71**
13. $|-64|$ — **64**
14. $|44|$ — **44**
15. $|36|$ — **36**
16. $|-41|$ — **41**
17. $|-8|$ — **8**
18. $|9|$ — **9**
19. $|214|$ — **214**
20. $|-510|$ — **510**

Simplify. Show your work on another piece of paper. Write your answers here.

21. $|25| + |-15|$ — **40**
22. $|-63| - |12|$ — **51**
23. $|-52| + |-8|$ — **60**
24. $|-3| \times |-7|$ — **21**
25. $|24| + |-6|$ — **4**... — (written **4**)
26. $|7| \times |-6|$ — **42**
27. $|-16| + |-9|$ — **25**
28. $|43| - |-20|$ — **22**
29. $|43| - |-20|$ — **23**
30. $|-15| + |3|$ — **5**
31. $|5| \times |-4|$ — **20**
32. $|-20| + |-34|$ — **54**
33. $|-12| - |-7|$ — **5**
34. $|-22| + |2|$ — **11**... (written)
35. $|-2| \times |20|$ — **40**
36. $|70| - |-51|$ — **19**
37. $|-18| + |-3|$ — **6**
38. $|-40| - |-17|$ — **23**
39. $|8| \times |-8|$ — **64**
40. $|50| + |-5|$ — **10**
41. $|36 - 50|$ — **14**
42. $|-6 \times 5|$ — **30**
43. $|-7 + -2|$ — **9**
44. $|-36 + -6|$ — **6**
45. $|5 + -10|$ — **5**
46. $|-11 - -3|$ — **8**
47. $|40 + -4|$ — **10**
48. $|-50 \times -2|$ — **100**
49. $|-12 + 15|$ — **3**
50. $|4 \times -7|$ — **28**
51. $|-81| \times |-16|$ — **1296**
52. $|-301 + 296|$ — **5**

Page 94

Page 95

Integers — Skill: Integers and Exponents

Name _____

Evaluate. Show your work on another piece of paper. Write your answers here.

Total Problems __42__
Problems Correct _____
Percent Correct _____

1. 3^{-4} — $\frac{1}{81}$
2. 4^0 — 1
3. 12^{-1} — $\frac{1}{12}$
4. 9^{-2} — $\frac{1}{81}$
5. $(-5)^2$ — 25
6. 8^{-2} — $\frac{1}{64}$
7. $(-3)^3$ — -27
8. 10^{-3} — $\frac{1}{1000}$
9. 19^0 — 1
10. $(-4)^{-2}$ — $\frac{1}{16}$
11. $(-6)^{-2}$ — $\frac{1}{36}$
12. 30^{-1} — $\frac{1}{30}$
13. $(-3)^{-4}$ — $\frac{1}{81}$
14. 17^{-1} — $\frac{1}{17}$
15. 4^{-2} — $\frac{1}{16}$
16. 16^0 — 1
17. 2^{-5} — $\frac{1}{32}$
18. $(-6)^2$ — 36
19. 11^{-2} — $\frac{1}{121}$
20. $(-5)^{-3}$ — $\frac{1}{-125}$
21. 22^{-1} — $\frac{1}{22}$
22. 14^0 — 1
23. $(-2)^{-4}$ — $\frac{1}{16}$
24. $(-9)^2$ — 81
25. 5^{-3} — $\frac{1}{125}$
26. 4^{-3} — $\frac{1}{64}$
27. 18^{-1} — $\frac{1}{18}$
28. 3^{-3} — $\frac{1}{27}$
29. $(-13)^2$ — $\frac{1}{169}$
30. $(-10)^{-2}$ — $\frac{1}{100}$
31. 24^0 — 1
32. 2^{-6} — $\frac{1}{64}$
33. $(-2)^{-5}$ — $\frac{1}{-32}$
34. 15^{-2} — $\frac{1}{225}$
35. $(-2)^{-6}$ — $\frac{1}{64}$
36. $(-10)^{-3}$ — $\frac{1}{-1000}$
37. 12^{-2} — $\frac{1}{144}$
38. 18^0 — 1
39. $(-4)^3$ — $\frac{1}{-64}$
40. 26^{-1} — $\frac{1}{26}$
41. $(-8)^{-2}$ — $\frac{1}{64}$
42. -4^5 — -1024

Page 95

Page 96

Expressions — Skill: Solving by Substitution

Name _____

Evaluate the expressions. Use a=6, b=5 and c=4.

Total Problems __48__
Problems Correct _____
Percent Correct _____

1. $b + 9$ — **14**
2. $a - c$ — **2**
3. $a + 8$ — **14**
4. $\frac{12}{c}$ — **3**
5. $\frac{15}{b}$ — **3**
6. $c - 1$ — **3**
7. bc — **20**
8. $a + c$ — **2**... (written 2)
9. $4b - a$ — **14**
10. $4(b + c)$ — **36**
11. $8 + c$ — **12**
12. b^2 — **25**
13. $c^3 - a^2$ — **28**
14. $\frac{33}{a + b}$ — **3**
15. $6a + -8c$ — **4**
16. $ca + b$ — **29**
17. $\frac{26 - a}{c}$ — **5**
18. $a^2 + b$ — **41**
19. $\frac{2b + 2}{a}$ — **2**
20. $\frac{a^2}{c}$ — **9**

Evaluate the expressions. Use x=2, y=7 and z=-5.

21. $z - y$ — **-12**
22. $2y + x$ — **16**
23. xz — **-10**
24. y^2 — **49**
25. $4xy - z$ — **61**
26. $xy + 1$ — **15**
27. $28 + y$ — **4**
28. $6z$ — **-30**
29. $3(x + y)$ — **27**
30. $2xyz$ — **-140**
31. x^3 — **8**
32. 3^x — **9**
33. 10^x — **100**
34. xz^2 — **50**
35. $\frac{y - z}{x}$ — **6**
36. $\frac{16 - x}{y}$ — **2**
37. $y^x - 6y$ — **7**
38. $4^x - y$ — **9**
39. z^2 — **25**
40. $yz + 40$ — **5**
41. $\frac{25}{-z}$ — **5**
42. x^y — **128**
43. $10y + z$ — **-14**
44. $-3xz$ — **30**
45. $\frac{x + -z}{y}$ — **1**
46. $\frac{77}{-y}$ — **-11**
47. z^3 — **-125**
48. $x^2(x + y)$ — **36**

Page 96

Math IF8771

Equations — Skill: Equations

Name _____

Is the given number a solution of the equation? Show your work on another piece of paper. Write yes or no here.

Total Problems __38__
Problems Correct ____
Percent Correct ____

1. $13 = x - 20$; 7 — **no**
2. $88 = 8x$; 11 — **yes**
3. $a - 15 = 8$; 23 — **yes**
4. $\frac{n}{15} = -3$; -45 — **yes**
5. $9x = -7z$; 8 — **no**
6. $22 = y + 14$; 7 — **no**
7. $9 = \frac{x}{8}$; 81 — **no**
8. $20a = 80$; 4 — **yes**
9. $-4 = x + 23$; -27 — **yes**
10. $16 = b - 4$; 20 — **yes**
11. $-13c = -65$; 6 — **no**
12. $6 = \frac{a}{-11}$; -95 — **no**
13. $-12 = \frac{m}{6}$; -70 — **no**
14. $6 = c + 28$; 22 — **no**
15. $y - 6 = -1$; 7 — **no**
16. $c + 10 = 33$; 23 — **yes**
17. $r - 18 = 26$; 44 — **yes**
18. $3a + 5 = 14$; 3 — **yes**
19. $\frac{c}{-9} = 8$; 72 — **no**
20. $8a = -64$; 8 — **no**
21. $\frac{y}{7} = -6$; -42 — **yes**
22. $49 = 7m$; 7 — **yes**
23. $b + 11 = -8$; 19 — **no**
24. $n - 9 = -6$; 3 — **yes**
25. $-6y = 60$; -10 — **yes**
26. $40 = x - 11$; 29 — **no**
27. $5 = \frac{n}{-21}$; -105 — **yes**
28. $-5 = r + 26$; -33 — **no**
29. $\frac{a}{-13} = -4$; 52 — **yes**
30. $20 = 4n + 12$; 3 — **no**
31. $3 = c - 22$; 26 — **no**
32. $12c = 48$; -3 — **no**
33. $a - 35 = -12$; 23 — **yes**
34. $19 = \frac{x}{-5}$; -85 — **yes**
35. $m + 15 = 4$; -11 — **yes**
36. $-75 = 15x$; -3 — **yes**
37. $-99 = -33b$; 3 — **yes**
38. $40 = 5x + 15$; 5 — **yes**

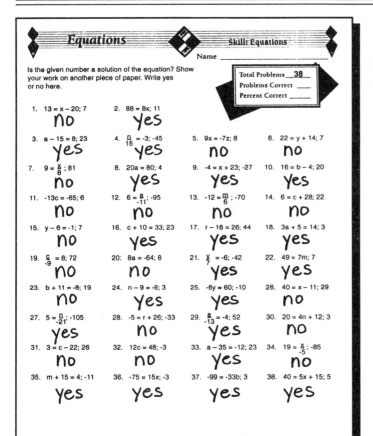

Equations — Skill: Addition and Subtraction

Name _____

Solve.

Total Problems __40__
Problems Correct ____
Percent Correct ____

1. $5 + x = 8$ → **3**
2. $m - 11 = 19$ → **30**
3. $-6 = -a + 3$ → **9**
4. $a + 20 = 33$ → **13**
5. $-4 = 13 + b$ → **-17**
6. $150 + b = 163$ → **13**
7. $n - 14 = -11$ → **3**
8. $x + 8 = -5$ → **-13**
9. $21 + c = 30$ → **9**
10. $18 - x = 3$ → **15**
11. $-15 = x - 20$ → **5**
12. $18 = x + 13$ → **5**
13. $x + -9 = 15$ → **24**
14. $-15 = c - 7$ → **-8**
15. $44 + x = 56$ → **12**
16. $19 - c = 11$ → **8**
17. $n + 14 = -11$ → **-25**
18. $6 = a - 25$ → **31**
19. $y + 7 = -14$ → **-21**
20. $b + 25 = 4$ → **-21**
21. $b + 9 = -11$ → **-20**
22. $-20 = d - 8$ → **-12**
23. $x - 10 = -8$ → **2**
24. $-14 + y = -3$ → **11**
25. $12 - y = 1$ → **11**
26. $19 = c + 30$ → **-11**
27. $b - 13 = -25$ → **-12**
28. $4 = y - 16$ → **20**
29. $45 + a = 22$ → **-23**
30. $-20 = a + 11$ → **-31**
31. $13 = 38 + x$ → **-25**
32. $-45 = d - 50$ → **5**
33. $-14 = a - 39$ → **25**
34. $8 + y = -30$ → **-38**
35. $11 - y = 5$ → **6**
36. $15 = -22 + y$ → **37**
37. $-5 = 16 + x$ → **-21**
38. $a - 63 = 7$ → **70**
39. $-7 + y = -4$ → **3**
40. $-16 = c - 22$ → **6**

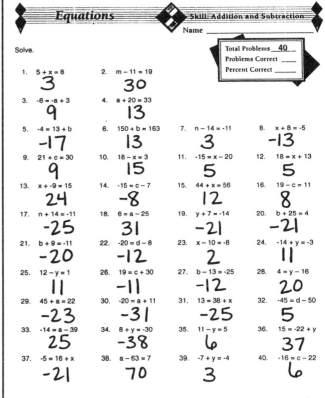

Equations — Skill: Multiplication and Division

Name _____

Solve.

Total Problems __40__
Problems Correct ____
Percent Correct ____

1. $4x = -20$ → **-5**
2. $\frac{n}{6} = 3$ → **18**
3. $64 = 8y$ → **8**
4. $11 = \frac{a}{-4}$ → **-44**
5. $\frac{n}{-14} = 2$ → **-28**
6. $49 = -7x$ → **-7**
7. $-10 = \frac{b}{4}$ → **-40**
8. $36 = 4y$ → **9**
9. $6 = \frac{c}{7}$ → **42**
10. $3a = -45$ → **-15**
11. $\frac{x}{-11} = -9$ → **99**
12. $-5x = 80$ → **-16**
13. $-48 = -12c$ → **4**
14. $\frac{c}{-8} = 9$ → **-72**
15. $7b = -77$ → **-11**
16. $\frac{x}{5} = 13$ → **65**
17. $-8y = 120$ → **-15**
18. $-12 = \frac{x}{-6}$ → **72**
19. $120 = 20n$ → **6**
20. $\frac{n}{-10} = 13$ → **-130**
21. $-8 = \frac{y}{11}$ → **-88**
22. $-52 = -13m$ → **4**
23. $15 = \frac{a}{9}$ → **135**
24. $60 = 6x$ → **10**
25. $-39 = -3n$ → **13**
26. $5 = \frac{m}{8}$ → **40**
27. $\frac{n}{-12} = -4$ → **48**
28. $2a = -90$ → **-45**
29. $81 = 9b$ → **9**
30. $\frac{x}{25} = -8$ → **-200**
31. $-10m = 110$ → **-11**
32. $\frac{-y}{9} = -9$ → **81**
33. $12 = \frac{x}{7}$ → **84**
34. $-63 = 21x$ → **-3**
35. $8y = 56$ → **7**
36. $-4 = \frac{m}{20}$ → **-80**
37. $-99 = -11a$ → **9**
38. $4 = \frac{b}{21}$ → **84**
39. $72 = 9c$ → **8**
40. $\frac{a}{-13} = 2$ → **-26**

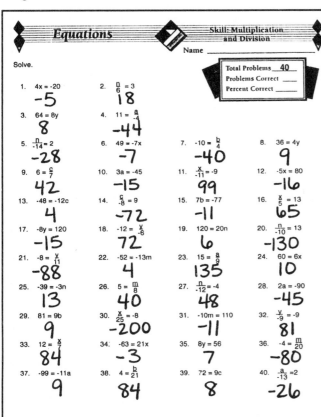

Equations — Skill: Two Operations

Name _____

Solve. Show your work on another piece of paper. Write your answers here.

Total Problems __38__
Problems Correct ____
Percent Correct ____

1. $3x + 4 = 25$ → **7**
2. $\frac{x}{4} + 3 = 11$ → **32**
3. $8 = 6x - 4$ → **2**
4. $\frac{n}{-5} + 6 = -5$ → **55**
5. $-55 = -8n + 9$ → **8**
6. $5x + 1 = 21$ → **4**
7. $-20 = -11s + 24$ → **4**
8. $\frac{r}{8} + 5 = 4$ → **-8**
9. $7x - 11 = 3$ → **2**
10. $8r - 7 = 17$ → **3**
11. $20w + 5 = 85$ → **4**
12. $12c - 16 = 44$ → **5**
13. $13r - 11 = 28$ → **3**
14. $\frac{c}{-3} + 16 = -5$ → **63**
15. $3x - 8 = 28$ → **12**
16. $\frac{c}{8} + 9 = 15$ → **48**
17. $-33 = -6r + 9$ → **7**
18. $7x - 3 = 18$ → **3**
19. $8n + 21 = -43$ → **-8**
20. $63 = 9a - 27$ → **10**
21. $8 - 2r = -12$ → **10**
22. $\frac{x}{7} - 5 = 6$ → **77**
23. $9s + 13 = 85$ → **8**
24. $22 = 11 + \frac{x}{-4}$ → **-44**
25. $\frac{a}{-5} + 2 = -13$ → **75**
26. $20b - 93 = 7$ → **5**
27. $\frac{n}{-12} + 8 = 10$ → **-24**
28. $7a - 28 = 21$ → **7**
29. $\frac{n}{10} - 3 = 8$ → **110**
30. $40 - 7x = -16$ → **8**
31. $-28 = -9x + 17$ → **5**
32. $16 = \frac{c}{20} + 19$ → **-60**
33. $12r + 33 = 81$ → **4**
34. $\frac{n}{15} - 13 = -18$ → **-75**
35. $61 = 16 + 15a$ → **3**
36. $18 = 22 - \frac{n}{5}$ → **20**
37. $\frac{x}{-15} - 160 = -32$ → **-1920**
38. $21x + 36 = -378$ → **-20**

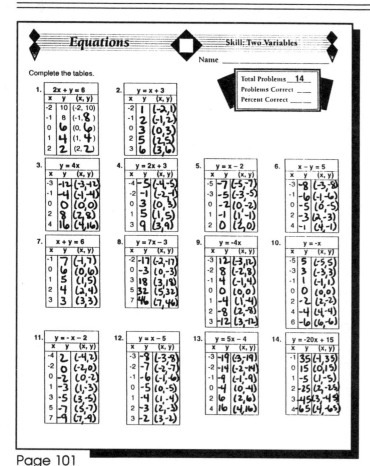

Page 101

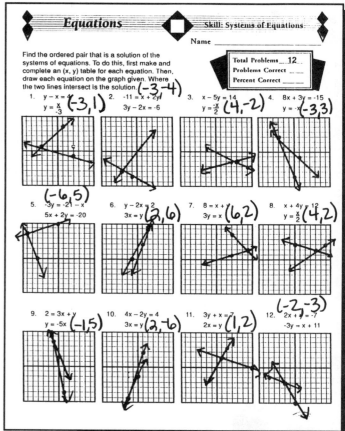

Page 102

About the Book ...

You've taught the skills, but how do you make them really sink in? With practice, of course. This book provides thousands of practice problems and addresses only one basic skill on each page. If your students need practice, this book is the answer!

About the Author ...

Andrea Miles Moran lives in Stamford, Connecticut, with her husband and son, Miles. She received a Bachelor of Science degree from the University of Missouri-Columbia and a post baccalaureate teaching credential from San Diego State University. She taught junior high mathematics before moving to New York.

Credits ...

Author: Andrea Miles Moran
Project Director: Mina McMullin
Typesetting/Graphic Design: Emily Georg-Smith
Editor: Jill Kaufman
Production: Janie Schmidt
Cover Photo: ©Comstock, Inc. 1994
Cover Production: Annette Hollister-Papp

Math IF8771